CLOUD NINE
CONOR MURRAY

WITH TOMMY CONLON

CLOUD NINE
CONOR MURRAY

WITH TOMMY CONLON

Reach Sport

This book is dedicated to my grandad, the late Con Roche, who paved the way in our family and lived to see me carry on his legacy.

Reach Sport

www.reachsport.com

Copyright © Conor Murray 2025.

The right of Conor Murray to be identified as the owner of this work has been asserted in accordance with the Copyright, Designs and Patents Act, 1988.

All Rights Reserved. No part of this publication may be reproduced, stored in a retrieval system, or transmitted in any form, or by any means, electronic, mechanical, photocopying, recording or otherwise without the prior permission in writing of the copyright holders, nor be otherwise circulated in any form of binding or cover other than in which it is published and without a similar condition being imposed on the subsequent publisher.

Published in Great Britain and Ireland in 2025 by
Reach Sport, a Reach PLC business,
5 St Paul's Square, Liverpool, L3 9SJ.

www.reachsport.com
@Reach_Sport

Reach Sport is a part of Reach PLC.
One Canada Square, Canary Wharf, London, E15 5AP.

Hardback ISBN: 9781916811102
eBook ISBN: 9781916811119

Photographic acknowledgements:
Conor Murray personal collection, Alamy, Inpho, Sportsfile.
Every effort has been made to trace the copyright.
Any oversight will be rectified in future editions.

Production: Christine Costello
Editor: Simon Monk
Cover Design: Chris Collins

Printed and bound by CPI Group (UK) Ltd,
Croydon, CR0 4YY.

CONTENTS

Dramatis Personae	viii
Foreword	1
Introduction	6
Slán go Fóill	11
The Well	23
Con Roche	35
Phone Calls from Declan	49
Lessons in Italian	64
Bollockings	75
A Lonely Night in Lahinch	83
'A poor man's Mike Phillips'	92
A Big Mac in Maynooth	109
My Kind of Town	120
There is an Isle	128
The Erasmus Scholarship	135
The Beach Boys	149
Aftershocks	162
Close But No Cigar	175
Leading The Pack	201
Slip Sliding Away	212
Last Tango in Paris	229
Spirals	243
Trolls	267
Final Curtain	280

DRAMATIS PERSONAE

Archie – Stephen Archer
Axel – Anthony Foley
Besty – Rory Best
Bossy – Isaac Boss
Bundee – Bundee Aki
Church – Cian Healy
Craig - Craig Casey
Donners – Donncha O'Callaghan
Dougie – Doug Howlett
Drico – Brian O'Driscoll
Dumper – Tony McGahan
Earlsy – Keith Earls
Faz – Andy Farrell
Fla – Jerry Flannery
Gats – Warren Gatland
Jamo – Jamison Gibson-Park
Johnny/Sexto – Jonathan Sexton
Kearns – Rob Kearney
Keats – Ian Keatley
Killer – Dave Kilcoyne
Leams – Denis Leamy

DRAMATIS PERSONAE

Lowey – James Lowe
Paulie – Paul O'Connell
Pete – Peter O'Mahony
Prendy – Mike Prendergast
Quinny – Alan Quinlan
Redser – Eoin Reddan
RoG – Ronan O'Gara
Scans – Seán Scanlon
Strings – Peter Stringer
Wig – Graham Rowntree
Zeebs – Simon Zebo

FOREWORD

by Johnny Sexton

I CAN'T SAY THAT CONOR and I got off to the best of starts together, given that we turned the air blue late in the game against Italy at the 2011 World Cup. And we barely knew each other at the time. He had broken into the national squad only a few months earlier. He was just beginning his meteoric rise for Munster and Ireland.

But at that moment in time I wasn't really paying him much attention. I had my own business to take care of. I was locked in a battle with Ronan O'Gara for the ten jersey and I wasn't winning it. I needed to be making an impression with the game time I was getting. And, in all fairness, it would've been hard to make any kind of impression with the sort of ball this fresh-faced young fella threw at me that day in New Zealand! So, I got rid of it fairly lively and duly ate the head of him. In fact, I effed him and scotched him virtually from one end of the pitch to the other.

Then understandably he got a bit fed up and started returning the compliment in fairly unparliamentary language too! We were both deadly serious about it in the moment. In hindsight, it was a pantomime.

CONOR MURRAY

But if anyone had seen us caught up in that war of words in Dunedin, they wouldn't have predicted that we'd end up forming the longest Irish halfback partnership of all time. I definitely couldn't have foreseen it. And I had no idea either that I was about to team up with a player who would go on to become the greatest scrumhalf in Irish rugby history.

After that dodgy start we really began to click on and off the pitch during the 2013 British & Irish Lions tour of Australia. We still hadn't really warmed to each other at that stage. But on a Lions tour you tend to gravitate towards the Irish guys even though you mightn't have been close to them in the Irish squad. You end up going for coffees with them and suddenly they're one of your best buddies when you're a long way from home.

On the training ground, I was also getting to see up close the full repertoire of his talents. Obviously, any time you play with a new scrumhalf, the first thing you're looking for as a flyhalf is the quality of his pass. The better his service is, the easier it is for me to do my job. Then you're hoping he can kick the ball well enough to take a bit of the pressure off you. Murr was excellent at both those fundamentals. His pass off either side was fast and accurate; he had an amazing kicking game. On top of that, he was an unusual size for a scrumhalf. He was a big, physical nine. He had the power to break tackles and make sniping breaks with a big hand-off. And because he was so strong he was like an extra back row on defence. So, you were getting a lot of bang for your buck from one scrumhalf.

By temperament he was quiet and understated: never got too high, never got too low. He wasn't a man of many words. He wouldn't talk much at team meetings. But he set an example not just because of how he played in games but also through his

FOREWORD

professionalism in training. He was an immaculate professional. He prepared himself physically and psychologically in the right way, day after day, year after year.

And because he was that kind of chilled-out type of guy, maybe people didn't fully appreciate how tough and competitive he was. There was an inner core of steel beneath that smooth exterior. There had to be, to play at such an elite level for so long. Mentally he was very strong in high-pressure situations.

A few years into our partnership, I knew I could depend on him completely. He was consistently reliable. I don't think we studied much video together but we talked a lot before and after training sessions about our work as a two-man unit. In that way, our professional partnership evolved into a personal friendship.

As time went by, we needed fewer and fewer verbal communications on the pitch. What started out with two fellas who couldn't fire enough verbals at each other, ended up needing no words at all. That's the ideal, isn't it, where you get to a level of understanding that telepathy takes over from language? In our case, Conor is running to the ruck and I'm running to get into position and he knows what you want just by your body language. That's all it takes when there's so much trust and mutual experience built up between you.

We had hundreds of those moments but I suppose the most famous is the last play against France in 2018: the 41 phases, the 83rd minute, and the drop goal that sets us up for the Grand Slam season. I didn't call that ball. I just gave him a nod and he knew straightaway. In Paris that day, at the exact moment when everything was on the line, he knew and I knew. Nothing needed to be said. He threw me the perfect pass.

CONOR MURRAY

It goes without saying that he was a dream to play with. I was so lucky to have had him by my side during the Joe Schmidt era when we had a fantastic record in terms of titles and wins/losses. I played with a lot of very good nines for club and country but Murr set the bar. He has set the bar in terms of the standard that others have to chase. He went to a level that no Irish nine had gone to before and that's definitely the truth. Because at one stage he was at a level that no other nine in the world was at. Everyone will have their opinions but for me his performances against the All Blacks for Ireland in Chicago in 2016, and in those three Tests for the Lions in New Zealand in 2017, put him at the absolute pinnacle of his profession. In my opinion there was no one else in the world better than him in that position at that time.

The daft thing is, he was so consistently good for so long that some supporters and media started taking him for granted. Personally, I don't think he got the love he should have. There seemed to be a lack of appreciation for a player who was actually setting a higher standard than we'd ever seen before from an Irish nine. Part of our strategy in those years under Joe was to use the box-kick as an attacking weapon. It was a very successful tool in our armoury. But as is often the way with Irish sport when you have a bit of success, suddenly success isn't enough anymore. They want something new, or different or a bit flashier. I remember hearing occasional groans in the Aviva when Conor would go to the air. But the reason we did it so often was because he was so good at it. In terms of distance and hang time, he was so consistently accurate with it that we usually ended up getting the ball back. He'd have heard those groans too but he was mentally strong enough to ignore them. Sometimes

FOREWORD

I felt the two of us were on the receiving end together, which I liked in a lot of ways because it meant you weren't on your own. But I thought it was wrong to be honest.

Anyway, we went the distance from the 2011 World Cup until I bowed out after RWC 2023. Twelve years is a long innings in this game. That's a lot of passes, a lot of giving and receiving. A lot of craic too in terms of parties and celebrations and nights out in victory and defeat. During that time we crossed over from being professional team mates into becoming good friends. Laura and Joanna, our wives, have become great friends too. We both have families now and we've all the commitments that come with that as we move into the next phase of our lives.

But there's a bunch of us players who soldiered together for years and we intend to stick together socially in the years to come too. There will be dinners, nights out and plenty more laughs along the way.

Conor has left a legacy to the game here which I hope he feels proud of, in terms of his achievements, his performances and the standards he set. The game has been very good to both of us in return. It has given us far more than the caps and the trophies. It has given us a connection and a friendship I hope will serve as an enduring legacy of our shared past in green.

INTRODUCTION

THE END OF THE ROAD for me is nigh. At the time of writing I am 36 years and two months old – and counting. The clock is only going one way. I am ancient for a rugby player, for any kind of professional sportsman.

I also happen to be in great shape physically and emotionally. The athleticism hasn't deserted me yet. The game hasn't left me yet. Right now I'm mulling over a potential move abroad for one last season in the boots before I hang them up for good. It's hard to let go.

I know I'm dicing with Father Time here. I want to leave the game before the game leaves me. But I don't want to leave it if there's juice left in the tank. I'd prefer to use it all up because I love what I do. I'm still undecided.

But I'm very clear in my mind that I'm in bonus territory now. I could walk away from it all today a happy and contented man. I don't think I could've given much more to rugby. I certainly never thought I'd get as much back as I did. I have a clear conscience because I know I tried to extract the maximum from my God-given talent. I didn't waste it. I started early and I'm finishing late. In between, I've lived a beautiful life.

And unbeknown to me, I was accumulating a ton of stories and a ton of memories. I am delighted to be able to share so many of them now with you in this book. I hope it might offer

INTRODUCTION

a fresh perspective on the working life of a pro rugby player in this country.

One thing I know from personal experience is that people can end up judging you without knowing you in the slightest. Understandably, maybe, they fall into the trap of thinking they know you from watching you play a game. But any sportsperson can tell you there's a big difference between the public performer and the real-life individual. I kept the two things separate. I never had to think about that; it was just the natural way of my own personality. As a competitor, I played with all of my heart. I just didn't show those emotions externally. But they were there inside of me, pounding away. I found I functioned better when I kept them internalised and stuck to the mechanics of what I was doing. I needed to keep my brain clear. I needed to park the passion and get on with my work.

So, between my natural reticence off the pitch and my need to stick to the process on it, I may have ended up as a bit of an unknown quantity to people. I never doubted that I was respected as a player and competitor during that time. What was lovely to discover over the last few months was how much warmth and affection the rugby-supporting public felt for me. It all kind of came out when I announced earlier this year that I would be retiring from Munster and Ireland at the end of the season. The send-offs I got were full of warmth and kindness and good wishes. It has touched me deeply and I am really grateful.

I am happy now that I can open up a bit more in return through the pages of my autobiography. The reason I was a bit of a closed book during my playing career goes back to a lesson I learned early on. It was February 2009 and I was 19 going on

20. I'd been selected for the Ireland U20s team to play France in the Six Nations in Dubarry Park. I was rooming with Andrew Burke, my good friend and team mate at Garryowen. I was scrumhalf, Andrew was outhalf. We were both in the Munster academy at the time. This was a major occasion in our young lives. You were edging closer to the big time here. The game was going to be on RTÉ, there was going to be a good crowd there, this was a chance to make a name for yourself.

We're sitting on our beds in our hotel in Athlone and I'm making sure that I'm dotting every i and crossing every t. I've done my training thoroughly and I've taken loads of notes. And now I'm going through my notes, making sure I'll remember all the stuff I want to do the next day and telling myself I have to cross everything off that list before the match is over. Meanwhile, I have my headphones on, listening to songs that will hype me up, songs with powerful lyrics and motivational music. I'm also visualising the game in my head: we're gonna do this and I'm gonna do that and we're gonna smash them back and I'm gonna play havoc with them. Next thing, there's tears running down my face. Not roaring crying, but tears flowing. Burkey looks over at me and he's like, are you alright? I fob him off. Yeah I'm fine, I'm fine.

The next day I'm hooked after 53 minutes. I was so hyped up that I played the worst game of my life. I dropped simple passes, missed kicks at goal, got my wires crossed, and kept forcing things that didn't come off. And I can remember clear as day thinking to myself afterwards: "Right, that's enough of that. Just bloody well enjoy playing rugby. What are you getting so riled up for? You love rugby, you enjoy playing it, and you did not enjoy that whole experience one little bit."

INTRODUCTION

I didn't know anything about the psychology behind these things at the time but I knew enough to know that I would not be making the same mistake again. It obviously didn't suit me getting all psyched up like that for games. Just be your natural self, be true to your own nature, because I'm a relaxed type of person and therefore I should be a relaxed type of athlete. If it suited other lads to get wound up, no problem, I could see it worked for them. But it didn't work for me and it was obvious how I should prepare myself mentally from then on. It was an invaluable lesson and I've lived by it from that day to this.

But it doesn't mean you're not as passionate as the next fella. The passion in me to compete, to win, to be the best, is the exact same as the fella who wears his heart on his sleeve.

Now that I've got that off my chest, I can hopefully reveal a bit more about the life I've lived in a sport that gave me 125 caps for my country, a full career with my hometown team, four World Cups and three tours with the British & Irish Lions. It has been a golden era for Ireland with Grand Slams, triple crowns and championship titles. It has sadly been less than golden with Munster. I have enjoyed some incredible highs and endured a lot of crushing disappointments.

But now that it's over, or almost over, I find myself feeling a lot of gratitude for the life that the game has given me. I have been a very lucky boy. I've been blessed. There's been an unbelievable amount of craic along the way too because you're surrounded by blokes who, like yourself, are having a whale of a time. The stress and the comedy go hand in hand. We're playing serious sport but it's still sport and we're still playing games. We are good at being mature when it's needed and good at being immature the rest of the time. We are conscientious and responsible citizens one minute, silly and irresponsible schoolboys the next. It's not a real job but it suddenly becomes very real if you blow out a knee or your contract is not renewed or you're dropped from the squad. You are only ever a moment away from the fun and games turning around and slapping you in the face. It is incredibly precarious as a profession. That's why I feel so lucky to have lasted so long in this world that I love.

Soon enough, I will be back in the real world. I am married with a baby son now. And I am an old man still trying to wear a young man's shoes. So, the boots are headed for the hook on the wall very soon, never to be taken down again. That's life, that's sport, but what a rollercoaster ride it has been.

Not everyone gets the chance to tell their story in the pages of a book. It is a privilege for me to share that story now with any readers who might like to join me on that journey through Patrickswell, Thomond Park, Lansdowne Road, and all the foreign fields across the rugby universe that let me in to spin a pass.

Chapter One

SLÁN GO FÓILL

THE WRITING WAS ON THE wall but I had a feeling in my bones that there might be one final chapter. I felt I just might catch a break somewhere that would let me back for a few farewell games in green.

I'd earned my 120th cap against Fiji in the second last of the autumn internationals in November 2024. I actually came on for the last half hour and played on the wing; Jacob Stockdale had done his hamstring. But the overall picture was that I'd slipped down to third in the pecking order, behind Jamo and Craig. The changing of the guard was happening in earnest now. It was looking like I'd be squeezed out of it for the 2025 Six Nations. Fair enough, what will be, will be.

But there's a corner of my mind where I'm thinking, you never know, you just never know, you might get lucky one more time. I have been incredibly lucky my whole career. So much so in fact, I've gotten a bit of a slagging about it over the years. Lads would be saying that I always land on my feet. The toast falls butter-side up for me. Or, as one of the Munster boys said to me years ago, if I fell into a barrel of shit I'd come out smelling of roses. And I can't deny my good fortune. I have had the most amazing run, especially in a sport where horrendous injuries are an occupational hazard. The only thing I will add to that is, I think I've made my own luck too by taking maximum care with my fitness and conditioning from day one in the academy through every season since.

One of the reasons I ended up playing so many games for club and country was I minded my body religiously. I kept myself in top nick week in week out. And I reaped the rewards for it in my thirties when so many of my peers were constantly breaking down with injury after injury. Their bodies were just crumbling.

In fairness, there was probably an element of genetic luck here too in that my system could cope pretty smoothly with the athletic demands of Test match rugby. My musculoskeletal structure could take that level of stress in its stride. I've seen other fellas whose physical system was under so much strain in that environment that inevitably their hamstrings or calves or knees or ankles would buckle. I don't think that those games took quite as much out of me. I could recover quickly and be fresh again for the next match. I think that natural physical resilience allied to all the daily maintenance I did saved me from the sort of injuries that would take years out of another player's career. And it all contributed to the longevity that allowed me to play for Ireland up until the eve of my 36th birthday.

Still and all, I needed that bit of luck for it to happen because after the November internationals I was seriously contemplating the decision to call it a day with Ireland. I didn't want to be hanging on as the third wheel. I was too long in the tooth to be clinging on like that. After the Fiji game, Ireland would be playing Australia in the final match of the autumn series. When the 23 players were announced, I wasn't one of them. The Australia game was going to be the centre of the celebrations to

SLÁN GO FÓILL

mark the IRFU's 150th anniversary. They had commissioned a set of one-off jerseys for the match to mark the occasion. On the Thursday before the game, they brought in Ollie Campbell to give a speech to the squad and present everyone individually with his special edition jersey. One by one, the 23 players walked up to receive theirs and get a round of applause. There were seven or eight reserves left sitting in their chairs, myself included. It was a horrible feeling. It stung my pride. I'd been a first-choice player for club, country and the British & Irish Lions for most of my career.

One of our backroom staff, a really nice fella, came over to us after the presentations and he had the sympathetic expression on his face. He was like, sorry about that lads, really felt for ye there. He was being genuinely nice about it but it riled me up. I'd experienced this same feeling on the Lions tour in 2013 when I was the only sub left on the bench against the Queensland Reds in Brisbane. I didn't like the sympathies then and I didn't like them now either. I picked up one of the leftover special jerseys – it was an XXL, far too big for me. I left the room that evening convinced that I was going to bring the curtain down on my international career.

The only thing that stopped me was a voice in my head telling me not to pull the plug just yet. In a sport like rugby, almost everyone ends up getting games at some stage or another through the misfortune of a team mate. That's just a reality. And sure enough, in the middle of December, Craig did his knee playing for Munster against Castres. He was going to be out for four or five months. And just like that, I was back in the ball game. But you don't get to 35 without picking up some scar tissue, no matter how lucky you've been.

CONOR MURRAY

In December I'd been getting injections in my neck. It's a legacy injury from collisions with George North and Marika Korobeite in 2017 and 2018. I've suffered from intermittent seizures to the neck and shoulder in the years since. And I'm also getting an injection in my elbow because of a pure wear-and-tear problem. The consultant tells me it's the result of throwing a ball hundreds of thousands of times. Apparently it also affects quarterbacks in American football and pitchers in baseball. You end up with this sort of nodule on the point of your elbow that pinches the nerve and causes inflammation.

But by January 2025 I'm good to go again. I start Munster's Champions Cup games against Saracens and Northampton. Then it's off to Carton House for my last Six Nations campaign. Driving up to Maynooth for our first camp, I make a vow to myself to take it all in this time. Savour every moment. Enjoy it and soak it up. I've been blessed to get a last chance to go away and join the circus one more time. I'm really conscious of my family too. Mum and Dad and my sisters are going to get one last campaign because that part of their life will be coming to an end also.

They've had some great adventures following me around the world for the last 15 years. I'm delighted we'll all get to do it together one more time. And this time, of course, my wife Joanna and I will have our own special guest for these occasions. Little Alfie won't have a clue where he is but we'll bring him along and we'll take all the photos and in years to come we'll be able to show him that he was there at Daddy's last games for Ireland. That's the real meaning at the heart of this little bit of extra time I've been granted to wear the green. It will be a way of saying thanks to my family and friends for their support and

SLÁN GO FÓILL

because we know it's going to be the last time, make sure we treasure the memories.

Another beautiful bonus is that I'm now finding myself at peace with where I am. For a few weeks in November/December I was agonising about calling it quits but this reprieve has made me accept my situation. I haven't been dropped and forgotten about. They're bringing me back in and therefore I'll be going out on my own terms. And I have this lovely feeling of peacefulness about it. The timing is exactly right. It just feels right. Instead of frustration, I have this feeling of fulfilment and gratitude. Relief as well, knowing that it's coming to its natural end, but mainly a sense of fulfilment and gratitude for having had the privilege of such a long career.

I get six minutes against England, twelve against Scotland, two against Wales. At another time I would've had the hump about those stats but now I'm totally fine about it, not least because we've won all three games and I've been on the pitch at the final whistle. It always helps to be on the pitch at the final whistle. There's a two-week break between Wales away and our last home game of the campaign, against France.

The week before the France game we're at the national sports campus in Abbotstown for a training day. Simon Easterby has stepped up as interim Ireland head coach while Faz is on secondment as head coach of the British & Irish Lions. I've known Simon for years and I'm really pleased for him because he's been such a big part of the culture we've built with the international side. There's never been any bullshit with him, he's always remained true to himself. And now that he's in the spotlight, with all the pressure that comes with that, he doesn't change either.

CONOR MURRAY

The transition from Faz to Simon is seamless. We have a very happy camp and he's doing the job with his customary class. Anyway, this day in Abbotstown, Faz comes in for a social call at lunchtime. We're all milling around the campus restaurant getting our grub when Faz comes over to me and invites me to join him for lunch. So, we're having the old chit-chat when suddenly he asks me, what are your plans for the future? What are you thinking? Where are you going? I tell him that my club career is a bit up in the air because I'll be finishing with Munster in the summer and I'm not sure if I'll retire or play on. But with Ireland, this is the end of the road.

He knew that already: everyone knew it because it was pretty obvious, but he was very good about it anyway. With his usual emotional intelligence, he said some nice things to me and added that I had given enough to the cause to be allowed to finish the way I wanted it to finish. Very few players in any sport get to call it a day on their own terms.

Pete O'Mahony and Cian Healy were also checking out. Only the 376 caps between us when they were all added up. A day or two after I have the chat with Faz, we're back in Abbotstown and the media manager comes up to me and Pete and Church and asks us to say a few words to the IRFU's in-house film crew for their social media platforms. They've set it up in one of the rugby 7s dressing rooms that are empty at the time. You don't pass many remarks on these gigs because fellas in match week are always being dragged here and there for media stuff and sponsors' stuff and various PR jobs. We're asked basically to sit down on a bench in the dressing room and do a piece to camera announcing our retirements. It's fairly short and sweet. The IRFU put it up on their website on the Thursday morning

SLÁN GO FÓILL

and pretty soon it's going viral. The public reaction is really nice. We get loads of well wishes and thank yous and generous comments. I only read a fraction of them because we're busy, we have a game to play. But I do check out the video and there's Pete and Church and myself saying our farewells. But the bit that leaves a lump in my throat is the song they've chosen for the background music, Coldplay's 'Everglow'.

We transferred from Carton House to the Shelbourne Hotel that Thursday, as we usually do. And just walking down Stephen's Green with my gear bag there were loads of people calling out to me and saying thanks and good luck. After our team meeting that evening there was a presentation to Finlay Bealham, Caelan Doris and Jack Conan. They were going to be picking up their 50th caps against France. Faz and the backroom staff always do these little ceremonies with a touch of class. Usually they'll have players' parents and loved ones in for it.

The following evening, the Friday, the squad and coaching staff had our dinner together as normal and went back to our rooms. I was in Bundee's room with Jack and Robbie Henshaw talking our usual shite when Ger Carmody knocked on the door. Ger is the man. He's our team manager and all-round support guy. If you ever need anything, Ger will look after you. Nothing is too much trouble. He's been there for me from first game to last. Now he wants me to come with him somewhere or another. He rounds up Pete and Church too and we head downstairs and we follow him until we end up in this private dining room. My parents are there, and Joanna and Alfie, Faz, along with Paulie, Simon, all the coaches and our former team manager, another great friend to us, Mick Kearney. Pete's and Church's families are there too. Faz says a lovely few words.

There's a lot of emotion in the room, especially among our family members, because they're feeling the sadness too that it's all coming to an end.

But we three players have to keep our professional heads on because there is unfinished business. We're looking at making more history by doing back-to-back Grand Slams. Pete will be starting against France; myself and Church are going to be on the bench. We want to go out on a high in Dublin. Unfortunately, this wasn't meant to be.

We went out on a low. France took the game away from us after the first 20 minutes. We dominated territory and possession in that first quarter and came away with nothing. We were held up over the line a couple of times. Score then and I think we've got a different game on our hands. Instead, we get hit by a sucker-punch, a try by Louis Bielle-Biarrey and their tails are up. The intensity and physicality is a sight to behold from the seats. So, is the French speed and flair when they hit that top gear.

The defeat comes as a big anti-climax when we've been dreaming all along of another Slam. But what leaves a bitter taste for me is Fabien Galthie's comments afterwards. Antoine Dupont had to be carried off around the half hour mark with what turned out to be a cruciate ligament injury. It was a pure rugby incident. Dupont was cleared out at a ruck by Tadhg Beirne and Andrew Porter. It was completely legit. Unfortunately, his leg got caught and the knee got twisted. It's a common occurrence. I've had medial ligament damage done in similar situations. Galthie needed to be far more careful in his comments after.

He singled out Tadhg and Andrew and described their actions as "reprehensible". Maybe as head coach he felt he needed to be

SLÁN GO FÓILL

seen supporting his star player. But we're living in the social media age. When he singles out players like that, their partners and families get hurt in the fallout because of all the abuse that's targeted at the lads online. It has happened to a lot of us at one stage or another and it is a very unpleasant experience on a personal level. But worse again, it can be frightening and upsetting for those close to you.

I replaced Jamo with twelve minutes left in the match. There was a small bit of consolation in finishing my last Ireland game at the Aviva in my boots, on the pitch, wearing a jersey with a playing number on it. I was able to thank the fans on our walkaround as a player, not yet an ex-player. Joanna brought Alfie down from the seats to the pitch and I walked around with him. The wee man had already made his Lansdowne Road debut after the Fiji game but he was only a month old at the time. Now he was a veteran of five months and on his second visit! It was sweet to have that moment. Uini Atonio, the French prop forward, ambled over to us. Christ, he's a big unit. He is enormous. But he was as gentle as a lamb, smiling and asking me his name and admiring this little thing in my arms. It was a lovely little exchange.

The Italy game was a week later, so we stayed in camp. Meanwhile, loads of family and friends were getting ready to fly to Rome for their last hurrah. I suppose if you were going to bring the curtain down anywhere, Rome wouldn't be a bad choice.

On the morning of the match we had our units' meetings in the team room of our hotel. There was one last surprise for me on the occasion of my 125th and final match. My old mate Sexto had been visiting us on and off since the autumn to dip his toes in the coaching game. The amount of rugby knowledge that man has to pass on is phenomenal. He was part of the entourage for our trip to Italy too and at our backs' meeting that morning, he took the floor and spoke to the group about our times together in the nine and ten jerseys. Johnny's an emotional speaker anyway when his competitive spirit comes out. But he welled up on this occasion, I think because it was personal for him too.

We had soldiered together at halfback from the 2011 World Cup to the 2023 World Cup. We'd broken the Irish record for a halfback partnership at the 2019 World Cup. All in all we'd played over 80 times together. That's a lot of time in the cockpit. It's a lot of passes, a lot of effing and blinding and highs and lows. And, of course, an awful lot of memories. He said he'd loved playing alongside me. At this stage he had me nearly going too. Maybe there was a part of him saying goodbye to his own stellar career as well, among his fellow internationals and other team mates in the room who went back a long way with him.

The best that can be said about the Italy performance is that we won it. I was sent on with 14 minutes left. With that, I officially became the fourth-most capped Irish player of all time, behind Church on 137, Drico on 133, and RoG on 128. Now it's over, I think I can give myself a pat on the back. I'm totally at peace with what I've achieved. Obviously, I'm going to miss it. Fifteen years playing for your country – of course I'm going to miss it. I will surely have pangs of nostalgia when I watch the lads running out for the next big internationals in the autumn. I'll know what they're going through, I'll know the life they are living and I'll know that it is an incredibly special thing to be doing.

SLÁN GO FÓILL

I will miss the rush of adrenaline, the crowds, the anthems, the noise and applause, the combat on the field, the craic and the stories in the dressing room after. I will miss the five-star treatment we got at Carton House, the pleasures as well as the stresses of being in a high-performance athletes' environment. I will miss it all. I honestly expect I will go through a period of mourning, grieving what's gone and will never return. But I have the consolation of knowing that, whatever amount of talent I had, I squeezed every ounce out of it. I wasted very little of it. I got close to the absolute maximum out of it. That is a real bedrock comfort to have in retirement. The sense of fulfilment I have from doing right by my ability. I would have plenty of regrets if I had to admit deep down to myself that I wasted some of it. I have no regrets whatsoever on that front, thank God. I gave my all to the game and it gave an immense amount back to me.

It filled my heart to have Joanna and Alfie and Mum and Dad and my sisters and a few great friends at the Stadio Olimpico for the final farewell. In the dressing room afterwards, Pete and Church and myself each got our jerseys signed by all our team mates. That night there was a black-tie event in this magnificent old Roman building that was like a cathedral. We were bussed from there back to the hotel. A few drinks were taken at this stage. The three of us each had to sing our party piece on the bus. The lads wouldn't shut up until we stood up and did our number. My old standby is 'Summer of '69' by Bryan Adams. The lyrics had a bit of meaning for me on this occasion. "Jimmy quit, Jody got married ... Oh, when I look back now, those were the best days of my life."

Back in Dublin we jumped into taxis and headed across town.

CONOR MURRAY

McSorley's in Ranelagh was the destination this time round for our traditional post-Six Nations session. In a previous life, I'd have seen it out to the last glass. Pretty soon the pints would be getting replaced by shorts. I could see the writing on the wall here too. So, I slipped away fairly quietly while the lads were getting stuck in. If I stood up and announced I was going, I'd have got slated by 30 fellas telling me to sit down and have another one.

I was around long enough to know how to leave when you have to. Same as with your Ireland career, there comes a time to walk away from it all. Across town, Joanna and Alfie were waiting for me in our hotel. This was my beautiful future, that was my golden past.

At the end of one thing was the beginning of another. The next morning would be the first day of the rest of my life.

Chapter Two

THE WELL

I WAS IN CARTON HOUSE when I got the call that Dad had been knocked off his bike and taken by ambulance to hospital in Limerick where his condition was critical. It was Tuesday 7th February 2023. The previous Saturday I'd started the first game of that season's Six Nations and was due to start the following Saturday against France. In my world, everything was going well.

Then you get a phone call that turns your world upside down in a second. My father loved his cycling, man and boy. He'd been out for a spin on the roads that afternoon. He was on the hard shoulder of the road from Croom, only about a kilometre away from our home in Patrickswell. The driver of a truck that was pulling a slurry tanker behind it came up the slip road and failed to halt at the stop sign. He collided side-on with my dad and the impact was shocking. He was driven backwards onto the road. His back, and the back of his head in particular, took the impact of the tarmac. His feet were still clipped into the pedals. He blacked out instantly. The bike's titanium frame was cracked and his helmet was smashed. It absorbed a great deal of the force. The helmet probably saved his life. Passers-by pulled in and called the emergency services.

CONOR MURRAY

By amazing coincidence one of the first people on the scene was my cousin Lisa Woulfe who lives in Adare. Lisa rang my mum and then stayed with her uncle as he lay unconscious on the hard shoulder. She went with him in the ambulance to University Hospital Limerick. Mum was at work when she got the call. She headed straight to UHL. Dad was taken to Intensive Care where they sedated him and put him on a ventilator. The first scans confirmed what doctors already suspected: he had a serious brain injury.

In Carton House I told Faz the news and I imagine I was white as a ghost. I was in a state of shock, really. He told me to get on the road straightaway, I had to be with my family. It was a terrifying drive, I was sick with worry and fear of what I would see. At the hospital, I was taken to the room where Dad was being monitored and where Mum and my sisters Aisling and Sarah were sitting devastated. It was an awful sight to see him lying there with all these tubes hanging out of him and all these beeps going off on the electronic machinery around him. The whole scene was incredibly distressing.

We were told that his brain was swollen and he would have to be transferred to the neurosurgical centre in Cork University Hospital to get the highly specialised treatment he would need. Later that night he was wheeled out of UHL and taken to Cork. There he would be put into an induced coma in the hope that the swelling would abate. The next few days would be crucial.

We stayed overnight in the family room in CUH and the next afternoon I was seriously conflicted about leaving or staying. We had a family chat about it. Mum reckoned it was best I go back and rejoin the squad. We were all powerless to help at this stage and Dad would want me to be back with the team. So,

THE WELL

with the blessing of Mum and my sisters, I took my leave later that evening. I got back into my car and somewhere between Cork and Maynooth I burst into tears with the overwhelming shock of it all.

It was very hard to watch this strong, capable man who'd minded me and mentored me all my days, clinging on for dear life in that hospital bed. Like any good father, he'd been the centre of my universe for so long. It takes a lot of people along the way to mould you into a professional sportsman. But, generally, no one is more important than the people who nurture you from childhood and show you the true meaning of love and support. I am lucky to be able to say I had a secure and happy upbringing. Mum and Dad were there every step of the way for myself, Sarah and Aisling. We never lacked for anything. Dad was an electrician with the ESB all his working life, Mum was a pharmacist. They were known as Gerry and Barbara to everyone else. Between them they created a warm and stable home life for my sisters and me.

And, as luck would have it, I inherited some pretty strong sporting genes from them. On the rugby side, there was mum's father, Con Roche, and he must have passed on some of those athletic abilities to her because she ended up becoming a very accomplished squash player, having taken up the sport when she moved to Dublin to study pharmacy. It was a very competitive sport in Ireland back in the '80s apparently. When she moved back to Limerick she progressed into the Munster representative team and was good enough to get a trial for the national squad. She loved the game and continued playing it while working and bringing up a young family. She actually became a fully fledged Irish international at the over-40s level.

CONOR MURRAY

My granddad on the other side, William Murray, did a lot of what they called grass-track cycling back in the day. Dad tells me it was popular in rural Ireland and that William would compete in grass-track cycling events during sports days in places like Dromkeen and Castleisland. One of his sons, my uncle Michael, did a lot of road racing and won big local competitions like the Rás Luimní. He also competed in the big annual national event, the Rás Tailteann.

So, something must've come down to me from both sides because as soon as I could walk I was mad for running about the place. Then when they put a ball at my feet, I was mad for kicking it. And when I picked up a sliotar and hurley, I was mad for swinging at it. Rugby or hurling or soccer or Gaelic balls, I was always lashing them off walls or whatever target I could find. I remember Dad scotching me for knocking the paint off the garage walls and the varnish off the garage doors. He'd repaint them and revarnish them during the summer and by the following summer they'd be all grubby again from the sliotars and soccer balls and rugby balls.

Out on Lurriga Road, where our house is, on the way to the shops or to church, I'd have a hurley and sliotar with me or a rugby ball or a football and I'd be up and down the road all day playing kerbys or pucking the sliotar or throwing rugby passes. I'd use the streetlights for target practice, trying to throw the ball off the poles from mad distances or kick it off them or see if I could hit the light at the top.

We had a good-sized back garden and Dad built us soccer goals with metal uprights and crossbar and nets. My neighbouring friends would come round for matches. These were properly competitive. It could be three vs three or four vs four. There

THE WELL

was full-on horseplay. We'd be laying into each other. We'd be dunting and shouldering each other into the hedge or flying into the tackles, two-footed challenges and all. A few of us were very alpha and some of the other lads would be trying to calm us down. Like, "You're not in bloody Wembley." But I thought I was in Wembley! I never wanted these games to end. I'd get the hump if one or two of the lads were called in for their dinner because it would ruin the game.

I'd be giving out shite to them for leaving. I'd nearly make them stay. They'd be like, but it's pure dark, we're finished, let's go play PlayStation. And I'd run into Dad and get him to come out and turn his van around on the driveway so it would be facing down the garden and he could switch on the headlights. Now we could have floodlit games.

My cousin Gearóid Balfry lived straight across the road from me. He was a regular at these scrimmages in the back garden. We'd be playing music and my songs were usually upbeat, high-energy songs with empowering lyrics. I didn't notice this at the time but Gearóid said to me that I was always singing songs that were a bit cocky or that made me look good, like 'Everybody Wants to Rule the World' by Tears For Fears. I was a bit embarrassed when he pointed it out to me but years later when I was playing for Ireland, it was a childhood memory that I recounted to a sports psychologist and he thought it was a telling insight. He reckoned I might have been "manifesting" my future ambitions without knowing it at the time.

My folks were happy to let me at it. Mum and Dad weren't hovering over me watching my every move. They weren't planning a future career for me in professional sport. They supported me completely without ever being pushy. They didn't even think about steering me in one direction, like getting me to specialise in one sport. I played whatever I liked whenever I liked. When I started playing for teams they came to as many games as they could and stayed in the background.

I was tiny and skinny before I got a growth spurt in my mid-teens. In my second-to-last year at St Munchin's I was on the squad that won the Munster Senior Schools Cup in 2006, the team that Earlsy starred on, but I didn't get a minute of playing time in the cup games. In my Leaving Cert year I was on the team but we weren't competitive that season, although John Broderick as always did his best to get the most out of us. John was our Irish teacher in the classroom. In the dressing room, he really knew how to galvanise a team. He was my first proper experience of an emotional coach who could reach into your heart and get your blood pumping. I loved playing for him. Brian O'Donoghue taught us science. I distinctly remember Brian taking me aside one day in my final year and talking up my talent. He said I was the sort of player who was good enough to catch a ball if I only got my fingertips on it. Meaning, I think, that the game came easy to me. I wouldn't need my full hands around the ball to secure it, my fingertips would do. It was a nice little confidence booster at the time and it stuck with me. But outside of Munchin's no one in rugby was really showing me the love. I was selected for the Munster schools representative squad that year but didn't get any playing time in the inter-provincial games.

My teens were almost over before I began to emerge from the pack. In the spring of 2008, I was picked for the Ireland U19 team for a couple of friendlies against Italy and France. Pete O'Mahony captained that side. Jack McGrath and Ian McKinley and my good mate Andrew Burke were also in the team. At this

THE WELL

stage I was a first year at University of Limerick (UL) studying construction management, which I hated. I decided I'd transfer to a course in business risk analysis the following year. But in the meantime I got a significant phone call. It was the late summer of 2008. I was playing golf with my dad in Castletroy. I can remember exactly where I was. I was coming down the ramp off the 18th green. It was Ian Sherwin, manager of the Munster rugby academy.

He was like, "Conor, we'd like to offer you a full-time academy contract."

Oh. Great! Thank you very much; I'd be delighted. So, I hang up and Dad asks who it was and I tell him and I must've sounded pretty casual because he's saying, do you know how big this is? Or, do you understand that this is brilliant? It would take a lot to get my dad animated. And he was never one to pester you with questions about how you were getting on. But he was in great humour now and decided he'd bring the family out to dinner for a celebration.

I guess I didn't fully appreciate at the time that it was a hinge moment in my life. I was still going to be doing my college studies alongside my academy training. The big moment of excitement came for me a few weeks later when I went into the Munster office in UL to sign on the dotted line and they gave me a free laptop as part of my academy gear. And not just any old laptop but the white Apple MacBook which no one else had at the time. So, the next day I rocked up to my classes on campus with my white Apple MacBook, prominently displayed, thinking I was Johnny Big Balls.

Needless to say, I spent a lot more time looking at rugby on my computer than studying business risk analysis. Ian Sherwin and Ray Egan and Fergal O'Callaghan, our S&C coach, were the professors I learned from. Later came Greig Oliver and his mentoring.

My three years in the academy would be the making of me. I had the time and space to develop physically and technically. Psychologically I was more mature than I realised at the time. I was just blessed with a calm temperament. I didn't overthink things too much. I'd have nerves before games, but they wouldn't undermine me during games. I would just get into my rhythm and play. I didn't lose my composure.

Generally, I'd stay calm and practical. I wouldn't get rattled in pressure situations. Big occasions where there'd be good crowds didn't get to me either. At the time I didn't know anything about sports psychology so, being calm just happened to be my natural state. I was absolutely blessed to have that gift because mental strength is so important. It is the big unseen question about any young up-and-coming talent. Physically and technically they might be superstars but they won't make it unless they have the temperament.

I've seen some incredibly talented players who were constantly let down by their nerves, or by overthinking things and working themselves into stress balls. Then their natural talent would get suffocated. They wouldn't be able to do themselves justice. And, of course, the higher you go through the levels, the more your bottle is tested. A major international match in front of a packed stadium is a frightening prospect. Pretty much everyone who is facing into one is feeling the fear. I was no different that way. I felt the fear. But somehow my mind would go calm at kick-off and I'd play away. I was very lucky to have that gift right throughout my career.

THE WELL

It'd be hard to know exactly where it came from but some of it must have come down from my parents and their parents. By the time Mum and Dad handed me over to the Munster academy, I was as well prepared as any young fella could have been. They couldn't have done any more for me. And part of your training as a professional is developing your ability to compartmentalise your emotions. You can't wallow for too long after a painful defeat because you've to turn the page and move onto the next game. Likewise you can't get too high after big wins either. You'd end up emotionally drained all the time if you're constantly swinging from highs to lows and back again.

So, you keep it in check. You stay in balance. You stick to the process. It's a cliché because it's true. You stick to the process and compartmentalise your feelings.

When I got back to Carton House that night and turned up for training the next day, my dad still in critical, I turned on my rugby brain and prepared for France. I started against Scotland too and came off the bench against Italy and England. I'd been part of this 2023 Grand Slam campaign while getting updates several times a day every day from the hospital in Cork. On the one hand my head was full of information about our next opponents, our tactics, our set moves and the multiple rehearsals of our plans; on the other it was navigating the worry and fear about Dad's condition.

The medics had put him into an induced coma in the hope that the swelling in his brain would come down. They opened his cranium and inserted a pressure monitor which they supervised very closely for signs of improvement or deterioration. He had bleeds on the brain. If the pressure swelled further they would have to operate on him. The hope was that the bleeds would cease of their own accord without surgical intervention. Eventually, thank God, the swelling started to reduce. It was a ray of light in what was still a very dark tunnel. Because we didn't know how much the brain damage would affect the quality of his life afterwards. It could be permanent for all we knew. We would find out more once he was taken out of the coma.

After two and a half weeks, he was eased back to consciousness. Dad had no idea where he was when he woke up. He had no memory of the accident. He had to be told about it. He had to be told that he'd been comatose in Cork University Hospital for the last two and a half weeks. He had to learn how to walk all over again. His speech and hearing were badly affected. The wonderful physios in CUH began helping him to take baby steps with the support of a walking frame. He had to do speech therapy and occupational therapy every day. His memory and his cognitive skills were severely impaired. But I think a part of the old competitive cyclist was stirred in him.

He was determined to make any bit of progress he could. Incrementally, there were little improvements. They sent him to the shop in the hospital one day on his own to buy three items, find out the price of each item and report back to the therapist. He did everything that was asked of him. After four and a half weeks of amazing care and kindness from all the therapists, he was transferred to St Camillus' hospital in Limerick to continue his rehab. All the time his progress was being monitored by his neurosurgeon. After two weeks in Camillus' he came home. Very sadly for us all, he wasn't well enough to travel to Portugal that summer for our wedding.

We are profoundly grateful to the doctors and nurses and

THE WELL

therapists who saved his life and started his recovery. But it has been a long haul and, two years later, he and Mum continue to deal with the after-effects. The collision changed his life. He has lost his hearing completely in his left ear and has partial hearing damage in his right. He suffers from constant tinnitus. He still needs regular physio for pain in his shoulder, elbow and wrist. His basic walking mobility is compromised. He can lose his balance if he gets off a seat too quickly. He loved his golf and going to rugby matches and now cannot do either. He has to avoid crowds because the noise aggravates the tinnitus.

There's also the psychological trauma of it all. It hurts me to see the quality of his life affected so much, at a time when he should be enjoying his leisure time, his retirement, and the fun with his two baby grandchildren. A lot of people have said to him since that he's a lucky man. Yes, maybe there was a degree of luck involved in surviving the impact at all. But it should never have happened. He didn't contribute in any way to that collision. He was in the wrong place at the wrong time and has paid a very heavy price. I think he was extremely unlucky.

In May 2025, the driver of the truck was sentenced to ten months in prison for careless driving causing serious bodily harm. The same person had been convicted of careless driving as recently as 2021. He had a previous conviction for drink-driving and another earlier conviction for a hit-and-run incident.

Dad has got back on the bike. I mean literally, he has got back on his bike and taken it out on the local greenway, away from traffic and motorways. There have been a few wobbles, he tells me, and his Stephen Roche days are definitely over. But we have to count our blessings too. At their last consultation, the neurosurgeon told him that when he first saw him unconscious in the hospital bed, he didn't think the day would come when he'd see Gerry sitting across the table from him and on the mend. He showed Dad two MRI scans side by side: the one they'd taken just an hour earlier that showed a clear brain and the very first one after the accident, which Dad says was like a starburst of brain cells. Everyone involved in his care had done the most incredible job to save him and us from a terrible outcome. We will never be able to thank them enough.

Dad is determined to get as well as he can in order to have the best quality of life for himself and Mum and his children and grandchildren. They have been through the mill, but they are two troupers. In my game we talk about resilience a lot. It is really important and I've been lucky enough to have a fair amount of it too. In the last two years I've seen exactly where I got it from. Sport is sport, but life is life and it is precious beyond words.

Chapter Three

CON ROCHE

YOU KNOW YOU'RE MOVING UP in the world when you can hand in your Ford Focus for an Audi. We're talking an Audi A1 here, not the top-end models, but I'm 21 and it's a brand-spanking new set of wheels. Even better, it's free. It's my first sponsored car. All the big names in Irish rugby have a sponsored car and I have mine now too.

Mind you, I loved my Ford Focus. It was the first car I bought with my own money. It was the 2010/2011 season and I was on a development contract with Munster, thirty grand a year if memory serves. It was a blue Focus; I had the Lexus lights put in, the boy-racer lights; I had the alloys and the go-faster stripes. All the lads in Patrickswell had cars like that, we were well into our wheels. Anyway, when the offer of the Audi A1 came in, sadly the Focus had to go. You can't get too sentimental in this business!

I was like a kid in a candy shop in those years. It was all happening and it was happening faster than I'd ever imagined it would.

I'd made my Munster senior debut in a pre-season friendly against Sale Sharks in August 2009 at Musgrave Park. The team were mainly academy players with a sprinkling of older hands.

I was 20, I replaced Toby Morland with ten minutes left in the game. They put me back in cold storage for the next eight months.

On 18th April 2010, I made my competitive debut against Connacht at the Sportsground in the Magners League. It was more a cameo than a debut, to be fair, a two-minute blood sub for Strings early in the second half. Three other rookies made their competitive debuts for us the same day – Simon Zebo, Danny Barnes and Declan Cusack. Declan was one of my house mates in a gaff we were sharing in Fr Russell Road in Raheen at the time with a few other up-and-coming Munster renegades; Dave Kilcoyne, Mike Sherry and Paddy Butler. Christ almighty, the craic we had in that place. We were young, free and single. We were all living the dream. We were professional sportsmen; we were getting paid to do the thing we loved, and a lot of our money was invested very wisely in pizzas, pubbing and clubbing – the proverbial wine, women and song. Then we squandered the rest of it, as George Best might have said.

My 21st birthday would be two days after the Connacht game – 20th April, a Tuesday. So, I got home to Patrickswell from Galway on the Sunday night and opened the door, only to find all my family and friends there, waiting to lay on a birthday party for me. "Surprise!" A load of the Munster lads were there too and, of course, the messing began when the beer started flowing.

I've always been the neat-and-tidy type; I like to have things orderly and stored away in their proper place. My bedroom was impeccable, so naturally nothing would do the lads only to turn it upside down. They were pulling clothes out of drawers and shirts off hangers and throwing them everywhere and for good measure, they took to signing their autographs on the wooden door of my wardrobe. Then came the moment for my big birthday present and all the lads were like, "It's a car! Has to be a car." I didn't have my own wheels at this stage. So, we're all gathered on the patio outside by the garden, but there's no sign of a car. Instead, there's a magician and I have to stand there and partake in all these various tricks he's pulling and it's all a bit corny. The lads can see I'm fairly underwhelmed by the whole thing and they're slagging me wholesale. In fact, the bloody slagging about the magician lasted for years. I got myself my own transport not long afterwards.

At this stage I was just another young contender, really. There were loads of us about and I wasn't anything special; I didn't necessarily stand out, and I didn't have the star quality that say an Earlsy had when he was coming through from schoolboys. But I was developing; I was consistently improving. In terms of the pecking order, though, I was way behind Stringer and Tomás O'Leary. Or so I thought anyway.

Strings was a Munster and Ireland legend, Tomás had several international caps. I was still playing a lot of club rugby with Garryowen. Toby Morland had come over from New Zealand on a short-term contract to cover for the two lads and was gone by Christmas. Duncan Williams was next in line to Tomás and Strings. Duncan was three years older than me. He'd been a schoolboys star too. He was an unbelievably talented scrumhalf, he had a repertoire of skills in training that I could only dream about.

So, as far as I was concerned, I was at best fourth choice. I knew my place in the hierarchy of nines and actually, I wasn't chomping at the bit, I wasn't making a big song and dance about trying to take their place. That's not who I am and it's not how it works anyway. Coaches see everything. You don't have to be in everyone's face going, look at me, look at me. Nobody likes the class swot anyway. And I was by nature fairly reserved and self-contained. I was just trying to be a good pro every day. But I was a learner, I was a developer; I was coachable, I would listen, and I kept getting physically stronger. The coaches probably saw the potential in me better than I myself did at the time.

I should say that while I was quiet, I wasn't a pushover either. Like, if I made a mistake in training and one of the established players gave me a bollocking, I'd generally take it without firing back because I'd know that they were making a valid point. And these fellas had the caps and the medals to back up what they were saying. Still and all, you have to stand your ground the odd time. Like the day down in the Cork Institute of Technology when we were training on the sports campus there. It's now the Munster Technological University of Cork.

Anyway, we had this set play where a pod of three forwards would come round the corner to take a pass off the nine. But the scrumhalf was always supposed to throw his pass to the middle man of the three. Then the fellas on either side of him could ruck in behind him properly. That was the move.

That day, two of the three were Paulie and Donners. And Paulie, of course, was famous for his attention to detail, he was an absolute stickler for detail: "You're hitting the middle man and we're going two rucks in." So, the three lads come round the corner off me and Paulie was the first fella, not the middle fella and, in my youthful wisdom, I decide to throw the pass to him because I reckon he's in more space. And because he's not expecting it, he drops it. And he goes fuckin' ballistic!

CON ROCHE

Just imagine his deep voice here as he goes nuclear. "The fuckin' middle man, you fuckin' bleep bleep bleep!" I have to bleep him out here! "The fuckin' middle man! How many times do I have to fuckin' say it?"

There's an awkward silence as everyone else looks down at their boots. But, out of nowhere, I find myself firing back at him,

"Yeah, but you can still catch the fuckin' ball." Jesus. It was out of my mouth before I knew it. I've no idea where it came from.

In hindsight, it probably shows I had a streak of steel in me that I usually kept well hidden, even from myself.

Soon as I said it I was thinking, uh oh, I'm probably going to get a dig in the head here now. I was shitting myself. I was shocked that I'd said it. I turned and walked away.

Paulie said nothing back; no one said anything, and everyone moved on to the next set play. Later, Donners came over to me and said something like, "Well done, kid." Because ultimately I think senior pros will respect you more if you stand up for yourself, Paulie included. It's one way of showing them that you have a bit of moxie about you. When someone from the opposition team is trying to take your head off for real, your team mates will know that you have a bit of gumption about you.

Knowing the man as I do now, I'd imagine Paulie, when he cooled down, just thought, fair enough, yeah, I did knock it on. Anyway, he took it on the chin and we got back down to work. These flare-ups are ten a penny on a training ground where there's all this testosterone and ambition flying about. I just happen to remember that one because I was so young and it properly rattled me and I learned a lesson from it.

I might as well throw in another similar yarn here while I'm at it, also back from the days when I thought boy-racer lights on a Ford Focus were a good idea.

It was February 2011, we were playing Aironi at their place in Viadana in the Magners. I replace Duncan in the 52nd minute, Quinny replaces Ian Nagle in the 58th. It was a terrible match in wet conditions in front of a tiny crowd. We were making hard work of it but more or less had the game put to bed by the last quarter.

Quinny at this stage is near the end of his career and he has nothing left to prove. I'm just a whippersnapper with everything still to prove. So, naturally, he takes exception when I don't pass him the ball. This is very late in the game, the result is in the bag, but being the grumpy bollocks he is, Quinny's not happy with me.

As I recall, we're going down the blindside and he has his hand up for the ball but I throw it to someone else and there's a knock-on or a turnover or something; I can't remember. But it doesn't matter because it's a shit game in shit conditions and it's practically full-time. But it matters to Quinny!

The ref blows full-time and Quinny is straightaway over to me, growling, "Just give me the ball when I've my hand out," he says in his worst pissed-off voice.

And this time I actually give myself a second to think before I reply. I decide I'm not taking it. So, I'm like, "You weren't the right option. Why should I give you the ball there?"

"You have to get the ball into my hands," he said.

I'm thinking, no I don't. I'm here to play my game, I'm not here to please you. And sometimes, when you pick up a ball on the blindside, you see the nearest opponent shooting up to tackle the player that's the obvious choice for your next pass. So, if you see that happening, you don't make that pass. In this situation I could see the tackle on Quinny was coming but maybe Quinny couldn't because he was looking at me to get the ball. So, I skip him and give it to the next fella and he's maybe tackled into touch or runs it into touch and the ref blows the final whistle.

"Why didn't you give it to me?"

"Because you were marked, fuck off." I felt I was within my rights. In fact, I was a little bit proud of myself that I didn't back down. I know it's only a tiny incident in the grander scheme of things, but looking back now, I can see it as a little marker that shows me going from being a young, insecure apprentice to being a proper grown-up who can stand his own ground. That's all it is, really, but I think they're significant developments in your mindset when you're young and still not sure of your place in an environment like this.

My career is on the cusp of major change over the next few weeks following that match. But on that day in Italy, I didn't know that. Far as I'm concerned, I'm still well down the food chain. I'm still only getting bits and pieces of game time. The most exciting thing to happen to me so far that season is an appearance against an Australian XV in Thomond Park in November. And it's only a friendly and I only get two minutes.

But it has a special significance for my family because Con Roche, my granddad, my mother's father, played for Munster against Australia in a famous game at the Mardyke in Cork in December 1947. The rugby writer and historian Edmund Van Esbeck was there that day. He recalled, "the heartbreak of seeing Munster put up a magnificent display before losing the match in the last minute, having led 5-3 before the Wallabies scored a try to steal the game." He added, "That was really the afternoon when Munster laid down the example that future generations of Munster teams would follow so gloriously in the years to come."

Here in 2010, I was lucky enough to be a member of the latest Munster generation to inherit that tradition passed on by players such as my granddad.

Con played second row, or number eight. He grew up in Cobh but moved to Limerick for work and that's where he met and married Joan Gleeson from the city. He joined Garryowen RFC and became a lifelong member of the club. He was part of the Garryowen team that had won the Munster Senior Cup earlier in 1947, which paved the way for his selection on the Munster side to face the touring Australians.

He got a final trial for Ireland but was never capped. I know he was proud to see his grandson follow in his footsteps 63 years later. We have a framed double photo at home, one in black-and-white from the 1947 game and one in colour from the 2010 match. I only got two minutes, but it meant a lot to him and to our family. It was the story coming full circle, I suppose.

Con died fourteen months later at the age of 88. But he had lived long enough to see me getting capped for Munster and Ireland and it means a lot to me to know that it made him happy in his final days.

On the same day we were slogging it out on that filthy afternoon against Aironi, Ireland were playing Scotland at Murrayfield. Eoin Reddan started at nine for Ireland and with Tomás carrying an injury, Strings was on the bench and came on in the second half. Ireland would play Wales in Round 4 of the Six Nations a fortnight later.

CON ROCHE

On the weekend in between, Munster would be playing Newport Gwent Dragons at Musgrave Park. Strings was back with us for this game but with Tomás still out, I assumed I'd be on the bench. But I was picked to start.

I made my full competitive Munster debut that day, 5th March 2011, six weeks before my 22nd birthday. We won handy; Doug Howlett scored two tries, I think I did fine, Strings replaced me in the 57th minute. I held my starting spot for the Cardiff Blues two weeks later. But it was the match a week after that, against Leinster at Thomond on 2nd April, that probably turned the page on my career.

Obviously, this was the big derby game and all our internationals were back in harness. So, I'm assuming that for such a major fixture, Dumper will go with the tried and trusted. Tomás had picked up a nasty eye injury in Ireland camp, so I wasn't sure whether he'd be available or not. But I was pretty sure that Strings would be back at nine.

That week we've a training day down in CIT and we're out on the running track about to do a walk-through and I'm just standing to one side with Sherry and a few other academy lads. Then Dumper names the team right there: Jones, Howlett, Murphy, Mafi, Earls, O'Gara, Murray, Wian du Preez, Damien Varley, Tony Buckley... And I was like, oh shit, I'm starting; I'm in.

The previous Leinster fixture that season was in October, with a crowd of over 50,000 at the Aviva. I watched that one in my street clothes. I travelled up to it with my girlfriend at the time and we had seats way up high and I was blown away by the whole occasion. I just loved every part of it. But I couldn't imagine myself being part of an occasion like that. It still wasn't on my horizon. Tomás started at nine that day. For some reason, I can still remember the lovely white boots he was wearing. Now, exactly six months later, I'm starting the return fixture in what's going to be a full house at Thomond Park. Christ, I better get my ass in gear. The lads have to remind me to join the first team for the walk-through to rehearse all our moves and set plays.

The place is heaving; I'm a bag of nerves, but I'm not frightened out of my wits either. When the game starts, I go into automatic mode and follow the play and do my job. Isaac Boss is my opposite number; Redser is on the bench for them. Leinster are absolutely stacked with famous names: Horgan, O'Driscoll, D'Arcy, Sexton, Healy, O'Brien, Heaslip.

We have a few marquee names ourselves and one of them, RoG, of course, nails the winning penalty with just a few minutes to go. A week later we're away to Brive on a roasting hot day. Management must've thought I did okay because I'm starting this one too. It's the Amlin Challenge Cup quarter-final; we'd been knocked out of the Heineken Cup by Toulon in the group stage in January.

The Brive game is bedlam and between the heat and the speed of play, I've never been so physically wrecked in my life. Fitness-wise I'm fine, but I just don't have the stamina in the legs that you get after a couple of seasons at this level. I'm hooked after 48 minutes. They take me out of the firing line altogether for the next game, away to Scarlets, with Strings starting and Duncan coming on in the second half. I'm back in for the next one against Ospreys and last an hour. Then it's Harlequins in the Amlin Cup semi-final, where they rock up to Thomond Park and they do a proper number on us. Strings and Tomás are back for the following match with Connacht, so it looks like Dumper

CON ROCHE

is holding me in reserve for the Magners League semi-final, against Ospreys again, a week later. Sure enough, I'm in for that one. So, the penny is starting to drop with me now: apparently, I'm the number one choice at scrumhalf for Munster.

A few days before the semi-final, I decide to treat myself to a new pair of boots. I'm absolutely buzzing with all the excitement of the previous weeks. So, I go into a sports shop in town and purchase a class-looking pair of white Adidas soccer boots. A week later I'll be inundated with free boots from Adidas, but for now, I'm happy to have these boy-racer boots.

On the Friday, I arrive at the dressing room in Thomond for the captain's run. I'm early and RoG is sitting at his locker next to me. But just as I'm taking my gear out of my bag, a red warning light goes off in my head. I'm looking at my white boots and the thought strikes me that if I produce these now, RoG is gonna think I'm a bit of a flash wanker with my fancy white boots. My antennae have shot up – I know I'm going to get a ferocious slagging if he sees them. So, I keep them in my bag and tog out. I put on my runners and smuggle the boots out under my tracksuit top and head onto the pitch where I very discreetly start smearing them all over with mud. Job done, or so I think. I head back in, take off the runners, put on the boots and RoG takes one look at them and goes, real droll, "New boots, is it?"

The dressing room is filling up at this stage and Paulie hears RoG's remark and suddenly he's looking at them too. Christ almighty, you can get away with nothing in this dressing room, absolutely nothing! The lads have called my bluff, totally outed me.

Paulie is like, "Jaysus, you're only in the door a couple of weeks and you're already wearing white boots!" I was morto,

I could feel myself going red. I should've known there was no fooling fellas like that.

I survived with the white boots and was retained for the Magners League final – our third clash with Leinster that season. Leinster had pulled off a stunning comeback to win the Heineken Cup against Northampton a week earlier, so we'd a fair idea they'd be mentally a bit vulnerable coming to Thomond. We planned our ambush accordingly and won it fairly decisively in the end. I was kept on for the full 80. Less than three months after making my full competitive debut, I was winning silverware with the team I'd dreamt of playing for since I was a kid.

Funnily enough, a standout memory I have from that match is a mistake before half-time. We're going down the blindside and there's an incident at a ruck and we have a penalty and I notice that Redser is standing at pillar for them, querying the ref's decision. He's a bit distracted so I just tap and go and barge through him and I have a linebreak. Dougie is on my outside and he has 20 or 30 metres of clear space in front of him – the try is on if I pass it. And if I was a few years older and wiser, I'd have whipped it out to him, but I'm raw and giddy, so I try to dummy the next defender and it doesn't work and the chance goes abegging. Dougie didn't give me a bollocking, although he was well entitled to. He wouldn't be that type; he'd be more the type to go like, don't worry about it. He knew that I knew. What a legend.

In fairness to myself, I did play well in that game. It was probably my coming-of-age performance. I was just involved all the time. I was making tackles, getting my hands on a lot of ball, sniping and probing. I was generally feeling every bit the equal of anyone else on the pitch, no matter how famous they were.

It was during these final three months of the 2010/11 season that I fell head over heels in love with this whole new scene. I mean, I was playing the same sport I'd always played, but everything just went up to a different level when you broke into the first team. You felt you were in the big time and I was absolutely relishing every second of it. It was all new to me and the more of it I sampled, the more I was like, bring it on.

Every week I was coming up against fellas who were household names in rugby union. At scrumhalf, I was coming up against the likes of Danny Care, Rhys Webb and Mike Phillips, my hero and role model as a nine. I genuinely didn't feel any imposter syndrome either. Every day spent on the training ground with the first team, I felt a little more comfortable in myself and my surroundings. I was finding out that I had the temperament to cope with big crowds and big occasions. I was definitely very nervous but never overawed.

Once the game kicked off, I would get down to work. I found I could concentrate on the nuts and bolts of the job without overthinking it. And after the Magners League final, I knew for certain I belonged at that level. It was proof that I'd earned my right to be there.

I look back and see photos of the celebrations afterwards and there's poor old Paul Darbyshire there in his wheelchair. Paul was our S&C coach, but by this stage he was suffering terribly from motor neurone disease. He died only three weeks later. I remember Paul fondly because the previous season, I was on the bench for a game alongside my good mates Andrew Burke and Dave Foley. And Paul pulls the three of us aside outside the dressing room in the Cardiff Arms Park and, in his no-nonsense north of England accent, he gives us a rousing pep talk.

"Lads, don't wait until after this game to realise you're good enough to be here. The three of ye are here because ye're fucking good enough to be here – and don't you forget it."

It was class. It filled us with belief in ourselves. That moment has stayed with me, not because of what happened to Paul afterwards but because of what he said to us that day and the way he said it. I will always remember him for that.

Chapter Four

PHONE CALLS FROM DECLAN

THE PHONE RINGS AND IT'S Declan Kidney on the other end. I've never met him and I don't know him, but I know his voice from all the times I've heard him interviewed on TV and radio. I recognise the Cork lilt straightaway. I can't remember where I was, but I'm certain I stopped whatever I was doing. This was the Ireland head coach ringing me in person. And he's asking me if I'd like to join them in camp at Carton House. Would I what?

This is the beginning of August 2011. I've just about come down from the buzz of winning the Magners League two months earlier. I've had a holiday in Ayia Napa with the lads and I'm back in pre-season training with Munster. I am more than happy with my lot. But now Declan Kidney is inviting me to a training camp with the international squad. And it's not just any old training camp because this is the start of the countdown to the 2011 Rugby World Cup.

Now, I'm not getting ahead of myself. I'm definitely not, because I reckon there were at least four scrumhalves ahead of me in the pecking order, maybe more. And just in case I would be in danger of getting ahead of myself, Deccie immediately tamps down any excitement on my part.

"It's just for a bit of experience," he adds, "see how you like it, see how you get on in training with the lads."

In other words, I'm not promising you anything; you'd probably be better off not to be making any assumptions at this stage. I'd learn in the coming months that that was his style anyway – keep everything low-key and understated. It suited me fine.

But you can't contain other people's excitement and, naturally, my family and friends are delighted with the news. I'm a mixture of anticipation and nerves. The nerves get worse as I set out on the road from Limerick. This is a whole new world I'm entering into; I'll know the Munster lads, of course, but this is another level altogether.

Carton House would become a kind of home away from home for me over the next fourteen years, but I distinctly remember coming into the long driveway that first day with a knot in my stomach. I'm driving past the golf club and I see a load of these famous Irish internationals standing around in their sunglasses shooting the breeze. I come into the car park and there's all these big jeeps and luxury cars that obviously belong to the players and here's me tipping along in my little Audi A1.

I am genuinely daunted by the scenario around me. Basically, I am driving into the big-time here and I find it scary. In fact, the thought goes through my head that if Deccie was to ring me up right now and tell me he's changed his mind, I'd be quite happy to turn around and go home. In my mind, I'm like, I've only started eight senior games for Munster. I'm red raw. I don't have the experience, it's too big a step up.

PHONE CALLS FROM DECLAN

All those doubts are swirling around as I park up and open the boot and gather my gear. It's why, from that day to this, I've always been conscious of new lads landing into camp and making an effort to try and be friendly with them. I've seen loads of rookies arrive over the years and some of them are like deer in the headlights, trying to navigate this environment.

It's a huge deal for them. They're meeting fellas they've only seen on television, famous players that they've maybe looked up to – and now they're supposed to be their team mates. I was unbelievably nervous. And, in fairness to Drico, he was one of the first to greet me in the function room. He actually complimented me on my performance in the Magners final, which was a lovely boost to my confidence. Then other lads drifted over for a handshake and a bit of small talk and I started to relax a bit.

Deccie was very considerate too. He made time for a little one-on-one chat. He was a nice man, emotionally intelligent, and with a good perspective on life, not just rugby. He'd ask you what you were doing outside the game, if you were studying, and what your plans were. He was good for conversations like that and throwing in a few funny analogies and observations. Deccie was a very smart man who cared about you as a person as well as a player.

The first game in the schedule of friendlies that August was Scotland at Murrayfield. I was brought over as cover, a non-playing reserve. Tomás was the starting nine; Bossy was on the bench and got the last 20 minutes. We lost 10-6.

Back in the dressing room I happened to be sitting beside Bossy. We got on well; he was a nice fella and I liked him. We're chatting away about the game and then he says something like,

"That'll be you out there soon, man." I remember him saying it because I was a bit startled when he said it. I wasn't thinking in those terms at all. I just didn't believe him. I just assumed I wasn't seriously in contention.

That evening at Edinburgh airport we're waiting for our flight when Deccie ambles over to me – or was it his assistant Les Kiss? – I can't quite remember. Anyway, one of them comes over and mentions something about having my passport ready for travelling because I won't be going back to Munster that week. We're playing France in Bordeaux the following weekend. It's a brief conversation and I rejoin the Munster crew.

Mick O'Driscoll asks me what was said there and I tell him and he's like, "That's your first cap next week." Just like that. "You'll be playing next weekend."

"I don't think so," I say, because in my head Tomás and Redser and Strings and Bossy are still ahead of me in the queue.

Mind you, I am going well in training; I'm actually flying it. There's no pressure on me at all. Sure enough, the team and subs are named later that week and I'm on the bench. Redser starts and I come on for my Ireland debut with 20 minutes to play. It's the 13th August 2011.

The atmosphere in the Stade Chaban-Delmas is unreal. You can hear it and feel it in the dressing rooms underneath. There's an awful long walk through this tunnel to get to the pitch. The two teams line up side by side before we begin the walk. I'm down the back and I'm doing a bit of star-gazing: there's Imanol Harinordoquy, Thierry Dusautoir, Vincent Clerc, Francois Trinh-Duc, Damien Traille. And there's Dimitri Yachvili, a world-class scrumhalf who is like a movie star to me. He's one of my favourite players. And there he is, just down the corridor.

PHONE CALLS FROM DECLAN

Man, this is incredible that I'm standing here beside them. The buzz of it all has lit me up properly inside. The national anthems are another goosebump moment, especially when three French fighter jets do a flypast trailing red, white and blue smoke out of their engines. In fact, I'm enjoying it so much I start smiling during the singing of the anthems. I know that all my friends and family will be watching back at home and it's just my way of saying, I'm all good here, I'm grand, don't be worrying. They got the message too, because they told me all about it when I got home. We lost the game. I don't remember much about it, but I do remember thinking afterwards that I've got an international cap now. It's nailed down; it can't be taken away. I've achieved that much at least.

The coaches have another look at me five days later in Donnybrook, an Ireland XV against a Connacht selection. Bossy starts and I get 33 minutes. Then I'm released to go back training with Munster. I'm back in Limerick when Deccie rings me to confirm there won't be a place for me in the World Cup squad. He says I've acquitted myself really well, I've got great exposure to this level and it will stand me in good stead.

I'm like, fair enough. I hadn't got ahead of myself anyway. I wasn't dreaming about World Cups. I just knew my place in the pecking order. So, I'm happy to bank the experience and pick up where I've left off with Munster.

On the Saturday, Ireland play France in the return friendly at the Aviva. I watch it on the telly with my house mates in Raheen. Ireland are beaten again and the general consensus is that this pre-tournament dress rehearsal is not going well at all. The bad omens continue when Felix Jones picks up a nasty foot injury that rules him out of the World Cup. And Tomás is struggling with his form too in this game. He throws a pass and it's intercepted for a try and he's replaced by Redser after 53 minutes. Straightaway I get a text from Seán Scanlon, my friend and team mate in the Munster academy.

"Keep your phone on," it says. But he doesn't know that I've already got a call from Deccie telling me I'm out of the reckoning. In my mind the decision is done and dusted. So, I go out on the town in Limerick that night with the lads.

Sunday morning I'm lying in bed recovering when the phone rings. Bloody hell, it's Declan Kidney again! Declan Cusack is in the bedroom next door to mine and I can hear him rumbling around, so I shuffle over to the window to try and get out of earshot.

Deccie's like, "How're you getting on?"

"Grand, thanks."

"Listen, there's been a slight change of plan. You're going to the World Cup."

Oh. Right. Jeez. Thanks a million. Feckin' hell. Okay.

"I know I phoned you last week, but . . ." But they've obviously had a rethink after the game the night before and Tomás is out and I am in.

I presume that Tomás has already got the devastating news. Him and Felix, it's devastating for them both. I know it is the nature of our profession and you eventually become hardened to it, but at the time I feel for Tomás because he has been nice to me since I was in the academy and I get on very well with him. I get on very well with Bossy and Redser too.

We're all competitive with each other, of course, but a bit like the goalkeepers' union in soccer, there's a bit of a scrumhalves' union too. It's a highly specialised job, so we have that connection

PHONE CALLS FROM DECLAN

in common. We speak the same language. Despite that, I have to be honest and say that me and Strings don't really have much of a relationship, not at the time and not since.

Deccie gives me the logistics down the phone: we're playing England next weekend, can you come up to camp tonight? As soon as the call ends, a big roar goes up from the room next door. Cusack, of course, has been listening in and got the gist of it.

"You're going to the World Cup, kid! Woo hoo!"

So, I run into his room and we're hugging and yelping and next thing I've a load of calls to make to reveal the good news. Then I scramble to get all my clothes and my gear together and head out on the M7 for Carton House, feeling a lot less dread about the journey this time.

The next day, the squad is publicly announced and my name is there in black-and-white. I'm in. I'm the bolter of the squad, the fella who is the surprise selection, the one that very few people see coming. But I'm not on the plane yet. First there's the England game the following weekend and you're never on the plane until you're actually on the plane. I'm selected for the bench, which means I will probably be getting some game time and you never know when bad luck will strike. Felix has already been on the receiving end of this desperate bloody lottery and in the England game it strikes again when David Wallace is horsed into touch by Manu Tuilagi and has his knee blown out in the process.

I get on for the last 18 minutes and come through unscathed. That's on the Saturday. The following Tuesday we pack up our bags in Carton House and are bussed to Dublin airport for the long haul to New Zealand. I board the plane along with the 29 other chosen ones and all my Christmases have come together.

It's my first time flying long-distance anywhere and my first time flying business class. One of the things I've discovered over the previous month is that you are incredibly well looked after inside this elite-level bubble. You are pampered and privileged. Everything is taken care of for you. It must be like a glimpse into the world of pop stars and movie stars. You are surrounded by luxury and prestige and people who are looking after your every need. You are treated like royalty, albeit that royalty and rock stars don't get mown down by the likes of Manu Tuilagi when they're going about their work, I suppose.

Queenstown on the South Island is our first base. The scenery, the mountains and lakes all around it, is stunning. There's loads of water sports and skiing and hiking and plenty of bars and restaurants for the tourists and backpackers. We get down to our training, but there's space in the itinerary for a few nights out as well. And the first night we're out, I remember a gang of us walking down the street and Besty turning round to me and going, "You haven't had your first-cap drinks yet, have you?!"

I'd been presented with my first cap at the post-match meal by some committee gent from the French rugby federation, but there was no ceremony or speeches or anything. Then we flew home, so there was no time to wet the baby's head in Bordeaux.

When I look back on photos from that time I'm still a bit baby-faced and I suppose Besty and the lads are figuring they'll have a bit of craic plying the rookie with drink. It's a time-honoured ritual and the rookie has to play along with it. I'm not averse to a few pints by any means, but nothing will do the lads only to get me properly shit-faced. So, we settle into a bar and Drico, the

PHONE CALLS FROM DECLAN

captain, gets me the first one – a glass of red wine. And there's no sipping allowed. I have to down it in one go. Then Paulie gets me a tequila – down the hatch too. And one by one they line up the glasses in front of me and one by one I knock them back.

A few hours later I am upside down. I've been into the jacks a few times for the old technicolour rainbow. Anyway, we roll onto another few bars and end up in a nightclub where I get chatting to a bunch of Kiwis, all mad into their rugby. At closing time they tell me they're going to a house party and would I like to come? At this stage I barely know my own name so whatever bit of common sense I have is long gone out the window. A party, you say? Sure why not. And I end up in this house up the mountain where the drinking and music goes on 'til first light.

I nod off for a few hours and wake up, still bladdered but suddenly in a panic. I've to get back to the team hotel pronto. But there's no one around except one of the fellas who lives there, so how the hell am I going to get back down the mountain? And it's only now I begin to realise that we are way up the mountain, very high up indeed. There's no public transport up here, that's for sure.

"Well there's a car in the garage; I can drop you back."

Fair enough. The descent down the mountain is like something you'd see in the Tour de France. We get into Queenstown, he parks up in a parking bay across from the hotel, I sneak into my room and conk out for the day. The next morning I'm up for training, right as rain, mad for action. Your system can take any amount of punishment at that age and bounce back, no bother at all.

Our first match is against the United States at Stadium Taranaki in New Plymouth on 11th September. The team and subs will be announced at a squad meeting a few days before. As we're gathering for the meeting, Deccie just casually hands me the laser pointer that they use for these PowerPoint presentations. Usually it's the outhalf who goes through the menu of plays – lineouts, scrums, moves, phases etc. And I'm looking at him and he's like, "Just go through the menu."

That was Deccie, he liked to do things like that to keep you on your toes, or say something a bit out of left-field. And this was his way of telling me that I was in the team. He hadn't announced it, but that was the hint he was dropping to me.

I had about five minutes prep before the meeting started. All of a sudden I was rattling with nerves. I'm a young lad surrounded by all these legends and veterans. Needless to say, I made a balls of it. I stayed sitting in my chair, pointing the laser at the screen and going, "These are the lineouts, these are the scrum moves, blah blah blah." Then Deccie announces the first fifteen and the bench and sure enough, I'm in from the start. It's my third cap and first start in an Irish jersey. As we got on the bus afterwards Geordan Murphy came over to me joking, asking how my hands were because they'd been shaking so much when I was aiming the laser pointer at the screen.

It's pissing rain that night in the Taranaki and we don't play well, but we eventually get the job done against a USA team managed by Eddie O'Sullivan. I played well enough and made a couple of half breaks. At one stage, we had a move in midfield, I went back to the blindside and threw a ball to Stephen Ferris standing on the touchline. Except it wasn't Stephen Ferris, it was the touch judge. I got my wires crossed. It must've been all the rain. Or maybe I just hadn't gotten over the fright with the laser pointer.

PHONE CALLS FROM DECLAN

Next up is the big clash of the pool, Ireland against Australia at Eden Park. Redser is recalled to start and I'm on the bench. My mother and my sister Sarah make the long haul out to be there. Australia were favourites, but our forwards smashed them up front and laid the foundations for a famous win. I get on with 22 minutes left. We're leading 15-6 with time almost up when I get my moment of glory. Tommy Bowe has just made an intercept nearly under our posts and gone 90 metres before he's tackled into touch. The Aussies have to go the length of the field if they're to score and they're trying to break out ten metres from their own line when Jamie Heaslip rips the ball out and it pops up into my hands. I throw a nice shimmy to step the tackler in front of me and leave him for dead.

It's just a run and a dive into the corner now and the massive Irish crowd in the stadium erupts. Donncha Ryan and Seán Cronin are standing in their bibs in the in-goal area and they're hugging me when I hear the bloody sound of Bryce Lawrence's whistle. Well, fuck it anyway. Bryce has cut me off in my prime. He's penalised Jamie and it's a penalty to Australia. Christ, it would have been so sweet, that try. I am denied my Hollywood moment. I still think of it as the one that got away. But it's not all bad, I suppose, because the coaches will have seen it and filed it away as something I have in my locker. Anyway, a famous victory and a famous night in Auckland with the Irish, my mum and sister included. Happy days.

We play Russia in Rotorua and I'm rooming with Earlsy this week. I get the word that I'm not going to be involved in this match; Bossy is going to start and Redser is on the bench. A lot of the frontline players are also rested. Anyone not involved has permission to go out the night before the game. So, of course, we give it a good lash and I don't get back until three or four in the morning. I'm creeping into the bedroom trying not to wake Earlsy up, but naturally, I make a noise despite myself and suddenly Earlsy is wide awake and shouting at me, "Go to sleep, you dope!" The vexed head on Earlsy has me in stitches. I nearly had a seizure from the laughing. It can't have done him too much harm because he scores two tries against the Russians anyway.

The significant news out of this match, is that RoG starts and Johnny is on the bench. The two lads have been battling it out for the ten jersey. The rivalry between them is getting huge coverage in the newspapers and on the radio shows. Johnny is the coming man; in fact, he's in pole position going into the World Cup, but RoG is not giving it up without a fight.

In my later years I've come to admire him even more for the attitude he brought at the time because I can identify with it now. The international jersey is precious; it's the ultimate honour, it means the world to everyone who gets to wear it. I've had my own battles to hold onto the jersey in the autumn of my career, so I can understand more than ever why RoG wouldn't give up the fight back then.

RoG starts against Italy in the final pool game in Dunedin, and so do I. Bear in mind that this is all still a dream to me. I haven't woken up. I'm living some sort of boyhood fantasy here. I am having the absolute time of my life. With every passing day, I feel more and more like I'm one of the lads, a proper member of a squad that includes all-time greats, and they are treating me as an equal.

Off the training ground, the craic is fantastic, the slagging and the comedy and the beers. We're being mobbed by Irish supporters everywhere we go. The excitement back home in Limerick and Patrickswell is off the charts. And we're hearing that the whole country back in Ireland is following our progress. I mean, I'm just hopping with adrenaline all the time.

It's rubbing off on me in games too because I feel really alive and vibrant against the Italians. The closed roof in Dunedin means the stadium is electric with noise. The chanting and the songs are bouncing off the walls and the roof and reverberating back down to the field. We have a midfield scrum at one stage and a pre-planned move that we call 'Hen' for some reason. But it leads to me making a big break down the middle of the pitch with the massive Irish support roaring me on. So, I'm on top of the world. At least I am until Sexto comes on!

He replaces RoG in the 67th minute. We have broken Italy by then and we're cruising into a World Cup quarter-final. But Johnny isn't in cruise mode. He has a point to prove and he has twenty minutes in which to prove it. So, we're playing away and we're coming off a sideline ruck and the move here is called 'Spud'. It's basically just a pod of three forwards waiting and I've to hit one of them, not unlike the setup that day down in CIT when Paulie went ballistic with me. Now it's Johnny's turn to go ballistic because I, in my giddiness, decide to miss out the forwards and throw it to Johnny out the back. But again, he's not expecting it. He catches it but there's nothing set up outside of him for a play so he just has to hoof it down the pitch. And he goes proper insane with me. We're chasing after the ball and despite the roar of the crowd, all I can hear is Johnny giving me both barrels. "You stupid c**t! I didn't call the fucking ball! I told you to hit the forwards, you fucking idiot!"

We're running downfield and this is the running commentary

I'm getting! And we don't know each other very well at the time. He's Leinster, I'm Munster and, of course, RoG is Munster too. And I'm getting so much of a bollocking I turn around and start fucking him out of it back. In my mind I'm thinking, fuck off Johnny, RoG is my man anyway.

What I didn't appreciate at the time was the pressure he was under. Like, the tour is a honeymoon for me but for Johnny it's all the scrutiny and stress he's feeling from this ongoing controversy over the outhalf position. I'm sure that that played a part in his reaction. And even if it wasn't a factor, he'd still have been within his rights because I didn't follow the orders, I didn't carry out my instructions. You don't throw the ball out the back just because you feel like it; you have to get a call first before you can do it. You're supposed to stick to the game plan unless you spot an opportunity to do something different. This wasn't that opportunity. But hey, like I say, I was floating on air at the time; I was immature. You live and you learn.

RoG gets the nod to start the quarter-final and I get the nod over Redser. As a team, all I can say is we just flopped on the day. Wales were waiting in ambush for us. They had their game plan, they were emotionally primed, and they took the game away from us. That was one hell of a good Welsh side, in fairness. And one of their best players on the day is Mike Phillips, my opposite number, my favourite number nine in the world. It's a chastening lesson for us all that day. Everyone is deflated, in the stadium and back at home. It's a major anticlimax after the high of the previous four weeks. I'm gone after 55 minutes. The magic carpet ride has crashed back to earth.

Being honest, I must admit that the defeat didn't hurt me the same way it hurt a lot of the veterans. They had been knocking on this door for a long time. They knew how hard this tournament was and they had the scars to prove it. RWC 2011 was supposed to be their time, our time. But for me, I wasn't gutted because it was all new to me and I was just in a permanent state of exhilaration. The loss to Wales didn't knock the stuffing out of me because my whole future lay before me. It was stretched out in front of me as far as the eye could see. I was only getting started; there would be more World Cups to come.

Fast-forward twelve years, to RWC 2023, and my future is in the past. There are no more World Cups and no more chances left for me. Now I bitterly understand what the lads were feeling like back in 2011. Maybe it's true what they say, that youth is wasted on the young. You just don't have the experience to know better. You have to live it to understand it. You have to find out for yourself the hard way.

We get back to Dublin airport three days later. We're saying our goodbyes in the baggage hall and I remember Drico coming up to me and shaking my hand and saying, "Enjoy your new life." I was like, huh, what d'you mean? And he just goes, "You'll understand soon enough." This was another example of the voice of experience passing on his wisdom to a naive young fella who hadn't lived it yet. Drico knew better than anyone that your life changes when you get a bit of fame and success as a sportsman.

He was basically telling me that my life would never be quite the same again. And, of course, he was right on that score too.

That month in Australia meant closing the book on my previous life and opening up the first pages of a brand new novel.

Chapter Five

LESSONS IN ITALIAN

BACK FROM THE WORLD CUP in October 2011, I'm still on cloud nine. I'm starting pretty much every game for Munster and in the new year I'm selected for my first Six Nations squad. The new experiences keep coming thick and fast. The bubble has to burst at some stage, I suppose, but I don't know this at the time.

In fact, you think you're going great guns until you pick up a newspaper the day after a match and you discover they've given you a 4 out of 10 in their players' ratings. Or was it a 3? I can't remember now but I can still remember the dent it put in my ego.

It's the 2012 Six Nations. We'd beaten Italy 42-10 the day before in the second round. I'd been replaced by Redser after 54 minutes, a fairly early time to be getting the curly finger. Three weeks earlier I'd made my Six Nations debut against Wales at the Aviva. A late Leigh Halfpenny penalty tilted a tight match their way. Four months after they'd turned us over in Wellington, they had our number again. I must've done okay because I lasted 77 minutes. It was a huge occasion for me because, of course, I'd grown up watching the tournament and I felt the history and tradition of it all weigh down on me in the countdown to kick-off. It just had an aura and level of expectation about it that increased the intensity of the build-up.

I found it a lot more pressurised than the World Cup. That had been on the other side of the world, whereas this was the Six Nations in front of your own home crowd. But I coped with it the way I was learning to cope with every new rung on the ladder, by concentrating on the nuts and bolts of my job and shutting out the noise. We were due to play France in Paris the weekend after Wales, but it was called off at the last minute because of a rock-hard icy pitch.

Against Italy in Dublin, it was supposed to be a formality, but it was 10-10 in the 35th minute when the great Sergio Parisse strolled in behind the posts. They had a massive overlap on the left and one reason they had it was because we were all scrambling back and at the ruck on our tryline I stationed myself at the near post, so close to Paulie that he was pushing me away with his hand, telling me to get over to the far side and cover their numbers there. It was kinda like, what the fuck are you doing here? It was only when I saw it back on video that I realised how badly out of position I was. I wasn't the only one but, Jesus, they had about five men spare on that side. Looking at it on replay the penny dropped with me: fecking hell, I still have loads to learn. I'm learning on the trot here and I've a long way to go.

I mean, could there be a bigger sign of pure raw naivety than picking up the paper the next day and seeing all the headlines and getting lured into reading the reports? I think we were in the Shelbourne, or maybe it was Carton House, but all the papers are scattered on chairs and coffee tables and I'm drawn to them like a moth to the flame. The player ratings column, scroll down, see my name – Conor Murray 4. Or was it 3? And it stings when I see it. Like, really? Did I play that badly? We actually won in the end by 32 points.

I should know better. I should know that you're never supposed to read the match reports and you definitely should not go near the player ratings. But it's too late now. And it's given me a scare. How cold and impersonal it is, your name and number in black and white and the verdict on your performance handed down just like that. There's no arm around the shoulder here. It gives me a jolt; it tells me that people are watching your every move at this level.

The realisation hits me that you're only as good as your last game. It's one of the oldest clichés in sport. I've heard it since I was a young fella, but it becomes very real for me in that moment. I realise that it's a very harsh, judgmental world at this level, and people aren't going to spare you your feelings anymore. If you're any way off the standard, it'll stick out, it will be seen and noted. That little seed of insecurity is planted into me now. If I want to stay in this job, I need to consistently perform. That seed of insecurity stays with me for the rest of my career. I think every player who lasts at that level has it – I think you have to have it. So, in hindsight, the assessment in the newspaper probably did me a favour, even if it most certainly did not feel like a favour at the time.

Deccie, as usual, is decent about it. He just tells me I need to sharpen up a bit all round. The rescheduled game against France is a week after Italy. It's my first time to play at the Stade de France and the atmosphere is sensational. I'm loving it and I'm going well until I jump for a ball around the hour mark and come down on one leg and buckle my knee. The shot of pain

LESSONS IN ITALIAN

that runs through the knee feels like I've been electrocuted. I'm roaring and screeching in agony. The sound effects are picked up on the referee's mic. I only find out later from the doctor that his first impression was I'd busted my cruciate. But when the scans come back, they show I'm in the clear. It's just bone bruising and I'm a bit embarrassed with myself now after making such a scene! But Christ, it was sore and I did fear the worst. The damage is sufficient to rule me out of the last two rounds of the Six Nations.

So, for the England match I'm back with my house mates in Fr Russell Road and we've a load of friends over for beer and pizza. The rain is bucketing down at Twickenham and the longer the game goes on, the more it dawns on me that I may have dodged a bullet here. I've been sickened for the previous fortnight over missing out on Scotland in Dublin and now England at their place. But it starts to get ugly pretty quickly.

England are just demolishing our scrum and we're coughing up penalty after penalty after penalty. In that situation, your scrumhalf is on a hiding to nothing too. I remember watching poor Redser playing and like there was nothing he could do there; he was just under horrendous pressure at the base of every scrum.

One of the lads turns to me and says there are some games where your stock rises just by not being there. It's true too. I've been in that situation and you don't have any good options if your scrum is getting monstered. The best you can do is feed the ball in, knowing the surge is coming and pick the ball up as early as you can and get rid of it asap. The ref is on the verge of blowing for a penalty anyway so anything you do might be too late. You might be able to flick it out to your winger or just boot it downfield. Usually you won't have time to get it out to your ten, you won't have time to wind up your pass to him. There's a fair chance you're going to get scragged by their nine or get clobbered by a flanker. Deccie said afterwards that it had been "extremely painful" to watch what unfolded. England humbled us 30-9.

I'm back for the summer tour of New Zealand. Before we fly out at the end of May, an Ireland XV has a warm-up match against the Barbarians at Gloucester's home ground, Kingsholm. It's a beautiful summer's evening, the mood is relaxed, the Babas are throwing the ball around so we decide to do the same. The freedom from the constant pressure is lovely to experience once in a while; you're not so much competing as playing the game you love. It becomes just a game again, not a business.

Down to London the next day where we're joined by the Leinster boys. They're having their end-of-season party in a restaurant in Richmond and so we all join in. It turns into a brilliant night's craic. We're staying in an airport hotel at Heathrow before we fly out to Auckland the next day.

The fun and games continue back in our hotel room. Mike Sherry is in hilarious form and me and Earlsy are egging him on in front of a few of the Leinster lads who've never seen his comedy act before. Everyone is roaring with the laughter when next thing there's this big bang on the door. All of a sudden we're stifling the laughs. That knock on the door sounds serious.

I sneak up to the eyepiece in the door and who's there but Deccie. I don't open it. I'm just shushing the lads and we're there waiting for another knock. But after a pause he heads off and that's more or less party over.

In the airport next day Deccie sidles up to Sherry, nice and handy, and says, "Good night last night?" No big deal, just

LESSONS IN ITALIAN

putting him on notice! The boss in his own quiet way is saying, I heard the racket last night, I'm just letting you know that I know. Poor ould Sherry was well rattled! We were saying to him, Deccie misses nothing!

The All Blacks give us a bad drubbing in Eden Park. Julian Savea scores a hat-trick on his debut. New Zealand have two other debutants that day too, Brodie Retallick and Aaron Smith. They would still be there 11 years later on that harrowing night in Paris in the World Cup quarter-final.

The squad we faced in 2012 had won the World Cup seven months earlier. It was frighteningly talented and strong, from Dan Carter to Richie McCaw, Conrad Smith, Ma'a Nonu and all the rest. Kieran Read was unbelievable in this first Test. Sonny Bill Williams was an absolute juggernaut. These fellas are gods.

In my young career, this is the ultimate standard I've faced. It's the first time I've faced the Haka in the flesh too. I've only ever seen it on telly. I'm taking it all in but I don't remember feeling intimidated. I was more excited to be there. My adrenaline was pumping, I wasn't going to back down, I was going to give it a proper go. In my head I'm looking over at them and thinking, I'd fucking love to beat you. I would love to play better than you. We actually started well but once they got into their rhythm, you just didn't have space and you didn't have time. They played way faster than any team I'd ever known. One fella would steal a yard or two and next thing they've a line break and all of a sudden they're racing for your line. It's a whole other world of speed and skill and all-round class.

Fergus McFadden chases down a good kick from Sexto into the NZ backfield and scores our only try of the game. I loved playing with Ferg; he was a true team man. Late in the

CONOR MURRAY

Six Nations game against Wales in 2018 – our Grand Slam campaign – we were awarded a penalty but Johnny was down with a knock and, in that situation, Ferg would normally take over the kicking duties. He'd done it loads of times for Leinster over the years. I'm assuming he'll take it, but he comes across to me and just says, "You take it – bang it over, mate."

There was only seven points in it with five minutes to go, so there was a bit of pressure on the kick. There was full silence in the Aviva for it. Anyway, I managed to get it over with the help of the inside of the left upright. But as a gesture from a team mate, I really appreciated it. I suppose he was basically saying, I trust you to do it. It was just a sound thing to do. When I first came into camp, I was blown away by how much slagging Ferg would dish out to the big-name players like Drico and Besty and Paulie and Kearns. He didn't give a damn who they were and he was very funny.

Wet conditions in rugby are definitely a leveller and it had rained a lot in Christchurch before our second Test. I remember going into this game thinking we'd a better chance than the previous week because of the wet ground and greasy ball. That was an underdog mentality, but that's where we were as a culture at the time. Shit weather would make it a bit harder for the All Blacks to execute their super-slick running game. Plus, we were hurting a lot from the beating they'd given us in Auckland. We wanted a response, we wanted to get stuck into them, and the Irish-style weather made us feel a bit more at home.

I scored my first try for Ireland ten minutes into it. Our forwards mauled it up to the line, I had options left and right, I was scanning left and scanning right, then Johnny made a decoy run to the narrow side. That triggered a twitch left from

LESSONS IN ITALIAN

Tony Woodcock, their prop forward who was standing pillar at the ruck, and it was the half-yard I needed to dodge inside him.

I'm 23, it's my eleventh international and the try is proof that I'm settling into the job. It puts us 10-0 up. We are going at them hammer and tongs all over the pitch; lads are making big tackles, we're playing with a huge amount of passion and fight. It's a heroic performance, to be fair, and then Carter mugs us in the last minute with a drop goal to win it. We deserved at least a draw, but of course, deserving has nothing to do with it. We've been gallant losers – again. We end up with the same old story when it comes to Ireland versus New Zealand.

Personally, and God help my innocence, I'm convinced we have their number for the third Test. We've seen the whites of their eyes in this game, we've properly rattled them, we'll go the extra mile in Hamilton and make history. Of course, they all but wipe us off the face of the earth. Nine tries, 60 points to 0 and it's hard to know which is the more embarrassing, the sixty or the nil. It was a punishment beating from a team who'd copped a bit of flak for their performance the previous week.

They wouldn't let up, they kept the foot on the throttle, they couldn't score enough points. Drico was captain and after every try we'd have a huddle behind the posts, the usual ritual after you've conceded, but eventually he ran out of things to say. Peter O'Mahony had broken into the team earlier that year during the Six Nations. I remember Pete saying after this game that he was wondering if he'd played his last game for Ireland. The thought crossed my mind also. It was a feckin' horrific day.

There was a personal lesson for me too. Our hotel in Hamilton didn't have Wi-Fi in the players' rooms. Myself and Sherry had got wind that some of the lads would be stopping off in Thailand on the way home for their end-of-season holiday. So, we decided we'd do the same. But to book our flights and accommodation we'd have to go down to the team room for Wi-Fi.

This is a night or two before the third Test. I get on a laptop in the team room and I'm all giddy with excitement about the craic we're going to have in Ko Samui or wherever. We're going to make it to one of their famous Full Moon parties and all. Then, wouldn't you know it, who should appear over our shoulder but Deccie. And in his quiet, diplomatic way he asks us what we're doing. And in our youthful enthusiasm, we blurt out that we're booking our holidays for Thailand after the tour. Then New Zealand put the hammer on us a few days later and in the dressing room afterwards at some stage, Deccie shuffles over and sits down beside me. And he says something like, "Maybe in future have your holidays ticked off well before a big game. It's not a good idea to be doing something like that."

And, of course, the penny drops with me straight away. Oh Christ. He is so right. We were so naive and stupid to be booking a holiday so close to a major match. It wasn't just the booking of it; it was the distraction, the anticipation of it taking up so much of your headspace when you should've been totally focused on the job at hand. When Deccie saw us in the team room planning and talking about our holiday, he must've gone away thinking that these lads weren't getting ready for the game, their heads weren't in the right place. But he said nothing and then just very politely brought it up with me in the dressing room after. He wasn't angry at all, didn't raise his voice; he was just disappointed the way a parent would be disappointed. I was embarrassed by my part in Ireland's performance that day and embarrassed all over again by my silly thoughtlessness. It was

LESSONS IN ITALIAN

a major lesson for me in terms of mental preparation. I never allowed myself to get distracted again in the build-up to a big game. Keep your mind on the job at all times. I can remember that moment in the dressing room a lot clearer than the Full Moon party on the beach in Thailand, I can tell you.

I can remember the first yellow card of my career, too. It came against Wales in the 2013 Six Nations in Cardiff. We were fifteen points ahead with ten minutes to play. The Welsh were held up short at the base of the upright and from the recycle there wasn't much chance of stopping them legally, so as Lloyd Williams, their sub scrumhalf, went to pop the pass, I leaned across the ruck and tapped it out of his hands. It was fairly cynical, alright, but the Welsh were building up a head of steam at that point and I did the needful. Romain Poite blew his whistle and flashed the yellow and that was my day over. We held on to win by eight.

Gats and his Lions coaches were in the stand that day to run the rule over any contenders for the summer tour of Australia. Back in the hotel that night, we were having drinks in the reception area before the big banquet and Deccie sidles up to me out of nowhere and quietly tells me to button up the top button on my shirt. I look at him as if to say, what does it matter whether it's open or not? It's such a trivial detail. But he tips me off that there will be Lions selectors roaming about and they'll be looking at everything.

Like I said before, whether it's newspapers or whether it's coaches, you are constantly under scrutiny at this level and I'm only starting to realise it. And after the party in our hotel room in London, after he spots us booking the holiday flights in Hamilton, and now copping the loose button on my shirt, it's pretty obvious there's a reason why he's the boss. He has the eagle eyes! At the time I don't understand why it should matter but if he's telling me to fasten the button, it must matter, simple as that. He's actually looking out for me here rather than trying to discipline me: he thinks I have a chance with the Lions, so I should look the part. I shouldn't look sloppy in any way. So, I tie the button, straighten up my tie and head into dinner looking spick and span.

We subsequently lose to England, lose to Scotland and draw 13-13 with France in Dublin. I'm given the nod for man-of-the-match on television after the French game and one of the lads remarks in the dressing room that I've booked my seat on the plane for Australia. I'm far from certain about that but maybe there's a chance now. I'm a lot less certain about it after Italy turn us over in Rome. It's an absolute shock. It's their first time ever to beat Ireland in the Six Nations. As of 2025, it's still the only time they've ever beaten Ireland in the Six Nations. It's historic in the wrong sense of the word for us. It's just one of those days where things go from bad to worse. It's a feckin' disaster of a day. And to put the tin hat on it, I'm sin-binned in the last minute for tripping up a fella out of pure desperation. The atmosphere in the dressing room after is horrible.

A couple of weeks later, Deccie parts company with the IRFU. His time as Ireland head coach is over. He deserved to go out on a better note than that. I was lucky enough to catch the last few years of his international career. I learned a lot from him; he helped me grow up at that level and he was always decent to me. A lot of water has gone under the bridge since my early years in the green jersey, but they were formative years for me and Declan Kidney was a very good mentor to have at that time. If I'm casual with the top button of my shirt these days, it's certainly not Deccie's fault.

Chapter Six

BOLLOCKINGS

TONY MCGAHAN WAS REMINISCING ABOUT his time at Munster a few years after he went back to Australia. Dumper had joined as defence/backs coach in 2005. He took over as head coach from Deccie in 2008 and left in the summer of 2012.

A lot of young hopefuls had come through the ranks during his seven years in Limerick and some of them had gone on to become Ireland internationals. By 2014 he was head coach of the Melbourne Rebels, but was obviously keeping an eye on our progress back at his old stomping ground.

"We get great satisfaction out of all those blokes that we put through the programme and where they are now," he told the *Irish Examiner*. "You've got Peter O'Mahony, Conor Murray, Simon Zebo, JJ Hanrahan. Then you've got Archer, Sherry, Kilcoyne, Foley, Nagle. Those guys, Murray and Zebo, going on to become Lions: it's huge for them and whatever about [taking] pride personally, I'd just be so delighted for them.

"You think of all the bollockings they took and the work they put in to get there. We could easily have had O'Mahony on the [2013 Lions] tour too and that would have been three out of that group, which for one club is fantastic."

"Bollockings" is right! Dumper wasn't shy about dishing

them out. He had a great sense of humour too. But when you were a young fella trying to make your way, he'd frighten the shite out of you with one of his tirades.

He was a tough, uncompromising Aussie out of the old school. The language would be fairly choice and he wouldn't be mincing his words. Of all the players he named in that interview, the mention of "Sherry" had me smiling in memory of the day that poor old Mike was on the receiving end of Dumper's rough and ready ways.

Myself and Mike and the lads were graduating from the academy around that time. Tony and the coaches had their offices by the swimming pool in UL. Sherry, being a hooker, wanted to practise his throwing one day and he was looking around for a few spare rugby balls when he innocently walked into Dumper's office to see if there were any there. But Dumper was on the phone, so Mike signals to him, where are the balls? And Dumper just dropped the phone to his chest and shouted, "Fuck off, mate!"

Sherry had to back out with his tail between his legs! I think he was rattled for months after. But that was Dumper. He could be caustic with young fellas.

That's the way things had been done in sports for a hundred years. Rookies had to be straightened out with a few verbal lashings until they copped themselves on a bit. Like, he sent one of my mates in the academy home one day because he kept messing up a drill on the training ground. And we'd all be fairly nervous already for fear of making a mistake and getting called out. So, it becomes a kind of a circular thing whereby being nervous makes you more liable to make the mistake in the first place.

BOLLOCKINGS

A simple passing drill, for example, and if a fella dropped the ball he'd be effed out of it and told to do a lap of the pitch in front of everyone. It was a bit of a sink-or-swim sort of environment. Fellas who were borderline in terms of making it or not could easily end up in the line of fire. And they're the fellas who usually need a bit more TLC. It can be really intimidating when you're coming from the academy onto the senior training ground where you've all these battle-hardened professionals who have high standards and not much patience for a fella learning his trade. Then you have this Aussie hard nut who will fuck you out of it at the drop of a ball.

Personally, I liked Dumper and he was good to me. I got the lash off him a few times, but escaped lightly enough in comparison to a few others. Usually I was in his good books. I was quiet and kept the head down and Dumper probably took a shine to me. He was the coach who trusted me enough to put me in the senior team and keep me there. I'll always appreciate that.

In hindsight, people might think that it's a no-brainer for a coach to select someone who looks to have the talent for the job. But it's never a no-brainer the first time. Someone has to give you your chance. It's always a risk until you've proven yourself. I needed Tony to pick me, I needed Declan Kidney to mentor me and pick me. I'd never take for granted the people who gave me the start. In fact, I remember the week before I made my Heineken Cup debut, McGahan taking me aside in training in Thomond Park for a private chat.

It was November 2011. We were facing Northampton Saints in the game that will be remembered forever for RoG's famous drop goal in stoppage time after 41 phases of play. A few days earlier, Dumper had pulled me aside, told me I would be starting and that this might be the beginning of a long career for me. He went through my strengths and weaknesses, what I needed to work on and improve. And then he said, "If you look after all these areas you can play as long as you want to. You can have this jersey for the next ten years if you want it."

Then, as luck would have it, my Heineken Cup debut coincides with one of the most legendary performances ever by a Munster team in Thomond Park. It's just a sensational night. I am totally in dreamland after it. A week later, against Castres in Toulouse, RoG only goes and does it again, another drop goal in stoppage time to get us out of Dodge with the win. I remember on the flight home from that game, I happened to be sitting in the row behind McGahan and I was peeking round the head rest watching him watch the game back on his laptop. I'd made a wee break from a five-metre lineout on our own line. It was just a reactive play, I only gained a few yards, it wouldn't make any highlights reel, but I noticed him rewinding it and slowing it down and replaying it a couple of times. He didn't say anything, but I got the impression that he liked what he saw and it's weird how I can remember such a tiny little moment like that, but I do.

I was always hoping that my actions would speak louder than words because I wasn't much of a talker, I wasn't by nature an extrovert. I had internalised all my goals. I was ambitious and driven, but it was all kept inside. I'd written down my own goals in private and never declared them to anyone. But they were there and I felt that to turn them into reality, I would have to take every training session seriously. So, I kept my nose clean and worked as hard as I could every day. That was my formula.

I gravitated towards Felix Jones. He was only two years older

BOLLOCKINGS

than me, but he was a sort of role model because of how hard he trained. I mean, Felix was a lunatic trainer, he could never do enough sprints, enough fitness drills. And he'd be all out for every one of them. He'd never slacken off. He was setting the standard so I figured I should tag along with him because he was so enthusiastic and supportive.

Anyway, Munster went six out of six in the group stages that season. We put 51 points on Northampton in the return game at Milton Keynes in January 2012. Zeebs scored a hat-trick, that was his proper arrival into the big time. At that point, our campaign in Europe had massive momentum. But by the time we got back to it in April, something must have gone missing because we had Ulster at Thomond Park in the quarter-final and we made a complete balls of it. It must've been complacency on our part. I'd say Ulster spotted an opportunity to come in under the radar and set us up for an ambush. They executed it perfectly, to be fair. We were 19-0 down before we knew what hit us. Ruan Pienaar, the South African, was my opposite number that day and he was outstanding. He showed me the standard for an elite scrumhalf. He was just class, a really slick, calm, talented nine.

Our dressing room was devastated afterwards. We were shell-shocked. We all knew we'd blown a great chance of getting to the final and winning it. Even though I was only starting out, I sensed it too. It wasn't lost on me at all. I might have had another ten years in the jersey, as Dumper said, but the time was now. We'd a great team; we'd been in great form all through the group stages. The winners would have Edinburgh in the semi-final at the Aviva Stadium. It was all set up for us, or so I thought. I was reared on Munster winning big European games at Thomond Park. I just assumed this was going to be no different.

CONOR MURRAY

We got a fair old bollocking in the Monday review after that debacle, right enough. It was really rough. Jason Holland was our backs coach and he went through a fair few players for a short cut. He didn't discriminate that day between rookies and veterans. The coaches were still fuming. Every piece of bad play was put up on the film footage, stuff that would normally be glossed over in a league game or if we'd won. I had my mistakes pointed out to me in no uncertain terms. That was the first time where I'd really been hauled over the coals. I remember feeling really shit coming out of that review. I was brought crashing back down to earth. My little honeymoon period where I could do no wrong was over.

Dumper's Munster days were more or less over too. He headed home a few months later. Rob Penney took over and he was a completely different animal.

But I think there's still a bit of room left in the culture for a good old-fashioned eruption on the training ground. Obviously, everyone's a bit more careful these days and you have to be sensitive in how you address the young crop of players now. They're in the shoes I was in thirteen or fourteen years ago. It wouldn't be my style to come down heavy on them anyway. I'm not one for using coarse language to an extreme and I wouldn't go round effing them out of it just because I can. These are young fellas that haven't got the knowledge and part of my job nowadays is to pass on what I know. It's a transfer of knowledge and experience; it doesn't have to be a power trip.

In one training session recently, we were doing a defensive set-up and there was a scrum in the middle of the pitch and you had to count how many backs the opposing team had on one side and allocate our own numbers accordingly so that everyone

BOLLOCKINGS

is covered. We ran the play and one of our lads switched late to the blindside and left them with an overlap. I told the lad, "Don't ever change late. We've stacked up our numbers against their numbers either side of the pitch, we've made the decision, so don't ever move late." He wasn't familiar with the set-up; he hadn't done it before. It was a pure learning moment. There's no need to swear a fella out of it in that situation.

On the other hand, I'm a bit conflicted because also in my head I'm going, 'Jesus Christ, you've fucked up the whole defensive system because you've jumped from one side of the scrum to the other for no reason. What the fuck are you doing moving that late?' But I filter out that reaction and go into instructor mode and explain the mechanics of the move in a calm voice.

You have to be conscious of your language and your tone. But then again, there's always heat-of-the-moment stuff when you've got 40 fellas on a field with all that testosterone and competitiveness in them. You can't sanitise that out of the system either and you wouldn't want to. Fellas have to learn fast in that environment. They can't be too thin-skinned because it's a dog-eat-dog business. They have to toughen up and eat a fair amount of humble pie when they make mistakes because mistakes cost you games. The same day that I've instructed the young lad in calm and measured tones about that defensive set-up, I'm barking at another fella because we're running such a routine play that he should have it down. It's a very basic ruck move and he doesn't execute it and in the moment I rear up on him. He's then explaining himself like, "I didn't want to ruin the shape." And I'm going, "It doesn't matter about the fucking shape, just get round the fucking corner, basically."

The first approach is generally the right approach, but there will always be times when a player has to be called to order in the old-fashioned language of the rugby training ground, whatever about in the office! I must ask Sherry if Tony ever sorted him out with the balls that day. Anyway, you'd have to hope that Dumper's phone etiquette has improved a bit since then.

Chapter Seven

A LONELY NIGHT IN LAHINCH

I'D PREFER NOT TO GO there, but you've got to take a look at the whole picture, warts and all. So, while it's nice that there's a load of your highlights captured forever in the video footage online, you have to accept that a few of your howlers are going to be hanging around there too, like a bad smell. They are tougher to take when you're young because you're more thin-skinned and fragile in your confidence. But they are better to happen at that age because you will learn valuable lessons from the experience. I can say that now, but I most certainly did not appreciate it at the time.

After Ireland's summer tour of New Zealand in 2012, I've missed most of Munster's 2012/13 pre-season for holidays, rest and recuperation. But I'm keeping my journal going and I've set out my goals for the incoming season and chief among them is to get on the scoreboard more often. After breaking into the side late in 2010/11, I've had a full season since to grow into the role. Now I figure the next stage of improvement for me is to score a few more tries and threaten defences a bit more by running at them and keeping them guessing.

My first full season, I've been content to service RoG and let him get on with the distribution and decision-making. Same with our forwards: just pop it up to them and let them take it from there. It's a confidence thing and an inexperience thing. I don't feel at this stage that I've earned the right to be making calls like that. I don't want to be seen to be doing anything that might be deemed selfish or individualistic. I'm here to facilitate my team mates.

But it's dawned on me in recent months that I need to be taking on more responsibility myself. I've picked up enough experience in the meantime to trust my judgement a little bit more if the opportunities come up. And funnily enough, RoG must've been thinking the same thing because in late September 2012, we're playing Newport Gwent Dragons in a RaboDirect Pro12 game at Thomond Park. It's just my second game of the season, I haven't started one yet. I come on after 50 minutes. I'm not long on the pitch when we get a scrum inside their 22 on the right hand side, about five metres from the touchline. The usual call in this situation is to give the ball to RoG on the left, the open side, and I'm ready to obey orders; RoG can see me shaping up to throw it out to him. But the scrum goes down and the ref calls a re-set. RoG walks over to me very calmly and says, "Are you seeing that?" He's nodding at the right hand side. "The blindside there?" And I'm like, yeah yeah yeah. Actually I'm bluffing, I'm not looking, I haven't seen it, because all I'm worried about is getting the ball to RoG whereas I should be looking at all the options, where their winger is, what their nine is doing etc etc.

The move is obvious now that I see it. We're ten, fifteen metres from their line. They've only got their winger guarding the blindside and he's marking Dougie. It's a simple 8/9 play.

A LONELY NIGHT IN LAHINCH

Paddy Butler is our number eight. The scrum is re-set, Paddy pops it up to me, their winger stays out on Dougie and I shoot through the gap and run it in. Great! Delighted with myself.

Pundits and fans are probably saying it was an opportunist try. I saw the chance down the blindside and took it. But it was RoG's tip-off that planted the seed in my mind. I was so fixated on feeding him at all times that I wasn't playing as much heads-up rugby as I should have been. And maybe people might assume that he would want the ball all the time, that he'd want everything to go through him. But that wasn't true. RoG would want you to do whatever was right. You had leeway to do what you felt was right in the moment. And actually I had a habit early doors of going down really short sides when there was nothing on and I'd be tackled so there'd be no nine at the ruck and it would disrupt the whole thing. I got a few bollockings for that and rightly so.

RoG and Johnny were both generals, like American quarterbacks, but they weren't demanding the ball the whole time. They were just trying to orchestrate scores for the team and if there was a better way of doing it at a given moment, then do it. If there's a possible opening on the blindside, the players on that side should be calling for the ball. I just had to learn how to pick and choose my moments. Johnny gave me a great insight one day that stuck with me: once we stay on our feet, once we're not tackled, we can control the game, we can manipulate defences. Obviously you are going to get wrapped up in tackles from time to time, but the more we stay on our feet, the more we can influence the game.

Experience is a word used so often that it sometimes comes across as an abstract kind of concept whereas in practical terms, it's an older player in a game situation telling you something useful and pragmatic. Then you put it into action and it works and you bank it in your mind. It's not theory, it is knowledge put into practice. I'm immediately a more experienced player after scoring that try against the Dragons. More confident too.

The score in itself didn't matter all that much, we were well on top anyway. What mattered was the lesson I took away from it. I don't need to be slavishly playing every ball out to RoG and he doesn't want me to be doing that either. I should be playing what's in front of me and backing myself a bit more to take the initiative. It's probably not a match that has lingered long in the memory for anybody else, but I remember it for that little breakthrough in my mindset. It's another moment in your growth as a player and if you're lucky you'll have loads of those moments in the early years of your career.

And, if you're lucky, you'll have a few bad moments too in those years. I know it's a bit of a cliche, but you actually do get big growth spurts out of adversity. And they're bloody horrible at the time and the last thing you want to hear is that you'll learn from them and they'll make you a better player. The one I have in mind is still up on YouTube.

It's three weeks after the Dragons match and it's a bit more high profile because it's the Heineken Cup against Racing 92 in the Stade de France. It's a shocking day weather-wise and the pitch is a bath of mud and water. There's loads of blunders on both sides because of the conditions. But, with eight minutes to play, Zeebs scores a brilliant try and Ian Keatley converts to nudge us in front by a point. We have a real gritty win in Paris on the cards. A few minutes later Ollie Barkley drills a long low kick from inside their own half. I'm in the backfield and try to trap it with my foot and miss it and the ball skids on to nearly

A LONELY NIGHT IN LAHINCH

our own five metre line. Now I've to run back another 20 metres to retrieve it but the ground is so heavy that my legs are wasted by then. They're drained from pulling them out of the muck all afternoon. Still, I should have enough time to get back and clear my lines. I shape to kick as the first tackler arrives, but he sells himself so completely I can't resist dummying inside him and now the next chaser is on my case. Stuart Barnes is on co-commentary with Sky Sports.

"Oh what's he doing?" Barnes wonders, as I'm tackled on our 22m line. Good question. Racing players pile in and I'm buried and then penalised for not releasing. They have a very kickable penalty.

"Oh, that is terrible from Conor Murray." The home support is cheering away as I pick myself up from the bottom of the ruck.

"Okay you can miss the ball trapping it, but then he's ambling along, he sells a dummy without any conviction, the side step without any speed and he has just handed the game back to Racing and the left boot of Ollie Barkley." Hard, but fair from Stuart there. Barkley lands the penalty to edge them back in front and Mirco Bergamasco adds another one in the 79th to wrap it up.

Rob Penney, being the gent he is, doesn't go hard on me in the dressing room. He's very aware of how awful I'm feeling. He's like, "Don't worry mate, these things happen, we've got your back." Rob was very good like that. I really needed a bit of empathy in that situation and he showed it and I was very thankful for it. There's these Jacuzzi baths in the Stade de France and a while later I was sitting in one of them, kind of lost in my own world, when RoG arrives in beside me and goes, "Jeez kid, that was some brain fart wasn't it?!" And he was sort of smiling ruefully as he said it. But it was the best thing anyone could have said to me in the moment cos it broke the ice and he was basically saying, shit happens, it's not the end of the world.

The other lads were avoiding me because I suppose they were a bit embarrassed for me and wanted to leave me alone. But I find there's nothing worse than people saying nothing to you when you know you've fucked up. RoG knew exactly what to say – a bit of black humour mixed in with the truth helps the medicine go down.

Young players can be hard on themselves at that age, I guess cos we're insecure and our mistakes are seen in public by a lot of people. This one was live on Sky Sports so every Munster fan knew about it. Earlsy has had a talk with me too, just trying to reassure me. I remember him saying more or less that it was bound to happen some time. I'd cruised into the Munster team and then the Ireland team in no time at all and it was all going so well. So, a setback was bound to happen. You were going to be brought crashing down to earth at some stage. That's just the reality of professional sport. You have to suck it up and move on.

Obviously I know that now. But at that stage in your career you don't have the perspective and you don't have the thick skin to deal with mistakes. I'm still devastated by the time we get home. Everyone is walking on eggshells around me.

So, a few nights later, I take myself off in the car and drive down to Lahinch to be on my own. I just drive around for hours, beating myself up and running the incident around in my mind over and over and over. It's a fairly lonely few hours. But at some stage I stop feeling sorry for myself and make a sworn promise to myself that it will never happen again. That will never happen again. In fact, we're playing Edinburgh in the Heineken Cup in

A LONELY NIGHT IN LAHINCH

Thomond Park the following weekend and it gets into my head that I have to score a try in that match – I have to score a try – and ideally get man-of-the-match too.

As it happens, I did both. Naturally when I was being presented with the award after I gave the usual spiel about it being all about the team etc etc. Which of course it is, but I was on a bloody mission to atone for Paris, so scoring the try and getting the nod for man-of-the-match meant a lot to me individually. It was only then that the wound started to heal. Looking back now, I can see I beat myself up too much, but that's easy to say when you're 36 and you've pretty much seen it all and done it all. Being young means being vulnerable and it generally means you have to learn the hard way too. That was a big learning moment. And what was the big lesson? Not to try running the ball out of defence when the pitch is a bog and there's fuckin' nothing on.

Edinburgh. That season sticks out for me because we play them again in the Heineken Cup return fixture at Murrayfield in January 2013. I score again, around the hour mark, but the reason I remember this match is because I was in a state of complete exhaustion by the time Duncan Williams replaced me in the 69th minute. From time to time you'll hear professional cyclists talking about being "tanked" during say a gruelling stage of the Tour de France. I take it to mean that they don't have a single drop of energy left in their legs, the fuel tank is completely empty. I came off that day against Edinburgh tanked. My legs were gone. The pitch was really heavy too, which didn't help, but the main reason was our gameplan.

Rob's big idea was to get the ball to the edge as often as possible, as early as possible. Don't truck it up the middle, play touchline to touchline in as few phases as possible. But it was torture for the scrumhalf because you ended up running over and back and over and back all afternoon. You'd arrive at a ruck and feed the ball out and the next ruck could be out on the touchline and you had to sprint like the hammers to get to that one, and the one after, and the one after. You were basically a pendulum swinging over and back across the pitch. It genuinely happened to me several times that I spotted a gap in midfield and just didn't have the energy to try a snipe through it. I'd just pass the ball back and try and follow the play. You ended up being a long distance runner who just passed the ball at every ruck.

It was factored into the gameplan that if the team went wide-wide-wide in rapid succession that the nine mightn't be able to get to every ruck on time so the ten would go to scrumhalf and I'd stand in as first receiver and pass it to the pod in the middle and then we'd revert to normal. That was alright in theory. But can you imagine telling RoG to go to scrumhalf? He'd tell you to fuck off fairly lively! In fact, there's no self-respecting outhalf who'd be happy with that kind of arrangement.

I remember playing alongside JJ Hanrahan in one game that season and at one stage I'm dragging my arse trying to get to the next phase and I'm shouting at him, "Go to nine, go to nine!" And JJ's like, "Ah you're nearly there, you're nearly there, you might as well keep going." So, I had to keep fuckin' going!

When I was taken off in Murrayfield that day I sat down and was panting like an old dog for the next ten minutes. Duncan said to me in the dressing room after that he should've been on at least five minutes earlier because, as he said, "You were stuck to the ground, you just couldn't move. I've never seen you like that before."

A LONELY NIGHT IN LAHINCH

A week later we demolish Racing in Thomond and qualify for the European quarter-finals on 7th April. That's the famous day against Harlequins at the Stoop when Paulie makes his comeback after a long injury and bends the match to his will. It's a titanic performance from the big man. Danny Care is their starting scrumhalf and I'm very conscious that Gats and the Lions selectors will be keeping a close eye on everyone.

By now I have fully embraced RoG's lesson from the Dragons game the previous September: I'm playing more heads-up, I'm taking on more responsibility. Against Harlequins I end up taking on a bit too much responsibility for his liking. We get a penalty advantage at one stage and the drop goal is on and obviously there's no better man in the business for this gig than my partner at ten. But Gats is in the crowd and I'm thinking a drop goal will look well on my CV here. Not a great idea. My effort is so poorly executed that it goes underneath the crossbar and next thing I'm getting the glare from RoG. He doesn't say a word, but he says it all with his face: never, ever do that again when I'm around. Or to put it another way, yes, I've given you your head, but don't be losing the run of yourself either, Sonny.

It was another lesson learned from the great man. Clermont Auvergne beat us in the semi-final in Montpellier and sadly that was the end of the road for RoG. In the dressing room afterwards there was a lot of sadness. We all knew it was the end of an era. He said his goodbyes and mentioned us young fellas and said something like, "It's your team now, lads, take it from here and drive it on." I was so blessed to have gotten two full seasons playing alongside this artist of his craft. I learned so much, brain farts and all. I was the apprentice and he was the master. It was a pleasure and a privilege.

Chapter Eight

'A POOR MAN'S MIKE PHILLIPS'

WE GET BACK FROM MONTPELLIER on the Sunday, licking our wounds all the way home after having battled so hard against Clermont Auvergne. It's the end of our European ambitions for another season.

But I'm turning the page on it pretty quickly because team mates and friends have been speculating for a few weeks that I'm in with a shout for the British & Irish Lions squad. The formal announcement is going to be made on the Tuesday – 30th April 2013. I know I'm in with a shout, but they're bringing three scrumhalves and two of them are pretty much nailed on already: Mike Phillips of Wales and Ben Youngs of England. That leaves just one slot vacant and Danny Care (England) and Greig Laidlaw (Scotland) have every bit as big a chance as me, I reckon. Warren Gatland is the boss and, in all honesty, I haven't a clue where I stand with him. I don't know the man, he doesn't know me, it all depends on his subjective impression of each player that he's considering.

At this stage I've moved from my place in Raheen to a house in Annacotty that was Dumper's accommodation before he

'A POOR MAN'S MIKE PHILLIPS'

moved back to Australia the previous summer. Sherry has made the move with me from our old place and Scans has also joined us in Annacotty. On the Tuesday morning we have the telly turned to Sky Sports for the live announcement. I've a day off from training, Sherry has gone to get physio or something, so there's just me and Scans in the living room.

As the time comes my phone rings. It's Michael Corcoran, the rugby commentator with RTÉ. Michael is at the ceremony in the Hilton Hotel in London and he has some breaking news before the public announcement. "Are you on your own there?" Hang on a sec. I step outside onto the driveway and sit down on a kerb.

"You're in," he says. "Congratulations." Paulie is also in, as expected, but Zeebs has missed out. Michael throws out a few more names, but I'm not really digesting any more info. All I know is that I'm about to be announced as a British & Irish Lion. I go back inside, but keep the big news to myself. Then Andy Irvine, the tour manager, steps up to the podium and one by one he names the 37 chosen players. When he gets to the scrumhalves, my picture comes up on the screen. Irvine announces my name and Scans goes mental and I kinda have to pretend to go mental as well!

My parents had a holiday home in Derrynane on the Iveragh Peninsula in southwest Kerry. We'd go there every summer when we were growing up. In the summer of 2001 I became obsessed with the Lions who were touring Australia at the time. I was 12 years old. That was the tour that Drico lit up with his famous solo try in the first Test. I fell in love with the Lions in those weeks and nothing would do me but to get a replica of their jersey, the one with the ntl: logo on the chest. All the private school lads had it and I so badly wanted one too. My dad would be working during the week and come down to join us at weekends. He arrived one Friday night with the jersey, said it was the last one in Shaws in the Crescent Shopping Centre. I think he might have been hamming it up a bit for drama, but I was one delighted schoolboy.

I remember wearing it all summer long, playing tip rugby with it on the beach every day. Twelve years later I'm going to be wearing not a replica, but the real McCoy and I'm feeling incredibly proud and fulfilled when my name is read out on Sky Sports that day. It is another boyhood dream ticked off my list. Playing for your country is still the ultimate honour, but at an individual level, to be selected when they have a choice from four national squads is really special. It means you have done an awful lot right in your life and your career to reach this pinnacle.

We assembled in a hotel in London two weeks later to pick up all our rugby gear and formal wear and leisure wear and get the official squad photograph taken. Then it was up to the Welsh centre of excellence in the Vale of Glamorgan for a few days and after that, a transfer to Carton House. A lot of the lads were still away with their clubs. You're always wondering in advance who you'll be sharing with and when I got to my room in Carton there was no one there. But there were a load of bags on the floor with "Phillips" branded on them. I would wonder no more. It was the man himself, the Welsh master, my idol growing up, Mike Phillips. I was 24, he was 30 going on 31 and had seen it all and done it all. Over the previous couple of years I'd been compared to him several times by pundits and rugby writers in the newspapers. We were both considered unusually tall for our position and we were both pretty strong and physical too.

'A POOR MAN'S MIKE PHILLIPS'

As soon as we met we clicked. Mike was friendly and open and turned out to be great company. We had five days in Kildare before we were due to cross to London for the farewell dinner on the Sunday before shipping out to Hong Kong for our first port of call.

Gats is an old-school rugby coach when it comes to a good night out and sure enough we were all bussed into Dublin one evening for a getting-to-know-each-other bonding session over a few scoops. We headed for Kehoe's off Grafton Street and the place was hopping. My new roomie was soon in the middle of the craic and he was obviously familiar with all the comparisons being made between me and him because we were only a few beers down when the slagging started: "Ah, you're just a poor man's Mike Phillips!", "You're a mini-me!", "There's only one Mike Phillips!", etc. We were having a great laugh at this and Paulie was telling him he better look out, Murray's coming for your place, watch your back, Mike. When people are taking the Mick it's always a good sign that they see you as a peer, one of them, part of the group. I was loving it. And no matter how much science goes into your strength and conditioning these days, I think there should always be room for a night out on the beer. It'll do wonders for team spirit in a way that a session in the gym will never do. And, of course, with the Lions it's especially important because you've to get a huge bunch of strangers to bond together very quickly as a team.

Two years earlier at the World Cup, my first exposure to major league rugby was an eye-opener in terms of the scale of everything, the size of the budgets for travel and accommodation, the publicity and media profile. Here I was discovering that there was a whole other level again. The sheer lavishness of the operation was a bit overwhelming at the start. This felt like big-time sport on a grand scale. There was a heavyweight corporate dimension all over it. The amount of staff was one thing – physios, masseurs, doctors, coaches, logistics. There was just more of everything. And it was the best of everything too, money no object. You were given so much clothing, gear and merchandise, you didn't know what to do with half of it.

The farewell dinner, for example, was held in the Royal Courts of Justice in London, no less. It was like walking into a vast, ancient cathedral. The prestige and grandeur and history of it – it was a far cry from the Chicken Hut in Limerick, I can tell you. Everyone was dressed in their official blazers and slacks, shirts and ties, cufflinks and socks and boxer shorts. The whole outfit was designed by Thomas Pink tailors. Everything was high-end and top class.

At the Royal Courts of Justice it felt like a showbiz night that you'd see on television, like the BAFTAs or something. You had TV cameras and lights, loads of photographers, a lot of rich and successful business people. We were announced into the dining room. Every table was assigned two or three players to mingle with the corporate sponsors and their guests. The food and wines were five-star. The whole thing was like a glimpse into the world of how the other half lives, or the other one per cent, I suppose.

After the speeches were finished and the whole palaver was over you were left in no doubt, if you didn't know already, that you were part of something far bigger than yourself. You were being connected with a tradition that went back to the 19th century. You were joining a roll call that included most of the greatest players ever produced by the four home nations. The

'A POOR MAN'S MIKE PHILLIPS'

starry-eyed kid on the beach in Kerry in 2001 was learning twelve years later what wearing the Lions jersey truly meant.

A week later I was wearing it for real against a Barbarians line-up in the searing heat and draining humidity of Hong Kong. I took over from Phillips in the 57th minute. It was the hottest temperature I have ever played in. The humidity was hellish. The Lions were dominating and strange to say, but games like these can be the hardest to play in aerobically because you're attacking all the time, you're not playing pragmatically, you're running the ball at every turn. I was only on for 23 minutes but it felt more like an hour because it was all running, running, running. In the dressing room afterwards we were wringing out our jerseys like we'd been swimming in them. I'd never seen the likes of it. But I was very happy to have gotten to wear it in action. I was relieved to have gotten onto the pitch. I made a good break down the right hand side at one stage too and put Alex Cuthbert away for a try, so I was delighted with that. It took a lot of the pressure and the stress off to get a run in the first game of the tour. You didn't want to be waiting around for weeks before seeing a bit of game-time.

The social side of things was fairly lively too. I remember after one night out in Hong Kong, we were in the swimming pool next morning for a recovery session that involved us jogging up and down the pool in straight lines. One of the boys was still so langers he was going up and down more in an S formation than in straight lines. Then Gats decided to sweat the beer out of us with a ferocious pitch session in 30-degree heat and the humidity still savage. Trotting around was hard enough, never mind full-on running. We had these big cooling fans around the pitch that sprayed water at us and we had ice jackets and ice towels. We were all wearing our heart monitors and a few of them were showing the strain alright.

But everyone dogged it out because at that level you don't just have the most talented players from England, Ireland, Scotland and Wales, they'll generally be the mentally toughest too. It's one reason why they end up as Lions in the first place. I was still getting used to seeing such high-calibre brilliance everywhere you looked on the training ground. I mean, the standard was off the charts. The sheer size and power of fellas like George North and Manu Tuilagi, for example. George was freakish in power and speed. Seeing him in the gym was an eye-opener, doing these explosive exercises with these massive legs under him. Jamie Roberts, the size and power of him too. Stuart Hogg's speed, Justin Tipuric's pure class as a footballer, Owen Farrell and the way he could rip a pass, how silky it looked, his complete skill set.

Owen was only 21 at the time. He made a big impression on me, especially the day when he arrived late for a meeting at Carton House. We had a pitch session after and at the end of training, Gats calls us into a huddle on the field and he was like, "Good session", etc. Then he looks over at Owen and reminds him about being late for the meeting that morning and hands him a ball and a kicking tee and says he has to land a kick from where we're standing, or he'll be getting a punishment. We're all sniggering and laughing because the court sessions are part of the craic on tour and we have this system of fines and embarrassing punishments which are fairly arbitrary the way they're dished out. You'd be going round trying not to get fined, but in the end everyone gets hit with something.

Anyway, Owen takes the ball, sets it on the tee, takes his steps

'A POOR MAN'S MIKE PHILLIPS'

back and gets himself into his mental zone for the strike. It is not an easy kick by any means and he has 30 people standing around looking at him. He steps up and absolutely nails it. He gets a round of applause from everyone. And I'm like, fuck me, this fella is a proper baller.

You have to muck in on the social side during a Lions tour. I knew that already. I was aware from conversations with the likes of Paulie and other Irish lads who'd been on these tours before. You have to go in with an attitude of being really open because that's how you make it work. Be open to new relationships, try to avoid getting drawn into your own clique, mix in with the lads you don't know. So, you put yourself out there a bit more than you normally would with a new group of people. Socially you have to get out of your comfort zone and that's good for you as a person as well as a Lions player.

I found it easy enough. I knew beforehand that it was going to be such a class life experience that you had to make the most of it and give it your all. It can't be easy though for fellas who are just naturally shy and reserved. The beauty of team sport is that you'll have a blend of different personalities who all share similar levels of talent and have the same ambitions. But you can get a wide range of character types in that one group. There was one fella on this tour who was unbelievably talented and incredibly polite and quiet off the field. It was just his nature. He expressed himself brilliantly on the pitch and would barely express himself off it at all. You can't be forcing these lads to be the life and soul when it's just not in their nature. Then, on the other hand, you have the lads who are complete and total messers. These are the fellas who you're liable to find down the back of the bus acting the maggot and taking the mickey and holding court. There's a kind of a social hierarchy in a rugby squad and the lads down the back of the bus tend to be the alpha males, the big dogs.

Sam Warburton was the Lions captain and I'd imagine he found it a tough gig at first because he was still only 24 and there's a lot of responsibility involved in terms of setting the tone and leading from the front, not just on-field, but off-field too. The captain is supposed to be an inspiring speaker too and Sam struck me initially as someone who was more comfortable doing his leading on the pitch than in meetings. He was surrounded by battle-hardened veterans who were much more senior than him, including Drico and Paulie who'd been Lions captains in 2005 and 2009. I'd imagine it was daunting for Sam, at least in the early stages when he sat out the first few games with an injury. When you're playing it's a lot easier to do the talking and leading. Lads tend to switch off if you're not actually out there training and playing. So, it was hard for him to make an impression in the first few weeks. And he was a fairly clean-cut, clean-living type of fella, he wasn't a messer and joker.

On a team bus of any description, you'll always find the messers down the back. During this tour I ventured a good bit down the bus but stayed far enough away from them too in case I came into their line of fire! By evening time most days I'd find my social battery would be fairly well drained. You're hanging out with this big group of blokes from breakfast in the morning to dinner in the evening and all points in between. By the time you got back to your room you'd be glad of the peace and quiet of your own company, just to unwind.

I started our second game, against the Western Force in Perth. Ben Youngs replaced me after 65 minutes and started the next

'A POOR MAN'S MIKE PHILLIPS'

one, against the Queensland Reds in Brisbane. Ben played really well; he scored a try and stayed on for the full 80. In fact, I was the only unused sub that night and came away fairly down in myself. Fellas were coming up to me in the dressing room after saying a few consoling words and patting me on the head and telling me I'd be back in the ball game soon. It was nice of them to be so thoughtful, but I don't think it was helping my mood at all. I was keeping a journal at the time and I remember writing down in it that I did not want to be feeling so shit again after a game and the next time I got a chance to make sure I'd take it. I'd gone from the high of playing in the first two games to feeling totally irrelevant in the next one and I did not like it one little bit. But it brought home a real powerful moment of clarity that stayed with me: basically that it was all well and good being part of this amazing adventure, but if you're not playing it's going to become a pretty hollow experience pretty quickly. That thought clicked in my mind. The competitive edge came out in me. I would have to take care of business first and forget about the buzz and the novelty of it all.

You weren't going to stake your claim for a place in the Test team against a selection of amateurs and semi-professionals, but I'd have to make the most of the midweek match against a combined Queensland-New South Wales XV in Newcastle. I started, scored a try, played 70 minutes, but as a contest it was a bit of a farce. In fact, I was in a ruck at one stage and one of their fellas was on the ground beside me and he goes, "Can I get your jersey after?"

"What?"

"Can we swap after?"

Jeez, okay, but can we get the game over with first?! There's a general etiquette that if a fella comes into your dressing room after a match looking for your jersey, you give it to him. I've heard of a few refusals in my day – the All Blacks are notorious for it – and it'd be very awkward to turn somebody down so normally you'd do it. In the end I was happy to swap with the lad. They all piled into our dressing room after and we all swapped and I still have his jersey somewhere up in my attic.

Meanwhile, Zeebs was on his way to Australia. He was called up as cover and landed in Sydney a few days before we played the Waratahs. I was out around Bondi beach with a few of the lads enjoying a coffee when my phone rings. It's Zeebs saying he's in his hotel room and he wants me to meet him first and then introduce him to the group rather than him having to walk in on his own. You never thought he'd be that shy! So, I meet him at the hotel and bring him round and introduce him to everyone and next thing, of course, he's laughing and joking and chatting like he's known them all his life. It then transpires that he's going to go straight into the starting team for the Waratahs. But he only has black boots with him and I've a lovely pair of whites and he nicks them. He likes his bright boots and so do I.

I hate wearing black boots. I never feel right in myself wearing black. It might seem silly, but there's a bit of logic to it, I believe. It's something to do with how colour reacts in your brain. I just feel better in orange, or red or white boots. It's that thing of 'Look good, feel good, play good'. Maybe it's just superstition. All the grizzled old forwards would be laughing at us, but them fellas would be happy enough playing in their wellingtons. I like my boots to be bright and sunny, I feel sharp in them. So, if Adidas bring out a new boot in black and send a few pairs to me, I'll just give them away.

'A POOR MAN'S MIKE PHILLIPS'

Zeebs does the whole 80 against Waratahs while Phillips starts at nine and Youngs comes off the bench. Obviously the selection committee is looking towards the first Test and moving the pawns on the chessboard accordingly. The Brumbies in Canberra is the final warm-up and in this one Ben starts while I'm on the bench. Phillips is a shoo-in for the starting fifteen in the first Test so they're holding him in reserve for that. Ben has won the battle for the place on the bench because he's in great form and so I'm going to be out of the reckoning, which is fair enough. I'm not frustrated or annoyed because I can understand the logic, but I am more than a little bit envious when the players are presented with their Test jerseys a few days before. It's a proper ceremony, the chosen lads get called up one by one for the presentation and it's definitely something I want to experience.

My chances recede a little further after we win the first Test. I'm sitting in my suit up in the stand watching Alex Cuthbert run in a brilliant try, and the team in general playing really well. My place is with the 'dirt-trackers' and we will have our final match of the tour between the first and second Tests, against the Melbourne Rebels.

I score the first of our five tries on the day and it's pretty obvious even before half-time that we're going to have a handy outing here. In fact, it's so obvious that Zeebs the bollocks decides to play a prank on me. There's about 20 seconds left in the half and we're 14-0 up and I arrive at a ruck on our own 22. We have possession, but it's all a bit static. Next thing I hear Zeebs shouting at me, "Half-time, half-time, kick it out, kick it out!" So, I pick up the ball and kick it into the stand only to see the ref signalling for a lineout to the Rebels! I was sure he was going to blow his whistle for the half-time break and I'm looking around me absolutely baffled. And then I see Zebo and he's cracking up, he's roaring with the laughing. I've just gifted the Rebels a lineout inside our half of the field and he thinks it's hilarious! It is now. I didn't find it so funny at the time! I'm trying to make an impression with the selectors and I make this elementary mistake courtesy of my buddy from Cork. Anyway, we end up winning 35-0 so everyone's happy and we're all laughing about it in the dressing room afterwards. I think even Gats sees the funny side of it, eventually.

We board the bus back to base, but now my body is shaking and trembling so much that the physios notice it and come over, wondering if there's something wrong with me. Turns out I'd overdosed on caffeine in the dressing room earlier. The Welsh boys have these caffeine drinks that they take before games and I decide to help myself to not one, but two of them, not knowing that they're rocket fuel. On top of that, I've already drunk two cans of Red Bull. It's no wonder I'm feckin' wired. I tell the physios what I've consumed and they're worried all of a sudden. They phone the hotel from the bus and tell our liaison guy there to have an ice bath ready for me when we get back. They reckon I've got dangerously high levels of caffeine in my system and they want to plunge me into ice to get my body temperature down. It works a treat and my system cools down and everything is fine, but I'll be steering well clear of the caffeine shots from now on.

It's kind of gone down in Lions lore that I got my own back on Zebo at our next players' court session. Everyone is there in the team room when I tell my story of how he stitched me up in the Rebels game. For his punishment he has to ring Rob Penney and

'A POOR MAN'S MIKE PHILLIPS'

ask if he can be Munster captain for the following season. He makes the call, everyone in the room is on tenterhooks hoping Rob will pick up. Rob had taken over as Munster head coach a year earlier. Zeebs gets through to him and he and Rob have a bit of small talk before he blurts out the question: now that Dougie has retired, would you consider me for the captaincy next season? Everyone is sniggering and chuckling, trying to hold in the explosion of laughing. It dawns on Rob pretty quickly that there's something fishy going on here and then the whole room just cracks up. In fairness, the whole set-up and punchline worked a treat and Zeebs was only too happy to play his part in the whole charade.

We're counting down to the second Test in Melbourne at this stage and the word is that Phillips is touch-and-go for it because of a knee issue. Then we get confirmation that he's out, so suddenly I'm back in the ball game. Ben will step up to the starting slot and I'll get my place on the bench. It's a tough old slog of a game, very tense and attritional.

Warburton is having a huge match. He is everywhere on the pitch. His leadership and class really come to the fore in this game. I'm sent in on 53 minutes and as it happens, I manage to get involved immediately by winning a jackal penalty at the breakdown. I haven't got many of them in my career, but this one gives me a real boost of confidence and from there to the finish I'm flying it. I'm kicking well from the hand and snapping my passes away and generally feel like I'm making a difference. I'm only on the field a few minutes when the Aussies fumble the ball loose in midfield, I shovel it over to Drico, he catches and in the same movement throws it between his legs to North. George is actually static when he gets it and Israel Folau is up in his face. And from a standing start, George somehow picks up Folau, throws him up on his shoulder and makes a few yards carrying ball and man. I don't have much time to admire it, but it's an amazing sight. Australia keep the series alive with a late try and conversion to squeak home by a single point.

On the bus back to our base, Zeebs is telling me I've done enough to start the final Test. I'm getting messages from home telling me people are raving about my performance. I reckon Phillips will start if he's fit, but maybe I have a shot at making the bench now: I don't know. That's how it turns out, but my promotion over Ben Youngs is only in the ha'penny place compared to the furore over Drico getting dropped, not just from the first fifteen, but the 23 entirely. Gats has taken a huge gamble and my bit of good news gets lost in the greater controversy. In the meantime we're let loose for a few days on the lash in Noosa on the Gold Coast. It's an incredible party town and we don't spare the horses. The jury is out on whether this is the right thing to be doing before a Test match of this magnitude, but it's part of the touring tradition and in this case it doesn't do us any harm. Alun Wyn Jones takes over the captaincy because Sam is out injured and he sends us out of the dressing room with our spines tingling after an incredible speech.

We are three points in front when I come on with about half an hour to go. But the tide of the game has been flowing our way and we put it to bed with three tries in ten minutes. Jamie Roberts scores the third one in the 67th minute and that seals the deal. I break lateral off the back of a maul and pop it to Jamie coming full throttle on a straight line and he's through the gap and streaking away for the score. The noise and atmosphere

'A POOR MAN'S MIKE PHILLIPS'

at this stage are giving me goosebumps. I'm hearing 'Bread of Heaven' ringing round the stadium and I have time to stop and think about what a great song it is. The last ten minutes are just pure pleasure because the work is done, we know we can't be caught, we have made our own slice of Lions history. I have seen all the old DVDs; I've been steeped in the whole mythology for the previous ten years, so to be out on the pitch with ten minutes left in the final Test, knowing you've won the series – I can honestly say it is one of the happiest times I have ever enjoyed on a rugby field. I could look around me and take it all in.

We were all chatting away among ourselves as the game petered out. It was special; it was magic. Back in the dressing room it's champagne all the way. Bottles of bubbly, singing and shouting and hugging and cheering – and then Daniel Craig walks into the middle of it all. James Bond himself. We're all queuing up for photos with him; I have mine somewhere in a box. I'm tipping back a bottle of the bubbly when Owen Farrell bumps into me and chips half my tooth off. Is there a dentist about the place?! A while later the media manager comes over to me and Sexto and says he needs us for a few interviews with the Irish reporters and broadcasters. We're already half-cut at this stage. The only problem is that the mixed zone is on the other side of the stadium, so we get a golf buggy over, still in our kit and our boots, and we end up being driven through crowds of Lions fans who go mad cheering and clapping when they see us. There's loads of Irish people too, with their tricolours and all, giving us the high fives along the way.

Australia as a country to tour is the best. I've been there several times; it's never less than brilliant. The next few nights in Sydney were outrageous craic. We were just on a permanent high. You could not wipe the smile off my face. In fact, I'd say I slept smiling, whenever I did manage to grab a few hours' kip.

I had the time of my life on that tour, going out as a rookie and coming back having made my name and played my part in a series victory. I find out for myself that it's true what all the old Lions players say: you make memories for life and you make friends for life. The 2013 tour of Australia is a memory that will keep me warm into ripe old age.

Chapter Nine

A BIG MAC IN MAYNOOTH

SOMETIMES ON IRELAND DUTY THE cabin fever would get a bit too much, even in Carton House. You were living in the lap of luxury and you had two golf courses on a thousand acres of land if you needed to get some fresh air and a nice walk to clear your head.

But even so, Joe Schmidt had this ability to turn the whole thing into a bit of a hothouse with his intensity and work ethic. And you'd be feeling the pressure yourself anyway because there was always pressure in your head, irrespective of who was in charge. Every game was pressure. Every day was a performance day, be it in the gym or out on the training ground. You couldn't really switch off. And then if you had a head coach who couldn't switch off either, it could all get a bit claustrophobic. Most of the time, I was fine; it didn't bother me. I was comfortable enough in my own skin.

But one night I just got an itch to break curfew. I needed a bit of a release. One thought led to another and suddenly I had this goo on me for a McDonald's, of all things. Jesus, I'd love a good old burger and fries and a fizzy drink to wash it down.

Obviously we were getting the best of food in camp. We were fed like kings. But in this spur of the moment, I had a craving for a hit of messy old fast food. Maybe it was the appeal of something forbidden; I don't know. Or maybe the temptation was nagging at me because it was so close at hand. It wasn't like I'd have to drive into Dublin. Maynooth was less than ten minutes away by car. And McDonald's had a drive-thru outlet there. So, I could be there and back in double-quick time. That was my cunning plan. I'd be back before anyone noticed I was gone. I'd bring my Ireland backpack with me and hide the bag of goods in there and enjoy it at my leisure back in my room. This was maybe eight o'clock in the evening. Usually at that time the ground floor of the hotel would be quiet enough; the staff and players would be back in their rooms, our work done for the day.

It all goes smoothly. Big Mac, large fries and a coke, please. I'm in and out of the drive-thru in no time. Back in Carton House I park up in the players' car park. I have my contraband in my backpack and I saunter inside and head for the lifts. Next thing, who appears out of nowhere, but Joe. I swear to God, you couldn't make it up. The last man on earth I want to bump into at that precise moment in time!

"Howya Conor!" Big smiley face on him. I can't believe it. I try to blabber something out.

"Joe! How's things?"

"Ah grand." He's like, "where were you?"

I gesture to my backpack. "I was just fetching something from my car."

"Oh, okay."

We're at the lifts now, the bell pings and the doors open and Jesus, he's coming into the bloody lift with me now. I'm trying to keep my composure, hoping he doesn't notice my body language. There's an awkward silence. The greasy food in my bag is starting to waft a bit and I can smell it. Unfortunately, so can he. He turns up his nose and in that distinctive accent goes, "What's that smell?"

"Smell?"

"Yeah, there's a funny smell."

"Dunno Joe, dunno." Christ this lift is crawling along. Then ping! It stops and the door opens and I have to check myself from running out of it. "See you in the morning, Joe," and I walk away, all casual like.

The doors close and I heave an almighty sigh of relief. I am one rattled boy. I get to my hotel room, but I can barely eat the grub. I cannot believe he's turned up just like that. Like a ghost, like he has a sixth sense. The one and only time I step offside and he turns up right there in front of me. Un-fuckin'-believable.

And, in my paranoia, I'm convinced he has me rumbled. He knows. He fuckin' well knows because he knows everything and he spots everything. I have never enjoyed a burger and chips less in my life. I'm looking at it thinking, this isn't worth it, this just isn't worth it. At that stage I'd have enjoyed a boring old chicken and pasta a helluva lot more.

But maybe in hindsight, he actually didn't know because it would have been inconceivable for Joe Schmidt to think that I'd have had a McDonald's in my bag. He would just assume that none of us would even dream of doing something like that. This is an ultra-professional environment. We are high performance athletes and he is a high performance coach. It would be unthinkable for any of us to prefer a milkshake to a protein shake. It just wouldn't cross his mind that it might be possible for one of his players to do such a thing. And yet here we were, me making small talk with him in the lift while inside I'm like a nervous schoolboy who is petrified that he's about to be caught red-handed by the headmaster. I'm supposed to be a grown adult here, not a child. But in this environment there is always a bit of that classroom dynamic going on: the players are the pupils, the coaches are the teachers and the head coach is the school principal that you're a small bit afraid of – and sometimes a big bit. After all, Joe was a schoolteacher before he went fulltime into coaching.

I was genuinely unnerved by that episode. Obviously it was only a tiny misdemeanour in the grander scheme. It wasn't like I'd broken out of my hotel room and gone on the piss. It was a burger and chips, a little treat to myself, but I can tell you it was the first and last time I ever did it.

Joe took over from Deccie as Ireland head coach in the summer of 2013. His reputation went before him at this stage. He'd managed Leinster to two Heineken Cups in 2011 and 2012. He had a high profile and a great CV. He was a shoo-in for the job. It was already well-established that he was a hard taskmaster, a stickler for detail, a man with high standards. The type of fella who was right up my street, actually. But like everyone else, I was apprehensive driving into camp for the squad's first coming together under the new boss. This was in the September of 2013.

It was a different atmosphere straightaway. It was straight down to business. He had us doing a walk-through of various moves in this smallish room, like a pre-function room where you'd be having drinks at a wedding before moving into the banqueting suite. And more or less immediately he's scolding fellas for not running lines properly or not punching onto the ball. But if you were to punch onto a ball here, you'd end up punching a hole in the wall and breaking the mirrors before you could slow down. It didn't matter, it was a two-day training camp and he was going to maximise every minute of it. The Leinster boys would have known that this was his form. But for the rest of us it was our first lesson in how he operated and how different the environment was going to be.

I was still on a high from the Lions tour that summer and after that first get-together was over I was booked for a massage. The masseur had brought a match programme with him from one of the Lions games. He asked me to sign it and I duly obliged and next thing Joe comes over and cracks a remark, something like, oh you're a big dog now, Jeez you're holding onto that aren't you?! As in, I was holding onto my big adventure with the Lions a few months earlier. He said it with a half smile, like it was a bit of banter, but of course, there was a bit of a dig wrapped up in there too. It planted a little bit of a guilt-trip on me, I was suddenly beating myself up, thinking that I shouldn't have been signing the programme because the Lions was over and I should've put it behind me. Obviously I was just obliging the fella who asked for my autograph, I wasn't looking into it any more than that – but Joe was!

I start against Samoa, the first of the autumn internationals, Joe's first Test match, and Redser replaces me on the hour mark. Three or four days later Joe announces the starting XV for Australia and Redser's in, I'm on the bench. I get the hump about this. I've been first choice for over two years and I've just come back from the aforementioned Lions tour where I've ended up getting a lot of game-time there too. But maybe I should have known from his previous remark that this wasn't going to cut the mustard with him. He was going to make up his own mind. Anyway, I approach him for a chat after the team meeting is over and it's the first time I've ever had a one-on-one with him. I'm not great in these situations: I'm not used to them, and I'm stuttering a bit with my words and Joe just cuts me off and says directly, "I'm not decided on nine yet." And that's more or less the conversation. He has put me back in my box before I've even had time to get out of it.

I go away and stew on it. It worries me because this is a stacked Ireland team and Redser is going to have the benefit of being surrounded by the best players. If the team performs well he has first dibs on the jersey going forward. But if I'm supposed to be the number one scrumhalf, why didn't he start Redser against Samoa and me against Australia, instead of the other way round? The answer, I tell myself, is because he knows and trusts Eoin from their Leinster days. And coaches, understandably, tend to go with the player they've worked with rather than opt for someone they don't know. It's just human nature, I suppose. I understand that more now than I did at the age of 24. As it turns out, I came on after 56 minutes, but it was a fairly shit day all round for us and the Aussies beat us comfortably.

A week later the men in black are in town. Thank God I'm named to start in this one. This is my 22nd Ireland match. I will go on to play another hundred and more, but this game stands out as one of my all-time favourites. And we didn't even win the damned thing. This was the one against New Zealand that got away. The whole country was on the edge of its seat watching. After over a century of trying, Ireland still hadn't beaten the All

A BIG MAC IN MAYNOOTH

Blacks. The record was played 27, lost 26, drawn 1. And now it looked like it was about to happen. We had a shot at history in our grasp. The atmosphere in the Aviva that day was sensational. It still stands out in my memory. The sheer hunger in the crowd to witness history was feeding into us down on the field. I was buzzing from the atmosphere. I lost myself in the ebb and flow of the game. I don't mean I was lost and struggling to cope. I mean, I became so immersed in the action that I forgot about everything else in the world except what was happening right in front of me. I was lost in a good way. Nothing else mattered. I was just completely absorbed in my work. We all were.

We hit the ground running, we had a try by the fourth minute. Great carries by Jamie Heaslip and Peter O'Mahony got us up to within three metres. I picked up and crashed between Wyatt Crockett and Andrew Hore for the touchdown. Nigel Owens kicked it up to the TMO to see if I'd lost control in the grounding of the ball. Brodie Retallick had tried to dislodge it as I was falling to the floor. One of the commentators working for NZ television reckoned I hadn't got downward pressure. Thankfully, the TMO reckoned I had.

We were up and running and the crowd was roaring. The first 20 minutes we were in dreamland. It still gives me goosebumps looking at it more than a decade later. Besty gets our second in the tenth minute. Then Kearns has his famous run-in all the way home from our 22m line. The crowd were lifting the roof off now. The place was absolutely rocking. I was in the middle of the field defending when Rob latched onto the intercept. I started running after him, but slowed down once I knew he was going to make it on his own. As he hit halfway, I swear to God I never, ever, experienced noise like it. And it just got louder and then hit a crescendo as he scored. I was stood in the middle of the pitch and my head was buzzing from the noise. The waves of sound were rolling down so hard it was like your head was vibrating. It was unreal, it was an out-of-body experience for me, so I don't know what it was like for Kearns.

We are 19-0 up on eighteen minutes. Then the All Blacks wake us up from our dream seven minutes later with Julian Savea's try. They are always going to have their purple patch. That's just inevitable with New Zealand. But it doesn't mean that losing to them is inevitable either. We're not accepting that on this day of all days. We're willing and able to dig in against them. And we do. We make them earn their yards. It turns into a long, hard battle. We're not giving them anything easy. It takes them until the 65th minute to get their second try. That leaves us 22-17 ahead. We have fifteen minutes to survive. Our lungs are heaving now. We are gulping down oxygen. We're under siege more or less for the remainder of the game. We're defending for our lives. We're running over and back, over and back, over and back. Just making tackles and getting back into the line again. Phase after phase after phase. We find out afterwards that the GPS stats for several of us exceed our previous records. It's the most running I have ever done in a game up until that point and it's still among the highest of my whole career. My calves were cramping up late on.

Bit by bit, metre by metre, the All Blacks get closer and closer to our line. Their skills and accuracy under pressure are famous for a reason. It doesn't get more pressurised than the 82nd minute of an 80-minute game. It's desperation time, but they stick to the process, move it through the hands one more time and Dane Coles, their sub hooker, is able to throw a dummy that takes out the last defender and get his hands free out of the tackle to pop it to Ryan Crotty for the touchdown. I have scrambled across; Crotty is out of reach to tackle him properly, but I give him a shove that knocks him down maybe five metres infield. Obviously the nearer he gets to the posts the easier the conversion will be. This is still going to be a tough conversion for the kicker. But Joe gives out to me afterwards for not bringing him down closer to the touchline. He's replaying it on video and saying I should have made him put it down here rather than there. And there was me thinking I'd done well enough to get anything on him at all. I was seizing up at that stage.

Anyway, the conversion. The upside of Joe's pernickety mindset is that no detail goes neglected. For the non-Leinster lads, this autumn campaign is our first prolonged exposure to his methods. We find out that he has done an in-depth profile of every opposing player we are likely to face, squad members included. Whatever habits a player has, we're told about them. He has a highlight reel on every one of them. The All Blacks, of course, get a granular inspection, one by one. And when it comes to Aaron Cruden, their flyhalf, he shows us footage of Cruden's ritual when lining up kicks at goal. Joe hones in on Cruden's foot shuffle. He does this tiny movement with his legs before breaking into his run-up. So, Joe warns us not to charge at him while he's doing his shuffle because that's illegal. He's still deemed to be stationary at this point. You can't charge until he breaks into his stride. "Don't go early," Joe warns us, "don't go early."

Right. We have that boxed off. And now in the 82nd minute we are lined up across our line, waiting to make the charge. A few of us remember Joe's instructions. I'm one of them. I shout, "Don't go yet, don't go yet." And what do we do? We go early. Cruden twitches his legs and three or four of our lads shoot off the line. They've gone so early they're nearly in his face by the time he kicks it. Those of us who stayed on the line are looking at each other in disbelief. Like, we've literally just said not to do that. This isn't Joe's team talk earlier in the week. We've literally just said it a few seconds before they do it. I mean, for fuck's sake. That's what kills me about this game. Cruden pushes his shot wide right. But Nigel has spotted the premature charge from our lads. I mean you'd need to be blind not to see it, it's so obvious. So, Cruden's going to get a second crack at it.

I sometimes think that half the battle in rugby is with fellas not listening to what they're being told. Like, are you taking this in or are you just nodding along and it's going in one ear and out the other? Some players only need to be told once. Others, you could be telling them 'til you're blue in the face and they still won't take it in. And what's worse, they'll then do the exact opposite of what they were told! This is a classic case in point. We wouldn't have won the match, but if Cruden's first effort stood, we'd have got a draw.

Fellas like Paulie and Drico who'd spent their careers trying to break Ireland's duck would've signed off with something to show for their heroic efforts against New Zealand down the years. If I still get goosebumps watching the first 20 minutes of this match, it still sickens me to watch the last few minutes. Cruden drills it between the posts the second time, the final whistle blows and they're celebrating and we're shattered. The contrast in the crowd is night and day too. All that ecstasy and noise in the first 20 minutes; now it's boos and silence. It's like going from a wedding to a funeral in the space of an hour. It's a devastating turn of events.

Being the last game of the autumn series, we headed out on the town that night. A load of us ended up in Krystle night club where we bumped into a bunch of the All Blacks. I was still a bit wide-eyed about moving in these circles. It was really cool having a few drinks with Aaron Smith, Beauden Barrett, TJ Perenara and others. The All Blacks still had an aura about them as far as I was concerned. You mightn't admit it in public, but privately you were probably still looking to gain their respect. And that was a brilliant team. Beating us meant they had gone unbeaten in a calendar year, the first team to do that since the game had gone professional. So, you were in the presence of greatness here. They were the gold standard.

At one stage I'm chatting to Perenara and he's like, "You're a good player, bro". Like I say, there was drink taken, but it meant a lot to me, coming from an All Black. You'd often hear it said that they wouldn't be able to name most of the Ireland players. But there's no doubting that we'd earned their respect that afternoon in the Aviva and it was very nice to receive that personal bit of validation, even if it was in Krystle in the small hours of the night. In fact, if memory serves, some of us ended up having breakfast there too.

Looking back on it now, it's probably a miracle that I didn't end up bumping into Joe coming out of there too. The one comfort I was taking out of the match was that maybe I'd helped him make up his mind about the nine jersey. This was a huge match and I thought I'd acquitted myself well in it. Not that it mattered what I thought, or even what TJ Perenara thought. It was Mr Schmidt who was most definitely running the show now.

Chapter Ten

MY KIND OF TOWN

THEY SAY EVERY PROFESSIONAL SPORTSMAN dies twice, the first time when he retires from the game he loves. In the case of Drico's Ireland career, he died with his boots on. We sent him into international retirement with the Six Nations title on the occasion of his 133rd and final game in green. It was 15th March 2014, and as his epic career closed, the Joe Schmidt era opened with silverware on that day in Paris. O'Driscoll had done so much to change the culture of Irish rugby over the previous 15 years. He had raised the bar and set a new standard for Irish players. I was a beneficiary of that and so were the rest of my generation. We had the fruits of it in our dressing room in the Stade de France that evening in the shape of our medals and my first trophy as an Ireland player. It was a huge win for us and for Joe. We were properly up and running.

Twelve months later we were holding up the same trophy again at Murrayfield on that famous 'Super Saturday' when we needed someone who was good at mathematics to keep us briefed as the final day of the championship turned into a points race. Wales had put 61 points on Italy, we put 40 on Scotland, then we watched with beers in our hands in the function room in Murrayfield while England put 55 on France in Twickenham.

MY KIND OF TOWN

One more converted try would have given them the title. It was an incredibly dramatic finish to a Six Nations tournament. England needed a 26-point winning margin over France. They got to 20. Jamie Heaslip's try-saving tackle on Stuart Hogg with five minutes to go in our game was suddenly huge. In fact, it became the difference. Usually, those last-ditch tackles don't prevent a player from scoring. It looked like Hogg would finish, he was over the line and fending off Jamie with his left hand while cradling the ball in his right. Somehow Jamie managed to slap it from his grasp as Hogg was falling to touch it down. And boy did it matter some three hours later.

The rest of the year would be all about the Rugby World Cup. The 31-man squad was leaked to the media a day or two before the official announcement. Joe was fuming about it because control was everything to him and this was something that breached his control. But in this day and age it's nearly impossible to stop leaks no matter how tight the ship is run. Myself and Redser were the two scrumhalves. Bossy was unlucky to miss out, so were a few other lads, and then there were one or two who got the rub of the green.

There are always winners and losers in these situations. One fella managed to talk himself into the squad more than play his way into it. He was never out of the team room, a bit like the class swot, chatting to Joe all the time and getting himself into the headmaster's good books as much as he could. Personally, I've no time for that carry-on. In fact, I fuckin' despise it. For me and for most fellas you lived by the rule of letting your game do the talking for you.

An early highlight of the tournament was getting to play at Wembley. I mean, the history and fame of that stadium. It's renowned around the world. As a kid I sat at home in Patrickswell watching the FA Cup final being played there every year. And there I was myself. But for atmosphere, nothing compared to the Millennium Stadium for the final group game against France. It was stunning, one of the most electric atmospheres I ever experienced. We lost Johnny, we lost Paulie and we lost Pete, but there was massive heart and spirit in us that day. The cracking Irish support kept our adrenaline flowing too. They were belting out the 'Fields of Athenry' and 'Olé Olé Olé' and you couldn't help but be inspired by it. That game remains an outstanding memory for me. And having won it, the big prize we'd earned ourselves was avoiding New Zealand. We'd have Argentina instead. We were going to be missing the three lads, and Seán O'Brien was suspended for punching Pascal Pape in the stomach. Plus, Jared Payne was ruled out with a broken bone in his foot. Still and all, we should have enough to get past Argentina.

We'd been forewarned about them. Everyone knew about the shock beatings they'd handed out to Ireland teams in 1999 and 2007. No way were we going to get done again by an Argentina team at a World Cup. But that's exactly what happened. We were too vulnerable without our marquee players, Pete, Paulie and Johnny. And O'Brien at his peak was just an awesome mix of explosive power and competitive courage. He feared no occasion and no team. But it turned out that Argentina didn't fear us one little bit. I think they sensed an opportunity, knowing we were missing so many of our big guns. But in fairness to them, they played out of their skins and totally deserved it. They got the ball early and often to the edge where they had speed and skill. They brought massive passion as well. They won by more than

MY KIND OF TOWN

double scores in the end. That was a dark day, a very fuckin' dark day. A dark few weeks in fact.

In the summer of 2016, I get my 50th cap. It's against South Africa in Port Elizabeth. My first was the friendly against France in Bordeaux before the 2011 World Cup. During those five years I've stayed injury free and I've managed to stay in the team. I'm 27 and all of a sudden I'm sort of a veteran. It has gone far more smoothly than I ever expected. We lose two and win one of the series in South Africa. There is no more than six points between the teams in any of the three games. The Springboks will test the mettle of any team that comes to South Africa. We've had the World Cup disaster the year before and a pretty mediocre 2016 Six Nations, but on this tour you can see the gap closing between Ireland and one of the traditional superpowers. There is real substance and genuine resilience in the squad that Joe is building. He is grafting incredibly hard to improve every single detail in our play. Everyone is expected to step up and improve, fringe players as much as regulars. In terms of standards it's a rising tide and our ambitions are rising with it.

Four and a half months later we prove it in Soldier Field, Chicago, with that famous first-ever win by an Ireland senior men's team against New Zealand. It has only taken 29 matches over the course of 111 years, but finally Irish rugby has broken its duck against the All Blacks. I think I had the game of my life that day. I don't know why it was this day of all days but I do know I felt absolutely brilliant in myself going into it. I was totally buzzing for it that morning. The weather definitely helped my mood. It was November, but the sun was shining in Chicago. It was America, the land of opportunity, and just being in America I think elevated my optimism. It was the home venue of the Chicago Bears. I could feel the razzmatazz that you get with big-time American sport. In my head I was thinking, this is showtime, this is major league, this is the NFL and I'm loving it. Myself and Zeebs went for a walkabout on the pitch before the warm-up. I don't usually go for the walkabout, but I decided to this day to sample the atmosphere and already there were thousands of Irish flags and jerseys in the stands. There would be a crowd of over 63,000 there come kick-off. And I remember saying to Zeebs on our walkabout, this is so cool, this is where you want to be. My whole bloodstream was popping with feel-good vibes. It would maybe take a sports psychologist to unravel all this, but all I can say is that I just felt on top of the world before that game. I was ready to let it rip. After half an hour I dummied a pass and Aaron Smith bought it and I sniped through the gap and ran it in from about 20 metres. Our subs were warming up in the in-goal area there and they mobbed me while the crowd erupted. It was a bloody great feeling. We led by 17 points at half-time.

There was enough know-how and experience in that dressing room to face up to the fact that the All Blacks would come back into it. They would have their purple patch because they're the All Blacks and that's what they do. Those of us who'd lost the three-Test series in New Zealand in 2012 were a lot more battle-hardened now. The message was to not go into our shells when the onslaught came. Don't be frightened by it, don't wish the minutes away, let's keep playing. That was the half-time mantra: keep playing, keep throwing your punches. And Joe also added, because he could see the future: don't be surprised if they score, but don't be surprised either if we score first in this second half. And if we do score, don't make a big deal about it, don't over-

MY KIND OF TOWN

celebrate it because we need to stay focused. Above all else, stay focused whether they score or we score. Three minutes into the second half Zebo goes over in the corner and we're 22 ahead. Do we do what Joe tells us? No we do not. We go fuckin' apeshit. I'm in jumping on top of Zeebs and so is Sexto and a rake of the lads. But in that moment, in a corner of my brain, I'm thinking that Joe is watching us up in his box and making a mental note of us celebrating when he explicitly told us not to! But we just couldn't resist it in the moment.

Then comes the onslaught, two tries in four minutes to reduce the gap to eight with 25 minutes still to play. That's a scarily long time when New Zealand are coming at you like sharks. Johnny limped off with a cramp and I had to take the penalty which put our lead back out to eleven. They started sending in the cavalry from the bench. Scott Barrett scored and his brother Beauden converted to leave it 33-29 with nearly 15 minutes left. The fat was truly in the fire now. This was the point where an Ireland team was supposed to crack. Not today. We had seen that movie too fuckin' often.

In the 75th minute Zebo kicked down close to their corner and we went chasing after it like maniacs. Malakai Fekitoa shovelled it back to Julian Savea and I was first in the chase line and I thought to myself, I'm going to absolutely nail him in the tackle here. I'm going to throw every ounce at him. And I did, I thought I'd properly floored him. But looking back on it on video, he was so strong that he was able to ride the hit and stay on his feet. His power was freakish. The first hit should've been enough, but I had to grab him and hang out of him to haul him down. Both of us were in the in-goal area and we ended up in a heap in touch, just under a load of fans in that corner who were looking down at us and going berserk. Anyway, it was enough to get us a five-metre scrum and it was off the back of that scrum that Jamie sprung and popped it to Robbie Henshaw for the try that sealed the deal. That's one of my favourite tries of all the Ireland tries I've seen scored when I was playing because the feeling was just so sweet. The relief just flooded through my system. We had it in the bag. I remember us jogging back to halfway after jumping all over Robbie and Kearns saying to me something like, don't lose focus, concentrate on the kick-off, keep our heads on the job. And I'm like, "Man, we're done! This is done! We've done it." And Kearns looks up at the clock and goes, you know what, you're actually right. Fuckin' hell, what a buzz.

Honest to God, I felt like Roy of the Rovers that day. Everything I did was the right decision, something good came of everything I did, it was like I could do no wrong. The game just came easy to me. In the middle of the maelstrom I remember thinking to myself, 'Jesus I'm loving this, I'm loving this.' I was just in a special place.

In the months that followed I was looking back on it and trying to analyse what I did in the build-up that week to get me into that flow state. How did I prepare? Maybe I can replicate that performance if I can pinpoint exactly how and why it all came together? But I suppose it was like trying to catch lightning in a bottle. Those conditions and those circumstances were unique to that day. Faz was our defence coach and I remember at the post-match function that night him coming up to me and he'd just got off the phone to Owen, his son. And Faz said Owen wanted to pass on his congratulations to me, he'd never seen a performance like that from me before. It meant a lot to me, coming from a fellow-professional of Owen Farrell's stature.

MY KIND OF TOWN

If I had to choose, I'd probably say it was my favourite day ever in an Irish jersey. In a team sport it's not that often you get a game where so many players reach those heights together. You might get a few in any particular game, but here, if you go through the individual performances, there was a load of us who played to our maximum. The unity of purpose in that squad that day was off the charts. Everyone piled in. There were huge performances all over the field. And this wasn't a day when there were any medals handed out, like we'd got in 2014 and 2015 for winning the Six Nations. But that didn't matter at all. I think the achievement of Chicago goes deeper because we didn't just win, we changed the culture a little bit.

After 111 years of trying, a team had come along that helped change the culture in Irish rugby. In 2022 a much-altered Irish squad went down to New Zealand and won a series there. That would've been unthinkable before Soldier Field. There have been plenty of ups and downs since then, but I reckon that first breakthrough victory started a new era for the sport in Ireland. It blew away the old sense of inferiority against the All Blacks that had been part of the culture of the sport in Ireland for over a century. It's a legacy that any of us who played that day will always be proud of.

Chapter Eleven

THERE IS AN ISLE

WE'RE 27-0 DOWN TO STADE Francais at Stade Jean-Bouin with five minutes left in the game. And it wouldn't be much of an exaggeration to say we're lucky to get nil. Stade have played with fourteen men for the entire second half, but it's they who look like they've the extra man. We are feckin' terrible.

In the 75th minute we manage to save ourselves complete embarrassment on the scoreboard. Zeebs puts in a grubber down the left touchline and somehow it bobbles along inside the white line. Niall Scannell chases it down and just about stays in play as he's tackled. I'm following behind, Niall throws it up to me and I break the last tackle to score. It finishes 27-7. It's 9th January 2016. It's our third loss in Europe in a row. Leicester Tigers have beaten us home and away in December. We are out of the Heineken Cup, now known as the Champions Cup.

In fairness to ourselves, we lost Andrew Conway to an injury after eight minutes, then BJ Botha three minutes later and Tommy O'Donnell after 22 minutes. It never rains but it pours. It's Axel's second full season as head coach. He took over from Rob Penney in the summer of 2014. Everyone knows we're not what we were as a Munster team. The glory days are over and we're falling further away from them. Most of our supporters were there for those glory days in Europe so they still have these really high expectations. In fact, most of us players still have expectations of winning another Heineken Cup. In hindsight, I think we were all a bit in denial about the real state of things at the club. It would take another few years of disappointment for the penny to finally drop.

But back then, people were still expecting great things because we're Munster. And when results are not up to scratch, there is anger and frustration. Nowadays it's more like apathy and acceptance. I don't know which is worse, to be honest. But in Christmas 2016, we are not in a good place. The atmosphere in Thomond Park reaches a new low when Keats is booed off the field in the Leicester game. It's a small minority of fans, but everyone hears it and everyone's a bit shocked by it. It's the first and only time I've ever heard a Munster player being booed by his own supporters at Thomond Park. That's just not part of the culture here. It doesn't happen, it's not supposed to happen. Everyone's heart goes out to him. It's an awful place to be for Keats and his family.

So, by the time we get to Paris in the new year, we're all feeling the pressure. Our morale has gone through the floor and that's reflected in the performance against Stade Francais. It goes without saying that the mood wasn't great that night back in the hotel. In a situation like this there's only one thing anyone can think of to relieve the stress and that's to hit the bar fairly hard. Now, you don't need to be told by a sports psychologist that a few beers isn't going to solve anything. Yeah, we know that. But they'll help us in the here and now. And funnily enough, there is a moment of genuine levity that stands out for me.

Tomás O'Leary, true to form, comes up with a quip in the middle of all the gloom. Tomás' career is winding down at this stage. He's been plagued by back injuries and he'll be moving on at the end of the season. He was on the bench that day at Stade Jean-Bouin. There's a load of us around the bar and the coaches and a few alickadoos are knocking around too. And next thing Tomás turns round to Axel and nods over at us and says something like, "Axel, sorry boy, they all let you down today didn't they, those fuckin' eejits."

It's a bit of a risky one, but it works a treat. Everyone is laughing, Axel included. There's maybe a bit of nervous laughter among some of us, but it breaks the tension. When someone makes a gag about something really serious, it kind of eases the mood a bit. That's the whole point of gallows humour, I suppose, and in fairness we've always been good at that in Munster.

We salvage a bit of pride the following weekend at home to Stade Francais with a 26-13 win, but we're just papering over the cracks really. We limp on through the rest of the season, losing to Ospreys, Glasgow, Cardiff, Leinster and Connacht along the way.

Axel and Fla have been doing the heavy lifting on the coaching front day in, day out so Munster management make a bold move to supplement them with a coaching ticket from South Africa. In June they announce that Rassie Erasmus will come in as Director of Rugby while Jacques Nienaber will join as defence coach. Our former team mate Felix Jones will begin his coaching career with us too.

As players we have no idea how this is going to work out but it's not really our job to worry about that. But early enough in the 2016/17 season it becomes pretty obvious to us that things are a bit frosty between the two main men. You can feel it in the atmosphere at team meetings and on the training ground. I mean, it was probably inevitable. Here's Axel, born and bred

THERE IS AN ISLE

Munster, and then this bloke completely unknown to us arrives in from South Africa – and he's not the shy and retiring type either. Rassie has a forceful personality and he has to be true to himself too. He has his own ideas and it's not a smooth ship at the top during that bedding down period. But that's okay, it's up to us to get on with it irrespective.

Nine months after that debacle in Stade Jean-Bouin we're back in Paris to face Racing 92 in the first pool game of this season's Champions Cup. The fixture is set for Sunday afternoon. We're staying in a Novotel and that morning we have our breakfast followed by a walk-through in the car park. No sign of Axel, but we crack on with rehearsing our plays and moves, as per every game day.

Back in the dining room for an early pre-match meal, I'm sat at a table when I notice George Murray, our video analyst, hurrying into the team room looking very serious. He has a word with someone and they come out of the room, very urgent, and more and more heads turn as they exit the dining room. Something is up. There's a vibe in the air now. I say to the players beside me, this feels odd, something is off. Then more people come in and out of the room and everyone is getting distracted. An ambulance arrives at the front door. Hotel staff are milling around looking very concerned. Eventually word starts circulating that something awful has happened to Axel. And shortly after it's confirmed that he's been found dead in his room.

We don't know how to take it in. You can't take it in. We're all just standing there moping around in a state of complete shock. Word comes through that the game has been cancelled. There's loads of people milling around the foyer and everywhere now. There's paramedics and official people and hotel managers rushing around. The phones at reception are hopping. There's another commotion when the body is brought to the ambulance and driven away to the hospital. It is a shocking scene that's unfolding all around us.

A squad meeting is called. Rassie confirms the unbelievable news. I can remember him sitting there, his eyes welling up and voice quivering, holding a white towel in his hands for something to grip onto, it looks like a physio's white towel. He is pale in the face. Everyone is pale in the face. We're all dumbfounded. At some stage, Brendan Foley arrives, Axel's dad, such a gent of a man, saying hello to everyone and him completely shattered, trying his best to hold it together. That image sticks with me.

The meeting breaks up. The senior players, myself included, are tasked with phoning all the squad players at home with the news. Everyone is on their phones ringing home. The news starts to leak out around Ireland. It brings Irish rugby to a standstill. Irish sport in general, I suppose, but for Axel's communities in Shannon RFC, in Killaloe, in Limerick, Munster and in rugby across Ireland – it is a black day for everyone who knew him.

Eventually, a load of us players head to a bar around the corner from the hotel. We don't know what else to do. We need a break from the intensity of the hotel. We needed to talk it out over a few pints. We just sat there drinking slow pints, sometimes talking, sometimes silent, sometimes gazing away into the distance.

At the funeral the players took turns shouldering the coffin from the church to the cemetery. Olive Foley's words to her husband in the church were stunning. What a champion she was and is. You knew from listening to her that Dan and Tony, their two broken-hearted boys, would be well minded in the long months and years after.

THERE IS AN ISLE

At the end of that draining week we had to face Glasgow Warriors in the Champions Cup. The order came down from on high that the fixture had to be fulfilled. I have never seen Thomond Park so raw with emotion before or since. There was a cloud over the whole city that week and it felt like all that grief was being funnelled down into the stadium now. It was incredibly sad and moving. You could feel it all around you, you were inhaling it into your body. The minute's silence on the field beforehand was laden with this intensity of feeling too. I was standing beside Zeebs and he'd be more outwardly emotional than I would and he was properly crying.

I'm not a crier, not usually, but I could feel myself welling up too. Then you've got to snap out of it and get your head sorted because there's an actual game of rugby to be played at the end of this massive outpouring. And we knew we had no choice, but to win this one. It wasn't even a question. It was a complete must-win game if ever there was one. Earlsy got sent off after 20 minutes, but that wasn't going to stop us either. We were never going to lose this one. If you could bottle that kind of attitude you'd never be beaten.

Two weeks later was the showdown with New Zealand in Chicago. As I said in the previous chapter, it was a privilege to be part of one of the greatest days in Irish rugby history. Ireland finally beat the All Blacks after over a century of defeats. But the image that's probably best-remembered from that day is the figure-of-eight formation we choreographed to face the haka, in tribute to Axel.

We all wanted to do right by him, in Thomond Park and in Soldier Field. I had my own personal memories of him. Axel had been coaching at Munster since he hung up his boots in 2008 so he saw a lot of young players coming through the system. I was just one of them. He was forwards coach with the U20s squad for our interprovincial series of games in September 2008. I was absolutely buzzing to be called into that squad because Axel was a god to me.

Only two years earlier I'd been in Cardiff with my dad for the Heineken Cup final when Axel captained them to that famous victory over Biarritz. Everything he said carried weight. And I felt that if he was coaching me I was getting a step closer to the big time. Even better, word got back to me that Foley seemingly really rated me.

Tom Hartery was a mate of mine from school in Munchin's and Tom's father John was steeped in Limerick rugby. John went on to become president of the Munster branch in 2013. You know the way you hang on every word of praise and encouragement at that age? Well, Tom told me one day around the time of the U20 interpros that his dad had been chatting to Foley and that Axel had told John that Conor Murray should be getting a run in the Magners League that season. My eyes were as big as saucers when I heard that news. "Jeez, he actually said that?" Apparently so. I was made up with that. If Anthony Foley rated me, that was a serious bit of validation for a 19-year-old to get.

Eight years later he was dead at the age of 42. Life is cruel. The game can be cruel too. I'd seen the stress he'd been under for the previous 18 months. I saw the toll it took. I wouldn't wish it on anyone. Maybe it's why I don't think I'll ever go into coaching. Axel loved Limerick and Munster rugby. It was in his soul. I prefer to remember the good times when he was king of Thomond Park.

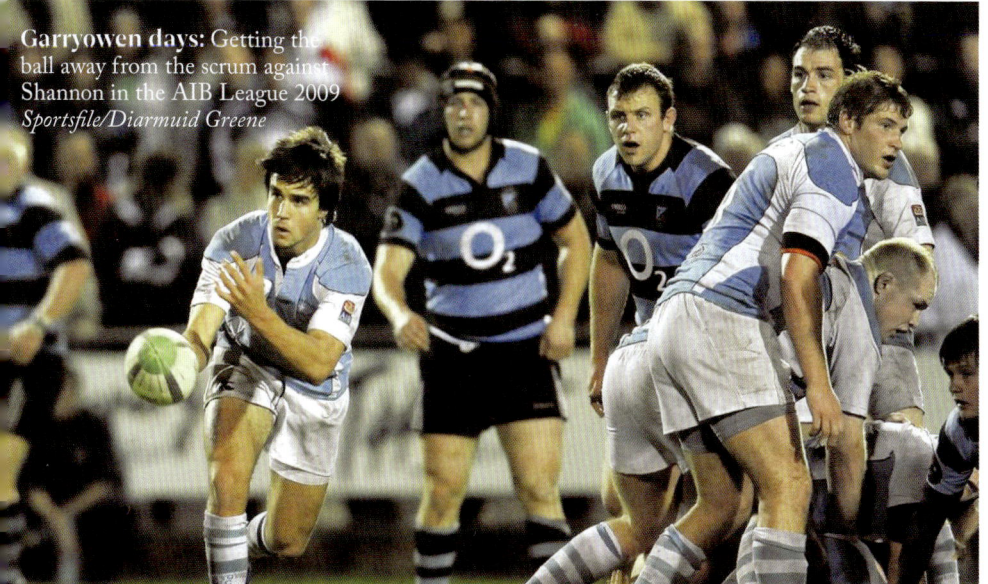

Garryowen days: Getting the ball away from the scrum against Shannon in the AIB League 2009
Sportsfile/Diarmuid Greene

Brace yourself: Facing Calum Clark of Northampton at Thomond Park in November 2011. RoG stole all the headlines with his famous last-gasp drop goal

High ball: Rob Kearney was incredible in the air. But this time Wales' Jamie Roberts beats him, and me, to it in Wellington at the 2011 Rugby World Cup

Spin the ball: Against Leinster at Thomond in 2013

Dream time: the Lions have won the decisive third Test against Australia in 2013 and I've played the last half hour at the ANZ Stadium in Sydney

Dream land: Scoring a try against the All Blacks at the Aviva. It still gives me goosebumps looking at it more than a decade later

Champs: Paulie, Pete and myself after we've pipped France in a thriller to clinch the 2014 Six Nations in Paris *INPHO/Dan Sheridan*

Catching waves: Trying to stay upright at Bondi Beach during the Lions tour in 2013. I'm a long way from Lahinch here

Boyhood dream: One of my first training camps with a Lions squad, in Vale of Glamorgan, Wales

Friendly rivalry: Zeebs to the left of me, Johnny to the right: and there I am, stuck in the middle during a Munster-Leinster Pro 12 match at the Aviva in 2012

Remembering how we stood: Axel and myself in conversation at Welford Road in 2015 *INPHO/Dan Sheridan*

Lions in Hong Kong: Mako Vunipola, myself and Jamie Heaslip line up before the Barbarians game in 2013

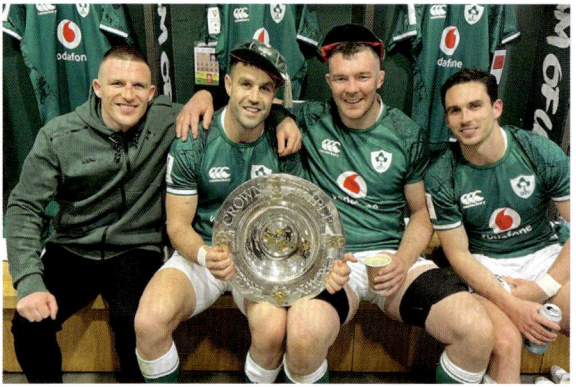

Hats off to us: Dressing room celebrations and 200 caps

Paris je t'aime: Hoisting the Six Nations silverware at the Stade de France in 2014 *INPHO/Dan Sheridan*

Family first: Holding the 2024 Six Nations trophy with Mum and Joanna by my side. I hope I've made them proud

Flash mob: Tommy Bowe has just scored the winning try against South Africa at the Aviva in 2014 *INPHO/Dan Sheridan*

Going crazy in Chicago: Billy Holland, Donnacha Ryan, Simon Zebo, myself and CJ Stander after Ireland's historic win over the All Blacks at Soldier Field in 2016 *INPHO/Dan Sheridan*

Taxi!: Pete gives me a lift as we celebrate the Grand Slam at Twickenham in 2018

Five years later: Tadhg Furlong and myself take our turn with the trophy at the Aviva in 2023

He shoots he scores: Johnny has just landed the drop goal in Paris that launches our 2018 Grand Slam campaign

Flying the flag: with Dan Leavy on our celebratory lap of the field in 2018

1 of 600,000: Getting my passes in during a Lions training session at the QBE Stadium Auckland, in 2017

Mum and Dad: Felt very proud to receive the 2017 Irish Rugby Players' award for Player of the Year alongside my parents

Tug of war: Trying to hold onto Caelan Doris during a Munster-Leinster URC match at Thomond Park in 2022

Veterans: Two happy oul' fellas at the Aviva in 2024

If the cap fits: Measuring Pete for the Triple Crown trophy in 2025

The next generation: Photos I'll hold very dear and can't wait to show Alfie when he understands it all!

Never say never?: When I hang up the boots, they'll stay hung up. I won't be taking them back down again to stand on sidelines shouting at players to do this, that and the other. I'll just go back to being a civilian

Chapter Twelve

THE ERASMUS SCHOLARSHIP

WITH AXEL'S PASSING, RASSIE TOOK full control of the operation. He'd shown proper leadership through that awful week. He led from the front, his natural authority came to the fore in a really impressive way. He was just one of those people who gives off natural confidence and authority. That was his style. His word was law, and that was part of his style too. As players, we liked it, or most of us did anyway. A manager or head coach who leads with confidence gives his players confidence. His conviction gives you conviction. It was pretty obvious from early on that Erasmus was going to be the general. And we would be happy to serve under him because you felt that he was going to take us places. We needed strong direction. We were struggling and we needed someone to inspire us.

Rassie was a blunt, hard-nosed South African. You could tell he was an old-school Springbok from his confrontational attitude. His own fingers were broken and mangled from his years in the trenches as a flanker. There was going to be no messing with this fella. He'd galvanise us with his speeches and he could scare us too if something pissed him off. One of his drills for instilling physical and mental toughness was getting us to bash our way through a tunnel created by players holding crash pads. He'd line up two lads a few metres apart holding the pads and two more behind them and two more behind them and so on. And your job was to try and batter your way through them until you got to the other end. The lads who were on the pads, he used to fuck them out of it if he felt they were going too soft on us so the lads would batter you back in turn. I really enjoyed this kind of stuff because it was instilling a really tough, abrasive edge into us.

When he went home to take over the Springboks, he turned them exactly into the kind of confrontational machine that was physically and mentally nearly unbreakable. To lead them to one World Cup triumph was a huge achievement, but to lead them to two back-to-back puts him up there with the all-time greatest coaches of rugby union. Obviously he hadn't carved out that level of reputation when he was at Munster, but this was the calibre of man we had leading us and I think if he had stayed, we could have done something special.

I really enjoyed working with his number two as well, Jacques Nienaber. They had a nice balance and chemistry to the way they ran the show, Jacques sort of being the good cop to Rassie's bad cop. And when Rassie was bad, you'd know all about it. We were reviewing a game on video one Monday morning in the meeting room in UL and Rassie was in the middle of making a very serious point when he noticed one of the lads wasn't paying full attention. This fella was smiling about something, as if what Rassie was saying was humorous in some way. Next thing Erasmus turned his guns on him. He called this player out.

THE ERASMUS SCHOLARSHIP

"Do you think that's fucking funny?" There's a pause while our fella realises what's happening. "Do you think it's funny?"

All heads have turned to him now and he's flustered, he doesn't know what to say, and his smile is turning to embarrassment. Rassie's like, "I'll tell you what's fucking funny. You can go back to your fucking club now for two weeks, because I'm not joking here, I'm not fucking around." Jesus almighty. The room was totally silent. You could hear a pin drop. I never left a meeting so quiet in my life. I remember we all left the meeting room and no one said a word. Yer man duly left and went back to his club for a fortnight.

In January 2017 we were away to Glasgow Warriors in the Champions Cup at Scotstoun. It was eleven weeks after we'd played them in Thomond Park on the day we said our final farewells to Axel. We'd hit a great streak of form in the meantime.

The first time I clear my lines in this game, I notice that a Glasgow player has come in low and targeted my standing leg in the tackle. It's a bit unusual because the normal thing to do is station a blocker at the ruck to try and charge down your kick. But this fella is coming from the blindside of the ruck and flying at my left knee. I'm just lucky it's not planted in the ground, it's airborne on the follow-through. This is an artificial pitch too, so if your foot is grounded it's going to catch even more because there's no give in the surface.

The second time it happens I'm like, there's something going on here. Again, I'm fortunate because my standing foot is off the ground when the hit comes and I just land on top of the tackler. Then it happens a third time and I erupt. I'm normally very quiet on a pitch. I rarely get into argy-bargy with anyone. But this time I'm spooked because I believe it's a gameplan now.

You're vulnerable when you're kicking a ball, you can't really see what's coming, you can't take evasive action. Your standing leg is supposed to be off limits because it's generally considered to be a cheap shot – and because the consequences can be devastating. If your standing leg is at full extension on the follow-through of a kick and some fella ploughs into it, you're looking at an ACL job, a cruciate rupture. It's a fucking disgusting act and it's not tolerated in the culture of the game. There's a lot of things tolerated, but that's not one of them. But here's the rub: after I get hit the third time I'm freaking out and one of their players – I won't name him – goes, "You better watch that knee of yours." Just like that as he's jogging past me: "You better watch that knee of yours." I've always wondered whether that was just sledging or proof that it was premeditated.

Francis Saili's try inside the last ten minutes got us the win and sent us into the knockout stages for the first time in three years. We had Racing 92 at home in the final pool game a week later. I was chosen for the midweek press conference between games. The day before a presser you're usually sent briefing notes in an email from your media crew. They'll be advising you about the subjects that are likely to come up and how to prepare your answers accordingly. But I was like, fuck that, I need to get this off my chest. I was still fuming. And at the press briefing in UL on the Wednesday, I tell the reporters, quotes, "I'm properly pissed off about that. I don't see any benefit in charging down someone's standing leg. I only see it as a danger or as a potential to get injured. I don't think it's a good tactic. You could put another label on that type of tactic. If my leg stayed in the ground – especially in that surface – you're looking at syndesmosis, you're looking at cruciate."

THE ERASMUS SCHOLARSHIP

Of course, they fed me a few more questions and I was happy to answer. It was so unlike me to get involved in any public spat, it just wasn't my style at all, but I felt it was too serious to let it slide. I explained that I'd raised it with the touch judge in Scotstoun after the first attempt, so the officials were aware of it. And part of the problem was that they didn't do anything about it. I made a broader point about player safety in general too. Someone would end up with a serious knee injury if it wasn't clamped down on. I said that Glasgow in my experience were the only team I'd seen doing it, but I wasn't necessarily blaming the players. "I don't know who told them to do it, but it's very dangerous and thankfully, I didn't get injured but if I had been injured I would've been going on more of a rant."

Gregor Townsend was Glasgow's head coach. He had his say a few days later. He denied it was a pre-planned tactic. Munster had a very strong kicking game and they only wanted to put pressure on it, he said.

"Conor Murray is an excellent player, one of the best number nines in the game. Maybe he didn't have his best game last week. Obviously, the pressure we put on them, they didn't enjoy. Rugby is a physical game and we have got to do things within the laws that involve tackling. We weren't penalised for anything [in that regard] last week."

Three or four days after the Racing game Munster's Irish internationals headed off to Carton House for our first camp of the 2017 Six Nations. As luck would have it, our first game would be against Scotland and a load of the Glasgow players would be involved with the Scottish squad. So, Joe Schmidt wasn't mad about the prospect of this story rumbling away in the background. It had nothing to do with him, but he knew he'd be facing questions about it in the media. So, early on in that camp he comes up to me for a chat. He's like, I saw that thing with Glasgow. And I assume he's wondering if I'm okay fitness-wise. But he says something like, you shouldn't have brought Gregor into it.

Now it's very seldom I'd push back against anything Joe says, but I push back against him on this one. I tell him exactly what happened, what the Glasgow player said to me, and I double down on my public comments. I said I'm not taking anything back. Joe hears me out and accepts my argument. He says, fair enough, I didn't know the whole story, that's okay. And he backs me up when he's asked about it at the presser.

"I totally understand Conor being disappointed with how it happened. You can't charge a ball down from the blindside [because] you have to go through the standing leg and the potential for injury there is clearly evident. If his foot is anchored he's going to blow his knee out."

The issue is put to bed until it resurfaces six months later on the Lions tour of New Zealand. After the first Test in Auckland Warren Gatland flags it up in public. The All Blacks have gone after my standing leg a couple of times in that match. And again I just flipped over in the air because my left foot thankfully was off the ground when the impact came. Gats emphasised that he wasn't making a big deal of it, but at the same time I think he wanted the word to go out to the match officials to keep an eye.

"The one concern for me was that there were a couple of times from Conor Murray where there was a charge down where someone dived at his legs. There were a couple of times where he's box-kicked and they've just pushed him to the ground after, so I don't know if it was a tactic. From my point of view, if someone pushes him afterwards, that's fine, but diving at his leg... I know other teams have used it in the past against Conor. It's just a safety issue for me. I'd hate to see someone dive at his leg and have him blow a knee and then wreck his rugby career."

Anyway, I don't know whether my public protest at the time registered with people, but I do know that it hasn't really been a problem since. In fact, less than two months after the Scotstoun episode, I'm not worrying about my knee at all because I've picked up an injury in my neck. I don't know it at the time, but it will trouble me on and off for the rest of my career.

It was against Wales in the Six Nations in Cardiff. I got run over by a ten-ton truck by the name of George North. It's the 31st minute of a game we will go on to lose 22-9. Wales have put together a series of phases, the ball is played left to George and I step out to meet him and, basically, I'm roadkill. I'm left lying on the ground in absolute agony. George has just trampled through me and over me like I'm a rag doll. The impact has crushed nerves in my neck and the pain that shoots down my left arm is so instant and so severe I'm sure it's broken. It has happened to me a few times since. You compress a nerve and the sensation it sends down your arm is that it feels like it's broken in half. The doctor comes running on and I'm roaring, "My arm's broken, my arm's broken." But he has seen the collision and he's like, "It's your neck, it's your neck."

"No, it's my fuckin' arm!" I'm scared to look at it, but when I do, I see that my arm is normal, the bone isn't bent at all.

The doc gets to work on my neck, trying to free the compressed nerve or whatever, and after a few minutes I decide I can keep going until they get me into the dressing room at half-time for a proper examination. We go into the warm-up room in the

Millennium Stadium at the interval and Joe tells me to pass a few balls, see how it's functioning. But the arm is shut down, I can't get any power into my passes. Joe goes, "Yeah, you've got some nice revolutions on the ball there. Yeah, I think we'll go with you second half."

I don't think Joe wanted to face facts in this situation. The arm was near enough dead. Pure adrenaline gets me through the first few minutes of the second half, but my passes are lacking zip and it's not working. I'm whipped off in the 46th minute just after North scores his second try; Kieran Marmion takes over. The following week I fail a fitness test at Carton House, not surprisingly because I can barely throw it ten metres, so Marms starts against England with Luke McGrath on the bench.

Back at Munster it's a race against time to get me right for the Champions Cup quarter-final against Toulouse on 1st April. I desperately don't want to miss that match. The French aristocrats in Thomond Park in a Heineken Cup knockout game? You wouldn't want to miss that one for the world. Rassie doesn't want me to miss it either, so he leaves the door open practically until the morning of the match. Normally these decisions will be finalised a couple of days before. But I'm ruled out and Duncan Williams comes in to start. Angus Lloyd had been brought in as scrumhalf cover before Christmas and he came on with a few minutes left. It was a Saturday evening kick-off and the place was heaving. The lads went hammer and tongs at Toulouse and ended up putting 41 points on them. It was like a blast from the past, that night, a return to the good old days.

We had three weeks to the semi-final against Saracens at the Aviva. But this injury is turning out to be a lot more complicated than I've expected. There's nerve damage there and I'm discovering that it can't be mended like a straightforward fracture in a bone. It's a lot more intricate and interconnected to my shoulder and arm. The damn thing isn't going away. My left tricep is starting to waste a bit. I'm trying to lift dumbbells with it and there's nothing happening. I have to drop down to a really light weight to get some action on the muscle. I'm trying to pass balls off my left and they're dying to the ground. The snap and rip in my action isn't there. And you have to pass a lot of balls off your left hand in any match. Any time you're hitting your inside centre with a ball it's off your left.

I'm sent to the Mater Private in Dublin to see a specialist. He's looking at all the scans and reports and he tells me I have a really bad compression of the nerve in my neck. Doctors usually give you the worst-case scenario when they're weighing up these things and he warns me that if I get another one of these compressions, I might end up needing one of those operations where they fuse a few bones in your neck. Jesus, that's news to me. Driving back to Limerick that evening I'm thinking that this isn't just a rugby decision here, it's kind of a quality-of-life decision too. If I do further damage is it going to affect me physically as a civilian?

Then you're back training the next day and everyone's buzzing about the game and you kinda forget what the consultant has told you and you're rationalising to yourself how you'll be okay to play. Like, even if I'm just 80 per cent right I might be able to get away with it. It's going to be such a massive occasion. You'd hate to miss it. Yeah, if I can get myself to 80 per cent I'll go with it. I'll take my chances. So, you go back passing balls off your left and reality bites again. I'm throwing spuds here. The ball is dying every time. I'm supposed to be ripping it 20 metres and it fades after ten and falls on the floor. But the coaching staff are willing me on. During the final week countdown Felix rings me and he's like, "Murr, doesn't matter, just to have you on the pitch will make a big difference." And I'm like, Felix, I'm not sure about this. "Come on Murr, I think you'll be good to go." Jesus Felix, I can't pass the ball.

Rassie is on to me all that week too. "Are you okay, will you play?" Then it's like, "Ah, you should be fine." There's a bit of the old South African machismo in his attitude and, in general, I think that's no bad thing. The downside is this old-school rugby mentality where you should play injured, no matter what the consequences are. Pain is for wimps and all that. Just play through the pain barrier and you'll be fine. It's kind of like a test of your manhood for him. Are you man enough to play through the pain barrier? But he doesn't know what the consultant in the Mater has told me and I don't tell him.

It's agreed that we'll wait until the day of the game. Rassie wants me togged out and on the field for the warm-up. It's all part of the mind games for him, giving Sarries the impression that I might be starting. Who knows, maybe he's playing mind games with me too, hoping that the atmosphere will lure me in to play. Sure enough, the place is a sea of red and the hairs are properly standing on my skin as we walk in after the warm-up. And it crosses my mind: do you know what, I'll play. But the arm is giving me another message. Say if we get a lineout down the left hand side and I've to rip a pass off my left, it won't get there. The basic power isn't there. I'll be a liability in defence too, trying to tackle with one arm limp. In general play I'll be feck all use either. Then you're letting the team down. Say there's an overlap on and I have to throw a ball over the top, it won't make it. And the tens of thousands of people watching won't care about the restriction in your neck and arm. They won't know, they'll just see the shocker of a pass you've thrown. Here's this supposedly top player making these schoolboy errors.

No one sees all the shit you've gone through in training to try and get yourself right. All they see is the 80 minutes on a Saturday. It's a tiny window into your overall working life, but it's all they see and it's all they judge you by. And let's be honest, they're not going to care much either if you do play injured and you aggravate the problem further and you're out for months.

My brain is wrecked from processing all these worries and anxieties. It's two days after my 28th birthday. And I think if I was four years younger I'd have succumbed to the pressure, I'd have been guilt-tripped into it. And I'd have succumbed to my own personal temptation to play in such a big match. But I'm a small bit older and wiser now and I make my final decision: I'm not playing. And I tell Rassie I'm not playing, end of story. Duncan Williams will start, there's no spare scrumhalf on the bench.

I believe I did the right thing. The neck has never been right since. I've been getting injections and physio on it from that day to this. After I retire I will probably need to get an operation on it. I'm glad I didn't risk doing it further damage that day. You have to think long term as well as short term, even in an industry where it's all about the short term. Everyone is under pressure to get the next result. But you'll be forgotten about pretty quickly if you end up just another casualty of the sport who is forced to retire young. In the eight years since, I've noticed a big shift in the attitude towards personal health and safety. The culture has changed. There's more of a consensus that players have to be protected. Physios and doctors have way more authority in that regard. If they decide that a player can't play, then the coaches have to accept that. It's taking the pressure off players to declare themselves fit when they're carrying an injury.

Now, I know there's different pain thresholds for different people and I'd even go so far as saying that some players will take the easy way out when in fact, they're just carrying a knock. We're all carrying knocks, all of the time. But overall I think the culture is healthier now and in my case, back in April 2017, I'm happy that I made the right decision for my own long-term wellbeing.

As it turned out, I'm not sure I'd have made much of a difference to the final result anyway. That was an awesome Saracens team. They were the defending European champions. They had world-class players everywhere you looked and massive amounts of power everywhere you looked too. They weren't one bit rattled by playing in front of this huge home support. They had a defensive system that was just suffocating. It was a complete blanket. There was nowhere to go with the ball. They beat us and they went on to retain their title. They were proper European champions and we were well off that level.

And as it transpires anyway, I'm still another two weeks away from being able to play again. I start the Pro 12 semi-final against Ospreys and the final against Scarlets, where they rock up to the Aviva and turn us over too. The old Munster aura that used to intimidate teams is just not there anymore. First Saracens, now Scarlets. Jacques had us playing this super-fast rush defence and Scarlets just dismantled it. It was a complete systems failure and Steff Evans had the game of his life for them. This was Saturday 27th May. The British & Irish Lions were already in camp a couple of weeks. The Munster contingent, myself and O'Mahony and CJ Stander, had to fly to London the next day to meet up with them. On Monday the touring party took off for New Zealand from Heathrow Airport. I happened to be sitting beside Jonathan Davies, the Wales and Scarlets centre. Jonathan was incredibly talented, we ended up voting for him as our player of the series. But on the flight over he was posting on his social media accounts loads of photos of himself and the Scarlets players celebrating their victory in the Pro 12 final. And I was just sitting there thinking, you could've done that another day Jonathan, couldn't you?!

We were in New Zealand when official confirmation broke that Rassie and Jacques would be leaving Munster. The rumours had been swirling around for months, but it was there now in black and white. We were gutted with the news, the senior players anyway, because we knew we had an exceptional head coach. He was like what you'd imagine Alex Ferguson was like at Manchester United. Rassie was going to be a one-man revolution. And I say this as someone who felt the cutting edge from him in person.

A week or so after Sarries beat Clermont Auvergne in the Champions Cup final, word breaks that Billy Vunipola is out of the Lions tour. Billy would've been a shoo-in at number eight for the Lions Test team. He was man-of-the-match in the Clermont game. Apparently he'd been nursing a shoulder injury through the latter stages of the season with Sarries. On several websites carrying the story, there's a photo of Billy with his jersey off and his right shoulder wrapped in bandaging.

CONOR MURRAY

I remember after we'd beaten Ospreys in the Pro 12 semi-final at Thomond Park, and were preparing for that brutal final against Scarlets a week later, Rassie was doing his video analysis at a team meeting. Out of the blue he puts up on the projection screen one of the online reports about Vunipola's injury. It might be from Sky Sports or somewhere, but it is accompanied by the picture of Billy with his bandaged shoulder. And Rassie's like, "That's what a proper club player is."

It was definitely directed at me. As in, Billy Vunipola had played through the pain barrier for his club, but there's someone in this room who didn't. There was no one else in the room who'd been touch-and-go with an injury for the Sarries match. Then he moved onto Munster business. It was done so quickly I wasn't sure at first what to make of it. But when I thought about it afterwards, he'd gone to the trouble of downloading a report about a player who had nothing to do with us, and not just any report, but the one with the image of Billy and his bandaged shoulder. It was a dig at me, it was definitely a dig.

All I can say about it now is, feck you Rassie and the horse you rode in on. It was only a few weeks before the Saracens game that he told us, the players, he was definitely staying. He said the same after the game too.

In the end he had bigger fish to fry than us and no one was going to stand in his way when he had his mind made up. You can't but say he was completely vindicated too in that decision after all he has achieved with the Springboks. Fair play and congrats to him. We were gutted he left and, as it turned out, with good reason too.

Chapter Thirteen

THE BEACH BOYS

IT WAS THE FOURTH WEEK of January in 2018 and the weather was so bad that our game against Castres in Thomond Park had to be postponed for three hours because of the monsoon rain. We won the match at a canter and qualified for the quarter-finals of the Champions Cup. That was on the Sunday.

On Monday morning we were off to sunny Spain with the rest of the Ireland squad for our Six Nations camp. There were nine or ten Munster lads in the travelling party. We were staying in the Oliva Nova hotel and golf resort, south of Valencia, north of Benidorm. Joe kept it all a bit hush-hush beforehand for some reason. But five days in the Spanish sunshine was exactly what the doctor ordered. We were there for business, not pleasure, but I can tell you, it's hard to keep your serious head on when you've escaped the Irish winter and you've got a beautiful beach for a playground literally at your back door.

Joe, of course, had his serious head on. But because we had played the day before, we were spared the first training session. So, while he put the rest of the squad through their paces that afternoon, all the Munster boys had to do was a recovery swim in the sea. Eventually we all drifted back to our rooms. I was sharing with Earlsy. Next thing we get a message on the Munster WhatsApp group. It's a photo of a tiny shack bar about a kilometre down the beach. A few of the lads have succumbed to the temptation! There hadn't been any mention of a curfew by the boss, but I guess he just took it for granted that no one would be going out drinking the first day we arrived in an Ireland training camp. Not that we were intending on doing that, of course. Definitely not. Myself and Earlsy have a look at the photo and a look at each other. It's the look that says, will we or won't we? Our dilemma didn't last very long, if you could call it a dilemma at all. Sure we'll just go down and have a look around. There's no harm in that. It'd be an awful waste to be cooped up in this room when we could be out admiring the Mediterranean Sea. We were gone out the door in jig time.

Down at the shack bar there's lads getting stuck into pints, proper pints, never mind your fruity holiday cocktails. Right. Sure, in that case me and Earlsy might as well have one too. But we'll only have the one, maybe two, max. I suppose you can take the lads out of Munster but you can't always take Munster out of the lads. Our excuse was that it was our day off and we didn't have any time to celebrate the win over Castres the night before.

In the heel of the reel we all lamped about eight pints each before we decided to call it quits. But on the way back to the hotel nothing would do us only to go running up the sand dunes and rolling down them, langers and laughing our heads off. The next day a few of the lads woke up with thorns in the soles of their feet and their biggest problem then was getting them extracted by the medical staff while making up excuses as to how they got the thorns in their feet in the first place. Amazingly, Joe

THE BEACH BOYS

was seemingly none the wiser about our escapade the evening before. Or maybe he was and just decided to let it pass.

We ended up having a great training week. It was one of the best prep camps I've ever been involved with. The whole programme ran like clockwork. At our first full meeting we were outlining our goals for the Six Nations campaign, but pretty soon, and very unusually, there was a kind of mass consensus. Everyone cut to the chase. The message was simple and clear. "We're winning the Grand Slam this year." A lot of heads were nodding in agreement and a lot of fellas reckoned it was time to be upfront about it.

Previous years, it might be mentioned in a vague, wishy-washy sort of way as something to aspire to. Here, it was laid out with conviction by speaker after speaker. We weren't to shy away from laying it on the line. We should put the pressure on ourselves to say it and not back away from it. We should open ourselves up to the pressure of the expectation and we should accept responsibility for how it goes. The Grand Slam was going to be our mission. We were convinced we were one hundred per cent good enough to do it. We'd won the 6 Nations championship in 2014 and 2015, we'd finished second in 2017, it was time now to shit or get off the pot.

And we doubled down on it knowing full well that we were volunteering to do it the hard way. We would be away to France and away to England, the reigning champions. Obviously, we kept it to ourselves, we didn't go public on it and we didn't bang on about it over the next eight weeks. We just had drawn a line in the sand and we were sticking to it.

And maybe it was that promise that we'd made to ourselves in Spain that steeled us through that famous endgame in Paris on

Saturday 3rd February. Maybe that's being wise after the event, I don't know. Teddy Thomas' try in the 72nd minute and Anthony Belleau's conversion had put the French 13-12 in front. So, we had eight minutes to try and make good on our promise. Then Belleau had a very kickable penalty in the 78th minute to leave us needing a try. But he missed it. That was a key moment and it had nothing to do with us. Their starting ten was Matthieu Jalibert, but he'd gone off injured after 30 minutes, replaced by Belleau. Maxime Machenaud, their scrumhalf and kicker, was replaced by Antoine Dupont in the 66th minute.

In the 76th minute Dupont sprang from the back of a French scrum, I tackled him and he twisted his knee in the contact and he had to be taken off. Machenaud came back on for him. That was controversial at the time. Machenaud was allowed back on because the French claimed that Dupont needed to come off for a HIA as well as his knee injury.

In the 78th minute, France were awarded the penalty that should have won them the game. Machenaud had earlier landed two penalties and you'd have fancied him to convert this one too. But it was Belleau who took it and he probably twitched. It was his Six Nations debut and he was only 21. We got away with it big-time. We were still in the ball game. We'd have one last throw of the dice. And that's where the famous 41 phases of play began that culminated with Johnny landing his immortal drop goal in the 83rd minute.

I have to confess when I saw the clock in the red and we were going through phase after phase that I doubted whether we'd get it done. It crossed my mind that our supposed-to-be glorious 2018 campaign was already over after one match. Partly it was because of the heavy ground and the rain that had

THE BEACH BOYS

fallen. It just made everything more laborious, trying to churn your way across the turf. And then the French were knocking us back time and again. All they needed was one mistake from us and that was the game. But we kept recycling it and fellas kept turning up to try and eke out a yard here and a yard there.

An awful lot of our lads made important contributions keeping that move alive. But every metre was so hard fought for that eventually you grind to a halt because there's nothing left in the tank. That's why me and Johnny pulled the trigger while we were still nearly 45 metres from goal. It was far from ideal. A part of me thought we were too far back. Another ten metres would've made it more realistic, but the French weren't going to give us another ten metres and our pack had given every ounce of effort at that stage. So, it was shit or bust now.

There were no words between Johnny and me. I was glancing over at him after every phase waiting for his facial expression to give me the signal. And on the 41st phase he gives me the nod that says, yeah I'm ready, I'm ready to try it. I'm well aware that my pass has to be plumb. He can't be reaching up for it or stooping down for it. I take one last glance over my shoulder at him, fish the ball out from the back of the ruck and rip it ten metres straight into the bread basket. From there Johnny's bottle and class take over. His connection is solid, the ball is on its way, it's looking good, it drops between the uprights and suddenly we're all going stone fucking mental. We've only gone and done it! It's a fantastic feeling. We've gotten out of jail. We've gotten out of Paris with a win at the death. The French are stunned. We're hugging and jumping on top of each other. We have pulled off a minor miracle here.

Back in the dressing room the place is flooded with happy

hormones. The pure bonding that a squad gets out of a win like that is priceless. The unity you get, the certainty that everyone is pulling in the same direction – the trust and morale go through the roof. We know for sure now that we're onto something good here. It could be special. Maybe our name is on the Six Nations trophy. It could be that maybe it's our destiny this year.

Did we somehow manifest that victory by making that vow to ourselves ten days earlier in Spain? By saying it out loud with such conviction, did we take away every excuse to fail? Because when you're behind on the scoreboard with the clock in the red away to France in shitty weather conditions, you have plenty of excuses to fail. No one is going to judge you too harshly if you don't get it done in those circumstances. But maybe we had left ourselves with no choice, but to win it after the promises we'd made in Spain. We couldn't go back on our word. So, we somehow found a way. I dunno. But I do know it is one of the best backs-to-the-wall victories I was ever involved with. The walls were closing in all around us and we managed to escape to victory with the final kick of the match.

Back at home the game is watched by a massive TV audience and when we get back to Ireland we get a full sense of how much the people are rooting for us too. The support is enormous. So, we better not mess it up now. In fairness, there's no chance we're going to mess it up at home to Italy a week later. We score eight tries. I get the second one after thirteen minutes. I remember years earlier RoG talking to me once in training about attacking patterns. He says if you touch the ball once in a phase of possession, we'll attack, if you touch the ball twice in the same phase we'll score, and if you touch the ball three times you'll score yourself.

THE BEACH BOYS

This try was a perfect example of that. It all happens down the narrow side. I get the ball from a ruck and play it to Dan Leavy. Dan plays it back to me on a wraparound, I pass it to Earlsy and it's quick hands then to Jacob Stockdale to Jack Conan and Jack back inside to me with a lovely, no-look pop and suddenly I'm in the clear, I have a free run-in from 25 metres down the left hand touchline. Jack is a proper footballer and a real team player. I'm smiling and looking at the crowd as I run it in. Kearns is on my inside running support and he's first over to congratulate me. He looks happy enough, but he's not exactly over the moon either because he was hoping to get the final pass from me! I think he was going through a bit of a drought at the time so in the dressing room afterwards he was like, you should've popped it to me. But there was no way a pass was necessary there. I was free, there wasn't any need, there's always a risk with a pass. So, I should in my shite have passed it!

Anyway, I was enjoying myself too much. Turned out I was enjoying myself just a bit too much because instead of dotting it down with my hands, I casually jogged over the line with the ball tucked in my right arm and as I flopped down it got sandwiched between my stomach and the ground and I winded myself. I was blowing hard, trying to get my breath back. So, as Johnny lined up the conversion, one of the physios came in to have a look at me. He has his earpiece in, he's wired up to Joe in the coaches' box. I can hear the crackle of his voice on the earpiece. He's asking what's wrong with me. And the physio replies something to the effect that Murr has winded himself touching the ball down.

Do I get any sympathy from Joe? No I do not! I can hear his reply through the physio's earpiece, "Well tell him not to facking showboat so."

It's hilarious when I look back on it now. It's not, "Well played there, son, good move. I hope you're okay." It's the boss in his no-nonsense Kiwi accent giving me a slap. "Well, tell him not to facking showboat so." I still get the giggles when I think about it.

Against Scotland after half-time we've a maul grinding its way to the line when I grab the ball and shoot through a gap and barrel over with the help of Bundee arriving to clear their tacklers out of the way. That's our third try and we're hunting the bonus point now for a fourth.

Around the hour mark we're putting them under heavy pressure. After sixteen phases we're two metres out from their line near the right corner. Jack McGrath has replaced Cian Healy about ten minutes earlier. Jack is stood outside me and he has an overlap here. A quick pop to him and it's a walk-in for Jack. But having already got in from six or seven metres in the 45th minute, I figure I can do it myself from two or three metres out. It's basically a classic case of white line fever. You're so near to the try line you just want to get it down. It's tantalisingly close. So, I go myself, but I'm held up short, my head is actually on the chalk line. Eventually they lift the siege and it actually takes us another ten minutes to get the bonus point try, through Seán Cronin.

We beat Scotland 28-8. I remember this game because of the feeling of control we had throughout it. I remember us feeling really in charge. It's not often you get that feeling when you're playing dangerous rivals. But we had it that day. Momentum is such a powerful energy. We've beaten France, Italy and Wales at this point and we're just on a roll now. We felt we had Scotland beaten before they even turned up, we were that confident in ourselves. Maybe that's the reason why I felt I could convert that chance myself when I should have given it to Jack. But Joe the bollocks thought there was another reason!

Myself and Joanna had started dating a few months earlier. This was one of her first matches at the Aviva. It was a whole new scene for her. But what has any of this got to do with Joe, you might ask? Well, it's because in the dressing room afterwards Joe is doing his usual debrief with all the lads and he comes over to me and says well done on the first try and then of course, he tells me I should've passed to Jack rather than trying to score a second one myself.

"But then you had your new woman in the stadium, didn't you?!" Said as a joke and with a smile, but a little sting in the tail for you as well, as per usual! I've said it before, I'll say it again: Schmidt would let you get away with nothing. Apart maybe from lamping a few pints in a shack bar in Spain. I wouldn't be surprised if he knew about that too. But we're four from four now in the Six Nations so that's long forgotten about and everyone is happy. And now we're rolling on to Twickenham for a Grand Slam showdown on St Patrick's Day.

I was fairly highly strung the morning of that showdown. I remember being in my hotel room in Richmond counting down the hours and thinking to myself, if I play well in this and we win, I'll be very happy. No, actually I don't care if I play well, I just want to win this. This is bigger than you, far bigger. It's nearly too big to rationalise clearly. Your whole career has gone into this, your whole life really for the previous ten years. We all know we've got a place in history on the line today. Get it done and we're in the history books forever. Only two Irish teams have done it before in over 120 years of trying. We can join the boys of 1948 and 2009 today. That's why I'm more highly strung than usual. You just want it over with. You want to be released from the agonising wait, but you have this ordeal to go through first. And I don't know if I'm praying to God or whatever, but I find myself saying to myself, if we win this today I will never ask for another thing. Just give me this and I will be contented, I won't ask for anything else, ever. And then when it's over and we're Grand Slam champions, you want this day to last forever. The morning hours felt like an eternity and now you'd love for this feeling to last for all eternity. You're in such a state of pure happiness that you'd love to be able to hold it in your soul forever.

For weeks after, you wake up every morning and the good vibes are still with you. You feel this lightness in yourself. You feel this deep satisfaction of a job well done. You're just in sunny humour all the time. A bunch of us and our partners head to Dubai for a week to continue the celebrations, myself and Pete and Besty and Kearns and Earlsy and Sexto. It's one of the great holidays. Everyone's on a high, everyone is so happy, not a care in the world, not a worry in your head, just this oasis of joy and fun and good times with great people. Lunch on the terrace, sunset beers on the beach, dinner in beautiful restaurants, a bit of a boogie on the dance floor. "This is living now," I keep telling myself, "this is living."

In the summer we head to Australia for a three Test series. We spend the first week on the Gold Coast. Because of the jet lag, a lot of us are awake at five in the morning so there's nothing for it but to go down to a café on the beach where there's young people already in the water, swimming and surfing or playing volleyball on the sand. You know, you could get used to this kind of lifestyle. It's a far cry from Derryknockane on a wet Tuesday night in the depths of winter.

THE BEACH BOYS

Most of the Grand Slam squad is here and the buzz is still high. It all comes down with a bit of a crash when Australia win the first Test in Brisbane. It's the end of our 12-game winning streak that stretches back to March 2017. We get our game heads properly on for the second Test in Melbourne. The Aussies are a fairly chirpy bunch at the best of times and we didn't want them getting too chirpy by winning the series. We got back in our groove at AAMI Park. Conway got us on the scoreboard with a try in the corner after six minutes. I've thrown him a long skip pass, he has to catch it overhead and by the time he's caught it a defender has come across and ploughed into him as he stretches to score. Poor old Conway is taken off injured a few minutes later and that's the end of his tour. What can I say? He reckons I threw the pass too high, or maybe I was used to throwing passes to wingers with a few more inches on them than the fella we know fondly as "the little thing"!

Tadhg Furlong crashed over in the 53rd off a ball I popped him but, to be honest, the decision wasn't really mine. Tadhg was screaming so loud and belligerent for the ball I'd no choice but to flick it to him. He'd have had my guts for garters if I didn't. Afterwards he was like, in his thick Wexford accent, make sure you fuckin' listen to me cos that's what I can do! I'm like, Tadhg, I never doubted you.

In the second half of the third Test in Sydney we took a pounding from the Aussies, but I think we were such a battled-hardened outfit by then that we had pure willpower in our muscle memory. We kept hanging in and holding out against them. It was an incredibly stressful, pressurised situation. But we hung tough and came away with a series win, Ireland's first in Australia since 1979. I made it my business to swap jerseys with

David Pocock afterwards, their fantastic flanker. I had actually met him twelve and a half years earlier when he was part of an Australian Under 19s squad that toured Britain and Ireland in the winter of 2005. They were scheduled to play a Munster U19s selection in Tom Clifford Park and local families were asked to host the visiting players. My parents agreed to take in two and Pocock was one of them. I'd have been sixteen at the time.

We're taking him home to Patrickswell this dark, December night and on our way there, maybe a few miles out, he asks if we can stop the car and let him out because he has to get his run in for the day. It's part of his daily fitness regime apparently, he has to get his run in. So, out he gets and we drive on.

An hour later there's no sign of him and naturally my parents are getting a bit worried. Next thing the phone rings. It's a farmer living three or four miles outside the village and he says, there's a young Australian fella here in our kitchen! He says he's supposed to be staying with youse? Turns out he'd got lost in the dark and ended up running down this farmer's lane and knocking on the door. We brought him back and gave him his dinner.

To this day my old man remembers the amount of food this young fella consumed. Mountains of it. And he even had a weighing scales with him to measure out his protein and carbs and all the rest. He was an incredible specimen of an athlete, even at that age. I remember looking at him and seeing the size of him, his power and athleticism, and thinking to myself, I'll never get to that level. Not a chance. He's in a different league altogether. And yet there we were together in Sydney twelve and a half years later swapping jerseys and chatting over a few bottles of beer in the Australia dressing room.

THE BEACH BOYS

The next day a bunch of us are flying out from Sydney to Vegas for our summer holiday at the end of one of the greatest seasons in the history of Irish rugby. A clean sweep in the autumn internationals, a Grand Slam in the spring and a series win in Australia in the summer. It was a golden season. From a beach in Spain in January to another one in Dubai in March and the Gold Coast in June, with a lot of brilliant rugby sandwiched in between, it was one hell of a magic carpet ride. As good as it gets really. And a sun lounger by a swimming pool in Vegas to put the tin hat on it, with no thorns in your life at all.

Chapter Fourteen

AFTERSHOCKS

BACK FROM VEGAS AND THERE'S still not a cloud in the sky for me in that golden summer – or so I think anyway. Next up, some good friends are getting married. So, I'm on my way from a wedding in Cork to a wedding in Doonbeg in Clare via the Tarbert to Killimer ferry. I'm waiting in this line of traffic to board the ferry, sitting in the car on my own, when next thing I heave a big sneeze and I get this sort of weird spasm through my neck and shoulder. Everything just tightens up. It's like a shot of a seizure that enters my body without warning and exits again. It's over in an instant. I'm not really in pain, but I'm a bit baffled. I check my neck and trapezoid muscle and they seem to be okay. I head onto west Clare for the wedding and a great night is had by all.

A few days later, myself and Joanna are off to Greece for our own holiday. And the second morning in Mykonos I'm jolted out of my sleep because of this spasm that's gripping my whole left side – bicep, tricep, forearm, pecs, lats, they're all visibly twitching and trembling. It's like a convulsion that I've no control of. I'm not flexing anything, my whole left side has gone into this involuntary series of tremors. Jeez, this isn't normal. Then the pain kicks in and it's severe. It's rippling up and down

AFTERSHOCKS

from my neck to my wrist. I'm thinking it will pass and I don't want to spoil the day with any moaning or grumping so we head out and try to carry on as typical tourists.

By lunch time it hasn't improved and I have to leave the café to walk around. Same at dinner that evening, I have to get up and walk out of the restaurant. It's not easing off at all. The hotel staff are very helpful. They contact a sports masseur who actually has a treatment suite of his own at the hotel and he comes round and checks me out. He calls round for the next few mornings and works on all the affected muscles, trying to massage away the paralysis and the pain. He offers me painkillers, but I can't take them because I can't take any medication unless it's approved by our doctors with Munster or Ireland. I tell him I'm a professional sportsman and those are the rules.

Oh, he says, I'm treating another professional sportsman here at the moment. Right, and who would that be? Sadio Mané, the Liverpool footballer. Grand. I hope Sadio is feeling a bit fuckin' better than I am at the moment.

I actually need to see a doctor at this stage because the pain is level eight or nine out of ten and it's been dragging on for three or four days now. So, I'm referred to a local doctor. In the meantime I've phoned one of our medics back at home and he gives me the name of an authorised painkiller and I turn up for my appointment at this Greek doctor's surgery. But he is very reluctant to give me anything. He doesn't know me and maybe because it's a holiday destination he's come across loads of young fellas coming in and chancing their arm looking for some prescription or another. He says he can give me an injection or put me in a neck brace. I have to tell him that I'm not allowed to take an injection and that a neck brace won't be worth a shite either. I don't think I said it quite like that. Anyway, he eventually agrees to write me a prescription for the authorised painkillers and I finally get a bit of relief from the hurt.

We finish out the holiday, but it's the end of my six months of pure bliss. It's back to reality. The game of rugby will always bring you crashing back down to earth. What I'd been enjoying was one of those rare spells in the sport where practically everything you touch turns to gold. That's not the normal or natural way in a business as unforgiving as this. And what I didn't know was that in Greece I was picking up the tab on a meter that had been ticking since the first Test in Australia over a month earlier. I had taken a ferocious hit after only three minutes of that first Test and now my body was calling in the debt.

The Aussie right wing Marika Koroibete had mowed me down as I waited under a high ball on the halfway line in Brisbane. It's one of those ones where you have to keep your eyes on the dropping ball so you're stationary, you can't take evasive action, you're wide open for what's coming, if the tackler gets his timing right. Koroibete gets it spot on. The ball lands in my arms and bang. He has nailed me at full velocity and it's totally legit. He literally lifts me off my feet with the impact and drives me back to earth on the follow-through.

Funnily enough, I got up and played on. I didn't need any treatment. I'm only substituted in the last three minutes. I play the full 80 in the next Test and the full 80 again in the last. If you're not a medic I guess it's hard to understand how the impact then led to such a delayed reaction. It's like your body has been hit by its own personal earthquake, but the first shockwave only arrives a month later.

Back in Ireland I'm put through the usual battery of scans and

AFTERSHOCKS

x-rays, not unlike the process after George North ran over me in the 2017 Six Nations. That was 15 months before Koroibete levelled me. So, the nerve damage sustained against North was compounded by this latest crash.

I discovered that the nerves in my neck, the discs at the top of my spine, were all damaged. Basically, the disc in my neck was bulging and compressing against the nerve. It was horribly painful. The pain spreads out from the epicentre of the nerve across your shoulder and travels down your arm. There's no way to lie in bed without discomfort. You're twisting one way and another trying to get some bit of relief. So, that affects your sleeping patterns then. It was a bit of a complicated mess. There was no easy fix and no way of knowing when I'd be able to function freely on a pitch without pain or impediment. As it turned out, the nerves in my neck and the adjacent spinal discs would need nursing and minding for the rest of my career. The damage in those areas was permanent.

Maybe I'm lucky that it wasn't fatal to my career. I was 29 at the time. That's a pretty good innings by modern day standards in this game. But there was no way I'd have wanted to call it quits back then. I'd have been devastated if a consultant had inspected all the scans and called me into his office and told me my neck was too vulnerable, I'd have to retire on safety grounds. Christ, it doesn't bear thinking about. Anyway, at the time I had good powers of recovery and I'd do every minute of rehab that was asked of me. There'd be no short cuts there. The constant cloud on the horizon was the medical staff not being able to give me a definite return date. With the dreaded ACL injury, at least you'll have a good idea of the timeline. With this one it was a case of wait and see and wait and see.

CONOR MURRAY

I missed the November internationals, including our win against the All Blacks, Ireland's first ever victory over New Zealand on home soil. It's another major milestone for this squad and coaching staff. I'm watching it from a corporate box with some friends and for some strange reason my face keeps flashing up on the big screens in the Aviva at various intervals. I don't know why or how, but someone in charge of the television coverage decides to keep cutting to my mug after some random sequence of play on the field. And I'm conscious of being seen to cheer and smile at every big moment for Ireland. But of course, inside, your feelings are a bit more mixed. It's the usual dilemma when a player is not involved and he has to watch his mates winning games without him. You're happy for the lads, but every fibre of your being wants to be down there in the middle of the action.

Maybe it's a bit like the actors and actresses who are nominated for an award at the Oscars. Someone else's name is announced on the stage and they have to sit in their seats with a forced smile glued to their faces. Mind you, Jacob Stockdale's try got me off my feet. It got everyone in the stadium off their feet, the kick-ahead, the chase and the plunge for the line. Jacob had the season of his life in 2017/18 and it couldn't have been better-timed for the rest of us; his tries made a massive difference that season.

A week later I make my Munster comeback as a second half sub away to Zebre in Italy. The pitch is a mudbath, the crowd is tiny and the game is a bit of a non-event. Around about the same time I'm sinking to my ankles in muck in Parma, Johnny and Pete and Besty are in Monte Carlo for the World Rugby awards. They've been flown out by private jet from Dublin

AFTERSHOCKS

airport, Johnny wins World Player of the Year, Ireland win Team of the Year and Joe wins Coach of the Year. It's a glitzy, glamorous black tie affair and – and Zebre in the rain is not. But I'm back in the ball game.

In the meantime I've had to put up in silence with something more sinister than the injury. In the months I've been off a stupid rumour has grown legs and gone floating around Limerick and Irish rugby circles. It's a small enough community at the end of the day and it doesn't take a lot for whispers to start circulating inside the bubble. It gets back to my family and it gets back to me. The word on the street is that Murray isn't injured at all. What's really happened is he's failed a drugs test and been suspended. But they're keeping it hush-hush so the injury story is just a cover, a smokescreen. Like most conspiracy theories it's complete bullshit. It's pub talk, pure gossip, fellas bigging themselves up by pretending they've got the inside track. I'm not sure how many people actually take it seriously, but when you're the one on the receiving end you can't help but take it seriously. It gets inside your head because it upsets your family and friends, the people who care about you. The boys in training have heard about it too, of course, and they look after me in the only way they can – by ripping the piss outta me at every opportunity. They turn it into one big laugh, which always helps.

In January 2019 I was invited by the commandant at Sarsfield Barracks in Limerick to give a talk on the day they were honouring the sporting achievements of the 12th Infantry Battalion. I knocked the rumour on the head in my comments that day. I didn't come out swinging because that wouldn't be my style, but I just pointed out that it had been a tough time for my family and it's the downside of being in the public eye.

Things are said about you that are completely untrue and you can do nothing about them. You can't control the narrative so you're kind of helpless when it happens. I have my say and it's reported in the *Limerick Leader* and I leave it at that. I move on. The best you can hope for is that it will blow over soon and usually it does.

I'm back in harness for the 2019 Six Nations and raring to go. England beat us in the first round in the Aviva and just like that we are former Grand Slam champions. We were hoping to go back-to-back. There was massive public expectation too. England were just too good for us on the day, simple as that.

We get back on the horse against Scotland in Murrayfield, they gift us a try on ten minutes and as it happens I'm in the right place at the right time to pick up the pieces. It's a Scottish back pass that goes wrong. The ball hits the deck, I'm chasing hard, the ball bounces into my hands and I've a free run-in. I flop over about ten metres left of the posts. Johnny has taken a knock and needs some treatment before taking the conversion. He pulls his shot wide on the near side and afterwards Joe gives out to me for not going under the sticks with the touchdown in the first place. Joe is never happy with me when I score a try!

To be fair, none of us are in a great mood in the Murrayfield dressing room afterwards. We've got the win, but we haven't played well, it's been a bit of a struggle. We don't know it at the time, but in hindsight, the defeat to England and the mediocre performance against Scotland are probably straws in the wind, signs that we're maybe slipping a bit from the highs of 2018.

Against Italy, I score again and knock over a couple of conversions too. But again it's another middling performance and the perception among commentators is that I'm not going great either. There's some degree of truth in it because I'm still working my way back to match fitness after the layoff. Plus when you've been around the block and played on Lions tours and all that, you're always going to be judged by a higher standard than you were in your early days. The expectation around you is always higher and so if you're not firing on all cylinders all the time, you're not usually cut much slack.

Eight years earlier if I'd scored two tries in two games and knocked over a few conversions as well, people would've been raving about you. But I'm at a stage now where anything below your best isn't good enough. In these games I'm probably doing okay but you're deemed to be doing poorly when in reality you're neither bad nor good, you're somewhere in between.

The narrative going around at this point is that I haven't gotten over the neck injury. Suddenly everyone's a medical expert too. Far as I'm concerned, the neck is fine, the shoulder is fine, but it's just another storyline that you've no control of. In Cardiff, Wales score an early try and pretty much dictate the game thereafter in the pouring rain. They take the Grand Slam title, it's a miserable day all round for us.

It's another performance that suggests we're not quite where we were the year before. But inside the camp there's none of that talk. It can't be entertained. We've a World Cup coming down the tracks in the autumn. We've worked too long and too hard to even consider the idea that we might be on the slide. We're one of the best teams on the planet. We've proven it right throughout 2018. This is only a blip. You can't sustain your top level game in game out. We'll come back in July and we'll be the best prepared Irish team ever to go to a World Cup. There are no alarm bells going off within the group. Maybe a few minor fixes are needed, but that's all. These are the kinds of things you tell yourselves when you've got the blinkers on. Having the blinkers on is a necessary part of any squad culture in my opinion. You have to shut down the outside noise. You have to stay focused on your goals. You have to find solutions to problems that are arising and within the camp there's plenty of self-criticism. That's a healthy culture to have. But you can't be getting distracted by people who are outside your environment. That's a basic principle of any operation like this in any sport.

We roll into the early autumn with a series of friendlies. In the second we take a hammering off England and I'm taken off with concussion. I was fully unconscious for a couple of seconds. It was just an accident, I was tackled from behind and got caught on the chin with a stray boot. We played England four years earlier in a World Cup warm-up too and I got dinged in that one as well early doors, trying to stop Joe Marler on the charge.

The previous November I took a bang to the head against Australia in Dublin. Each time I was taken off and minded. I was put through the HIA system and all the follow-up protocols. There's a huge amount of information and awareness around this issue now, far greater than at the start of my career. Averaged out over the course of 300 plus games, my head knocks thank God have been few and far between.

We attributed the ransacking from England to the heavy training load we'd gone through in our pre-season camp in Portugal. Maybe at this stage we were a wee bit in denial, but if we were, that's only in hindsight. In a situation like that you are always going to rationalise things in a way that suits your needs. We needed to believe we were on course for a big tournament in Japan. It's an amazing country and when we get settled into

AFTERSHOCKS

our team hotel, there's a lovely novelty about being in such a different place to our usual overseas destinations. But I'll tell you what, the novelty soon wore off when the home side turned us over in the Shizuoka Stadium.

For everyone else it is one of the greatest results in the history of the Rugby World Cup. For us it was a very unpleasant experience, a bit embarrassing actually. We were never less than professional in our preparation, but deep down I just don't think we could imagine being beaten by Japan. We were the number one ranked team in the world at this stage. We figured the Japanese would be up for it, but there's being "up for it" and then there's being absolutely manically up for it.

On the day they were manic with intensity and we just couldn't cope. We were gobsmacked. They were brilliant. They treated it like it was their World Cup final. They tore into us like their lives depended on it. And technically they were incredibly fast and slick. On top of that, they were whipped into a frenzy by their own crowd. The atmosphere was stunning, it was electric with passion and their players fed off it. Eventually an underdog team is supposed to run out of steam, but they didn't. They were inspired by their supporters to keep going and keep going. And they were thriving in the heat and humidity while we started wilting. For us it was like getting caught up in a typhoon. Hats off to those Japanese players. They'll always have that famous day in September 2019. Unfortunately we'll always have it too.

Long story short, that result sent us into a showdown with New Zealand in the quarter-final and they wiped us out. They were way better than us. We didn't really fire any shots. And just like that the dream of World Cup glory is over for another cycle. We've limped out of it with our tail between our legs. In the years after, a narrative becomes set in stone that Ireland peaked in 2018 and that we were on the downward slope when RWC 2019 came round. The other one is that teams had worked us out by then. They'd copped onto our gameplan and deconstructed it because Ireland under Schmidt had such a structured system in possession that we didn't know what to do after three phases. My own take is that the gameplan was still very effective, we just didn't execute it as well as the year before. There was nothing wrong with it, but we were starting to make too many errors. I think we could have won the World Cup with that system, but we just made too many mistakes in the execution. I know other players would disagree with me on that, but I would've loved to have seen us execute it to perfection and see where it took us. I think we could have won the big one with it because it had taken us to unbelievable heights, but we basically didn't do it justice in 2019, we just didn't perform to our level of the previous year.

So, maybe we did peak in 2018. The cracks started appearing in the Six Nations and got wider as the year progressed. But overall I'm still not able to be definitive about what happened. Even looking back on it from a good few years later, I still don't have clarity in my head. I don't trust easy answers anyway. I don't like black-and-white opinions. Things like this are usually more nuanced and more complicated. Yes, maybe our gameplan needed to evolve, which it very much has done since under Faz, but I still come back to the realistic opinion that we didn't perform with the plan that we had. We didn't perform on the biggest stage. It wasn't that the gameplan was suddenly no longer good enough, it was more that we as a collective just didn't play well enough.

Win or lose, you rarely got a show of emotion from Joe after a game. He was locked into the process and the execution and the nuts and bolts. But he did get a bit emotional after the New Zealand game. He himself had put a vast amount of work into it over the previous four years. So had his coaches and so had we and he was sad that we couldn't be the best version of ourselves when it mattered most. Plus, he was leaving. We all knew it was his last hurrah. After six and a half years, the show was moving on. But what a body of work he left behind him. Two Six Nations titles, one Grand Slam, a first-ever win over the Springboks on South African soil, a first-ever win over New Zealand, another win over New Zealand in Dublin, and a series win over Australia for the first time since 1979. In doing that, he spread the popularity of rugby in this country. He became one of the most popular people in Ireland himself. Any of us lucky enough to be part of those campaigns got to enjoy all those good times too. We had so many great days and nights, so many life experiences that have become happy memories.

Personally, he pushed my game to another level. A lot of the lads will say the same about their own development. He made us better players. He was so good in his coaching and his man-management that you could argue he made the team play better than it actually was in the beginning. Then at some point along the way we became as good as the level we were playing at. The sum was maybe greater than the parts in the first few seasons, but by 2018 the parts were as good as the sum.

He opened my eyes so much to what I could do better. The standards he set were non-negotiable. His work ethic was off the charts. He passed on this level of rugby intelligence that I'd never been exposed to before. He made me think about it more deeply and he helped take my confidence to new levels.

CONOR MURRAY

In December 2020 I was selected on World Rugby's Team of the Decade. Drico was the other Irish selection on that honorary XV. To be honest, it was a hell of an accolade to receive. I know that these debates are always very subjective, everyone has their favourite players and another selection panel would probably pick a very different XV, but if you look at the other names on that team of the decade, I was proud and humbled to be chosen among them.

Obviously a huge number of coaches and team mates had helped me develop over the years, but Joe Schmidt was probably more influential than any of them. And one of the reasons why he was so influential with me is that if he'd still been around when I got that award, he'd probably have told me not to "facking showboat" because there was more work to be done.

I was lucky to have him in my corner and Irish rugby was blessed to have had him too.

Chapter Fifteen

CLOSE BUT NO CIGAR

ON THE DAY OF MY 30th birthday Munster were playing Saracens in a Champions Cup semi-final in Coventry. We were knocking on the door again. We were one game away from the dream of a European final. We were two wins away from the dream of an open top bus parade through Limerick with the trophy that had last visited the city in 2008. This was 20th April 2019, the day of my big Three O.

A few weeks before, my mother had asked me if I wanted a party. And I was like, under no circumstances. We had a semi-final to play and then a final. If there was going to be a party at all, ideally it would be with the silverware I grew up knowing as the Heineken Cup. Never mind birthdays, I'd grown up believing that this was our birthright as Munster rugby people.

As a Munster player, it was going to be part of my life experience. I was going to play in finals and I was going to win a few of them. That was just built into your expectations. The boys of 2006 and 2008 had paved the way for us. They'd turned it into a crusade in that decade. It had fired my imagination. I was in the Millennium Stadium with my dad in 2006 when the lads lifted the big silver cup and the fireworks went off and our supporters raised the roof and everyone was in dreamland. These fellas were superstars, they were kings of Europe.

I wanted some of that. I badly wanted some of that. We all wanted it and we went chasing after it year after year after year. But now I'm 30, and the seasons have slipped away and I'm running out of chances to get the job done. Myself and Pete and the other veterans have been knocking on the door for too long now. Things are getting a bit desperate. So, no party please unless it's a Heineken Cup party.

But we're not good enough for Saracens. They suffocate us. They put us under relentless pressure. They are incredibly powerful and physical and domineering. They take the game away from us in the second half.

It's our fifth beaten semi-final in the eight straight seasons that I've been involved in the Heineken/Champions Cup; it's my fourth, having been injured for the 2017 semi against Sarries. In 2010/11 Munster failed to qualify for the knock-out stages for the first time in thirteen seasons. That was considered a disaster at the time. In 2011/12 – beaten by Ulster in Thomond Park in the quarter-final. In 2012/13 – beaten by Clermont Auvergne in the semi-final. In 2013/14 – beaten by Toulon in the semi-final. Then in 2014/15 we failed to get out of the group and in 2015/16, ditto. What was a disaster in 2010/11 just got a shrug of the shoulders now. In 2016/17 – beaten by Sarries in the semi-final; 2017/18 – beaten by Racing 92 in the semi-final; now in 2018/19 we were dealing with the wrong kind of three in a row.

So, if I wasn't mad about the idea of a birthday party in the weeks before we faced Sarries, I certainly wasn't mad about it after they'd beaten us 32-16 in Coventry. But back in Limerick

CLOSE BUT NO CIGAR

the next morning, Joanna, in her goodness, told me she'd been planning a surprise party for me on the QT, hoping against hope that we'd win the semi-final and then we'd have a double reason to celebrate. She breaks the news to me that morning as delicately as she can and I tell her to cancel it. I'm too down and too dark after the result. I really believed we were going to qualify for our first European final the day before and I'm still raw with disappointment and frustration. But, she tells me, she has ordered all the catering and all the bells and whistles and we can't call the whole thing off now. She's invited a few people around too. Oh, Jesus. All I wanted to do was crawl back under the duvet. Long story short, we ended up having the party in Earlsy's house!

I think Joanna had a chat with Edel, Keith's missus, and between them they hatched up a plan that all the food would go round to their house and they'd have a bit of a knees-up there. In fairness, I think the partners in general get a lot of practice dealing with the highs and lows that come with great results and bad results. Edel and Joanna had seen these mood swings before. Anyway, a lot of our team mates turned up at the Earls' and if it hadn't been there it would have been somewhere else because we were going to drown our sorrows one way or another. It would be the usual wake the day after a big defeat. We were far too familiar with that ritual at this stage. But in hindsight, I just should have gone along with the party plans in the first place. Joanna had gone to a lot of care and trouble, it was my 30th birthday and Munster were still out of Europe whether or not we had a party. I still get the occasional reminder about my carry-on that day!

There's always emotional fall-out from big games because you have to be all in emotionally if you're going to have any chance of winning. That's why we end up getting hurt so often and overjoyed so often. You'll have your bread-and-butter games where there's not much on the line and you won't be going to any extremes on the emotional spectrum. But for the big ones, you have to ride that rollercoaster and leave yourself open to the joy and the pain. And when you still have your innocence, the hurt cuts deeper and the euphoria runs higher.

By the time you've reached your mid-thirties, a lot of that naivety is gone. Same as in any walk of life, I guess. But when I was 22, for example, and we were winning the Magners League final against Leinster in May 2011, I thought all my Christmases had come together. I could not have been happier. I wasn't a wet week in the first team and here we were winning silverware just like that, just like Munster were supposed to do. Looking back on it now, all I can say is, God help my innocence. I'm in the dressing room after, grabbing the cup and getting the photographs taken and I'm top of the world. What's more, I feel like I belong here. I'm not suffering from imposter syndrome, I have my own quiet self-confidence, but there's no better validation for a young player than to win something. You've been tested in a final and you've survived. You've proven yourself to the big dogs in the dressing room. You have gained their respect. That's the most important thing for me. I have earned their respect. I've come through this rite of passage and we've won the cup and the future is going to be brilliant. I have loads of days like this to look forward to.

Toulouse the aristocrats of Europe arrive in Thomond Park in April 2014 and we blow them out of the water. The atmosphere is fuckin' ferocious and for our supporters it feels like the good old days. Munster are on the march again in the Heineken Cup. In reality, neither squad is the powerhouse it once was, but I don't know that and I don't care anyway because I'm living in the present. They have stars like Maxime Mèdard, Hosea Gear, Luke McAlister, Gaël Fickou and Louis Picamoles rocking up to our place in Limerick so this feels like big-time rugby to me. And we go to town on them.

At full time we do the usual post-match handshake and I'm going through their players one by one when I encounter their right wing, Yoann Huget, another high-profile French international. I offer my hand and he takes it and as he does he pulls me in and stamps down on my foot! Stamps down hard.

What the fuck? I push him back and he's like, "I get you, I get you, I get you!" Now I remember. Early in the game, Nigel Owens awards us a penalty in midfield, but one of their players has thrown the ball away and I run down to get it cos the opposition are always happy to slow down play when they've conceded a penalty. The ball rolls randomly to Huget's feet just as I arrive and I can see he's about to kick it away further so I stand on his foot to prevent him doing it and pick it up. As I'm running back, I can hear him shouting, "Number nine, number nine!" By the end of the game I've forgotten about it, but he obviously hasn't.

The weird thing is that he turns this into a bit of a running feud for the next few seasons. I come across him in France v Ireland games and every time he tries to stand on my foot! There's one post-match function where I bump into him and he brings up this thing about my standing on his foot and him standing on mine. Pretty childish stuff as far as I'm concerned and then only a couple of years ago Zeebs tells me he's listening to this French rugby podcast and Huget is talking on it and he brings up this yarn about the foot-stamping again. All I can say is, let it go, Yoann, let it go.

I'm on a high after the Toulouse game. We can beat anyone in this kind of form. But Toulon in the semi-final in Marseille is just a bridge too far. They have a team of superstars and we are a long way from home. But hanging tough in France is one of the legacies we've inherited from the team of the 2000s. Against all the odds, we keep scrapping and battling and Zebo's try in the 53rd minute keeps us in the hunt. I get a kick in the face for my troubles at one stage, courtesy of Juan Martin Fernandez-Lobbe at a ruck, and he gets ten minutes in the bin as a result. It's an accident, I think, but I'm not complaining that they're down to fourteen men.

It doesn't make much difference. Jonny Wilkinson keeps kicking his goals and ultimately, they have enough power and class to see it through. I remember being really disappointed with this defeat. Three weeks later our season peters out with Glasgow beating us by a point in Scotstoun to qualify for the RaboDirect Pro 12 final. It's the end of Rob Penney's two years and, in all honesty, I'm not sorry to see the back of his gameplan. Rob was a lovely man to deal with, an absolute gent, but as I mentioned earlier, his big idea of getting the ball from sideline to sideline had me in tears of exhaustion and frustration after too many games.

Axel will be taking over in the summer and we've a chance to turn the page with a bit of renewed optimism. But the decline continues. Axel promotes me to captain for a league game against Ospreys in Thomond Park in September of the 2014/15 season. The RaboDirect is now the Guinness Pro 12. We still

CLOSE BUT NO CIGAR

have Paulie and Donners in the team, two great survivors from the glory days, plus CJ Stander who's made a big impact since arriving from South Africa in the summer of 2012. Any of those lads could've done the job, but I think Axel was trialling different players for the role and I ended up wearing the armband this day. And we end up losing so it's early confirmation that I'm not really cut out for the captain's gig.

The baton was passed to Felix Jones for the next game, against Leinster at the Aviva. They're always a big scalp and we come away with it on the back of a really good performance. I'm sin-binned in the 78th minute for some sort of infringement at a ruck that I know nothing about. As God is my judge, it had nothing to do with me. In fact, it was Captain Jones! But we're both skinny with jet black hair and it's a classic case of mistaken identity by the referee. And Felix didn't fuckin' own up to it! So, I was left to take the lonely walk, but the game was in the bag and we were both laughing about it afterwards.

The TV people gave me the man-of-the-match award. I picked up quite a few of them in those early years. I used to be flattered by them. They were a nice little boost to your confidence and maybe your ego too. If you were taken off late in the game and you saw the sideline camera crew making their way to where you were sitting in the dugout, you'd know you were about to get the nod. Then the announcement would be made, your face would flash up on the big screen and your team mates beside you would be patting your head and joking and you'd be trying to look suitably humble. You're not supposed to be seen enjoying it because we're all team players. But when I was young and immature, I enjoyed the validation. Then you cop yourself on a bit as the years go by.

Firstly, there are times when you know you've played solid but like, was I really the best player on the field in that match? You might just have shown a few moments of individual flair and the ex-player in the commentary box has to give it to someone, so he gives it to you. That happens a lot. And if it's a young, emerging player, they will tend to gravitate towards him. It becomes cyclical like that. The next hot young talent picks up a few of these awards while you might have fellas elsewhere who've been far more influential over the 80 minutes.

In my early twenties these things mattered to me; now they don't matter at all. I'll know myself when I've played well and when I haven't. I don't really need anyone else to tell me, especially fellas on television who get so many things wrong so often in their analysis anyway. You don't need this kind of external validation because you've seen so much external bullshit along the way. There is so much noise for the sake of noise that the thing that's real and important gets drowned out. Eventually you come round to realising that your own opinion of a game you've played in is probably closer to the truth than all the outside noise. I know myself what's right and what's wrong and what's actually valued. I'm experienced enough to be able to filter out the superficial judgements from the real and genuine truths.

I mean, so much of that external judgement is plain wrong anyway. So, if you don't value their opinion when they're criticising you or criticising your team, you can't really value it either if they're praising you. That's not how it works. But when you're young and insecure you're looking for validation. In fact, you need it to a certain extent, and it's all part of the journey, learning which stuff is authentic and which stuff isn't. Like, I see

CLOSE BUT NO CIGAR

the young generation of players and they will love getting their man-of-the-match awards and I've been through that cycle as well, so I understand it. But, mostly, it's just a TV thing.

In January 2015, Saracens, with the Vunipola brothers and Owen Farrell and the rest of their big guns, thrash us by 23 points in Coventry and dump us out of Europe with a round to spare. It's the first time Munster have ever lost three Heineken Cup games in a row. Guinness Pro 12 included, we've lost five out of the last seven. It's Munster's heaviest defeat in Europe since losing 60-19 to Toulouse in 1996.

The whole situation is desperately stressful for Axel. Morale in the camp is on the floor. He had to come in after Rob and basically start over with a new gameplan and try and take us back to Munster's more traditional style. I've had this scenario happen over and over during my fifteen seasons as a senior with the province. From Tony McGahan to Rob to Axel to Rassie to Johann Van Graan to Graham Rowntree and now an interim head coach for most of 2024/25. Next season it will be Clayton McMillan from New Zealand in the hot seat.

The lack of continuity speaks for itself. A new coach on average every two seasons and with it, a new gameplan, new calls, new staff, new players: everything always seems to be in transition all the time. That's no way to build a successful organisation. It's just too unstable. You end up without an identity as a team. You end up without a proper, deep foundation that you can build a squad on. Sarries were the dominant team in or around the middle of the last decade. They won three European Cups and have won six Premiership titles under the leadership of Mark McCall. McCall has been running the show there since 2010. Compare and contrast.

CONOR MURRAY

We scramble to salvage something from the season in May 2015 with a dramatic win at the death over Ospreys in the Pro 12 semi-final. It's a chaotic game, but we just about survive and at least we're able to give Paulie a triumphant send-off from Thomond Park. Another link with our golden past has done his time and is moving on in the summer. Donners is moving on too and we're all thinking it'd be lovely to send them off with some silverware. But sentimental endings are hard to come by in this game and instead, Glasgow do a job on us in the final at the Kingspan Stadium. I've done my knee against Ospreys and Duncan Williams replaces me after seventeen minutes.

The final is a week later. I can feel that it's medial ligament damage, but I'm thinking to myself in the dressing room, I'll get it strapped up good and proper and play next week. There's no fuckin' way I'm missing a final, even if the leg is hanging off me. Then I bump into Joe Schmidt in the tunnel near the dressing rooms and he asks me about the injury because he's thinking about his World Cup squad for the autumn. I tell him what happened and that I reckon I will make the Glasgow game. And he's like, "No you won't." Straight up and abrupt as that. I'm like, what? And he goes, "You won't be playing the final. No facking way. You're not risking it."

I get the hump over that, but the subsequent medical scans end the argument anyway. Yes, it's a medial tear but it's a four-to-six week rehab job. I'm out of the final and I don't know how much difference I'd have made anyway because the Warriors are too good for us at the Kingspan and score four tries to our one.

Paulie and Donners take their leave of Munster and it's back to the drawing board for us at the start of 2015/16. This time we're eliminated from the knock-out stages with two rounds left

CLOSE BUT NO CIGAR

in the pool games. Stade Francais beat us 27-7 in Paris despite being down to fourteen men for the whole second half. This is January 2016. The alarm bells are ringing throughout the fan base, if they haven't been already. Everyone is talking about how far Munster have fallen. This is still one of the biggest brand names in world rugby. I suppose, on a far smaller scale, it's a bit like how everyone in football is talking about Manchester United's fall from grace over the last decade. It's just too big to ignore. In rugby circles our ongoing decline is the subject of constant conversation. This is one of those times when you can't ignore the outside noise, much as you would like to. It's just too big to contain. It's not a pleasant place to be for any of us who are inside the bubble.

The return leg against Stade is a week later in Thomond. A few days before it, RoG in his column in the *Irish Examiner*, argues that this is a crossroads moment, even though the game itself is a dead rubber.

"For the players," he writes, "if enough isn't enough after last Saturday, the thing is doomed. I would be confident there has to be a backlash. I have to see anger this week. I have to. Otherwise what we know and love, what we have identified with, what Munster almost trademarked, is no more."

Sure enough, we win the return leg, but it's really only a sticking plaster. One result isn't going to save the culture of an institution that's been kind of crumbling in slow motion for about five years already. The season fades away. The following October we all discover what rock bottom really means on that awful Sunday morning in Paris.

Then Rassie picks up the reins and we are inspired by the outpouring of love and emotion after Axel's death. We win 15 of the next 16 games. We make it back to the Champions Cup semi-final and the Pro 12 final. We lose both, but we've surely got a great launchpad for 2017/18. Then Rassie announces in the summer that he's going back to South Africa at the end of the year. But we've to crack on with the next pre-season anyway and get our ducks in a row for that.

You end up becoming fairly pragmatic about all these comings and goings. We still have a job to do every day. It's more in hindsight, when you have a bit of distance that you can see how all this volatility has affected us. But when you're in the middle of it you're only looking as far forward as the next training session and the next game. So, we know it's bad news that someone of Rassie's calibre is leaving – but we're not crying about it either. The show goes on.

As it happens, I've played some of the best rugby of my life on the 2017 Lions tour of New Zealand and I bring that form with me into the following autumn when I score one of my favourite tries of my career, against Racing in Thomond. It's a right old dog fight and there's still no score after an hour. Then their scrumhalf, Maxime Machenaud, takes the feed from their number eight off the back of a retreating scrum and I shoot up the blindside and charge down Machenaud's clearance. The ball ricochets nearly 30 metres straight back downfield on a greasy surface and I'm all on my own chasing after it with the crowd roaring in my ears. The bounce is handy, I gather it and slide home with a big grin on my face.

Van Graan takes over from Rassie a month later and once again it's on with the show. We quickly find out that we are dealing with two very different human beings. The outgoing boss was hard as nails, full of his own authority, a man to be

CLOSE BUT NO CIGAR

feared as well as respected. Johann was quiet, understated, sincere and courteous; he had a deep religious faith; you'd rarely hear him swearing. And he was totally invested in the Munster project. He poured a lot of himself into it. In terms of the overall ambience, it was a very different vibe to the Rassie/Jacques Nienaber regime. Johann brought in as his defence coach JP Ferreira, another South African, to supplement Fla and Felix, who was in the second season of his coaching career after injury ended his playing career.

That season we get the new manager's bounce under Johann. We have the mighty Toulon at home in a packed Thomond Park in the Champions Cup quarter-final. Their back line alone would make any Munster fan nervous: Chris Ashton, Josua Tuisova, Mathieu Bastareaud, Ma'a Nonu and Semi Radradra.

It's an incredible match. The momentum swings over and back. It's packed with drama. The atmosphere is sensational. But Toulon aren't one bit spooked by it. They have turned up to win. You can tell that straightaway. They have us under the pump big-time in the first 20 minutes. Then I score the strangest try of my career.

Jack O'Donoghue lifts the pressure with a storming charge up the field. Keats prods a lovely grubber into the left corner. They just about scramble back to retrieve the ball on their own try line. They form a ruck and then a second ruck. I'm there watching it when Guilhem Guirado, their hooker, picks the ball up one-handed and fumbles it. Does that mean I'm onside? Is the ruck over? Instantly, I come round the back and I'm waving my hand frantically at Nigel Owens, signalling a knock-on. The Toulon lads are just standing there. So, I pick up the ball and dot it down over the line. Nigel blows his whistle and comes over.

"There's no ruck there," I plead.

Nigel is like a Detective Inspector from Scotland Yard examining the scene of the crime.

"Time out, time out please, time out," he calls with his full Welsh authority. Detective Inspector Owens and his TMO, Detective Sergeant Jon Mason, go over the video replays time and time again. It drags on for ages. Eventually they come back with a verdict. Mason says, "When [Guirado] knocks that on, Conor Murray is onside." Bastareaud is the Toulon captain. Nigel goes over to explain the decision to him. "It is knocked on by your number two so the ruck is over, number nine was onside and the try is good." It's probably a turning point because Toulon have been dominating and suddenly they're 7-6 down. It gets us into the game.

After that it's hell for leather all the way until Conway turns it decisively with his fantastic solo try in the 75th minute. We're down 19-13 at this stage and running out of road. And it's still not over. We've to survive 20 phases in the last minute before Nigel blows the final whistle and the stadium erupts into 'Stand up and Fight'.

Then we don't really fire a shot in the semi-final. Unfortunately, it won't be the last time that this will happen in a big knockout match under Johann. The week before we face Racing in Bordeaux, he comes up with his big idea. Any time we get within 30 metres or so of their posts we'll have a pop at a drop goal. We'll keep the scoreboard ticking over with threes and in the meantime, we'll wear them down cos we'll be fitter than them. Eventually, they'll crack maybe around the hour mark and we'll be able to open them up from there. This was a new gameplan for us. It was sprung on us that week. But suddenly this was

CLOSE BUT NO CIGAR

what we were going to do. Obviously, it didn't work. They had three tries on the board in the first 22 minutes. We were more or less beaten by half-time. It's not often that a Munster team is a complete no-show in a big game, but we were on this day and it becomes a bit of a pattern on and off over the next few years. You can't pin it down to one factor, but putting a new plan on a team in the week before a major match is going to mess with your head. It's just not done.

If you don't have complete certainty about your identity and your gameplan, you're going to get found out against top opponents. You build certainty and identity over months and months of training and games. If you don't, you end up with confusion. You end up not doing the thing that is built into your DNA, which is to fight on your back when you go to France and take the battle to them. On top of that, I felt there was a selection error too, going with Alex Wootton over Zebo. Alex played really well that season, to be fair, but in my opinion you pick your big players for the big games.

Leinster beat Racing in the final to add a fourth European star to their jersey. A week later they had too much for us in the Guinness Pro 12 semi-final at the RDS, albeit we stayed in the hunt until the final whistle. But it's definitive proof that the relationship between the two provinces has been completely reversed during this decade.

Twelve months later, I'm not celebrating my 30th birthday. On the field, there's fuck all to celebrate. A month after Sarries grind us down in Coventry, we turn up at the RDS for another Pro 12 semi-final tilt against Leinster. Again, we're not good enough. The following season we're not good enough either. Against Racing in Paris in January 2020, we're good enough for an hour and then the wheels fall off in the final quarter and our race is run in Europe for another season. Felix and Jerry Fla leave the coaching staff and move onto greater things.

At this stage in my career I've stopped crying over results like this. I remember being teary-eyed and distraught after losing the quarter-final and semi-finals in 2012/13/14. After the semi-finals of 2017/18/19, I was in a state of darkness every single time for days afterwards. You'd get back on the horse for the next game, but every time your mind revisited those semis you'd have this shadow crawling over your mood. I always found those defeats long and hard to shake off. Eventually, you learn to put a shell around your heart. You have to, because there's only so much emotional punishment you can take. For the last four or five seasons I've sat in beaten dressing rooms after another big game and I've just kind of numbed myself out. We've given it our all out there and fallen short and you're like, again? How upset do I get this time? Do I let myself be badly upset again? I've been through this heartbreak so many times, so am I going to allow myself to be torn up about it again? I don't think so.

Here's where you have to learn to compartmentalise. In the week before the game, you are fully invested emotionally because that's the only way. And you're always conscious of your family and friends. You want to make them happy, you want to make them proud of you. So, you pour your heart and soul into the game and you lose, again, and eventually you learn to bring the shutters down and sort of turn off the tap. Because you can't be repeating that same pattern forever. It doesn't solve anything. It's not good for your mental health. And it's not good for your relationships either. Years went by where people would be afraid to talk to me after a bad defeat and it got to a point where I realised, this is just fuckin' stupid. It took me until I was 30 or 31, but I finally kicked that habit.

It also takes a long time for the penny to drop with us on another habit too. For my first seven or eight years, every pre-season we'd sit down as a collective and have a talk about our goals for the incoming season. Sort of like, what are we gonna do this season, lads? And every year without fail we'd say, we're gonna win Europe. Because that's what Munster are known for. That's our holy grail every year. It's the annual ritual: we're going to do it this season. A picture of the trophy is put up on the projection screen. That's what we're after and we can go the distance this year. Then eventually, maybe in 2016, when we've failed to get out of our pool for the second year running, a bit of realism takes over. As in, lads, we haven't even got to a final for how many years now? We can't even win the Pro 12. How about we tick a few other boxes before we start talking about the European Cup? It's the pressure of the expectation I suppose. The memories of '06 and '08 are still fresh in everyone's mind.

I have to hold my hand up and take my share of responsibility for Munster not achieving what those lads achieved back then. Players and coaches, the buck stops with us, especially with someone like myself who's been part of the set-up for so long. I'd like to think that in terms of my professionalism, my preparation, my fitness and conditioning, I've lived the life to a very high standard. Your responsibility to the jersey, to the Munster tradition, was always there in the background of your mind. I mean, when you saw with your own two eyes what winning the Heineken Cup meant to the people of your home place, you couldn't but do everything in your power to try and do it again. Not just for them, but for yourself. I wanted my name in those history books too. I wanted my photos with the trophy. And now it's not going to happen and it's a void in my life that I suppose I will always have to bring with me. I did a lot in my career, but the one dream closest to my heart, I didn't fulfil.

Personally, I happen to believe that we, the players and coaches, could have got more help from the organisation in general. I would argue that we were let down by recruitment decisions over the years. Munster's recruitment policy hasn't been near good enough in my time. I don't know if they tried to recruit on the cheap, but I do know that to win the Champions Cup you need a cohort of world-class players and I don't think we had enough of them. RoG was a world-class ten, with a huge personality and the pure willpower to drive his team to those legendary heights. He had an incredible forward pack in front of him, driven by another world-class player in Paul O'Connell. Did we ever replace them? Of course we didn't. They happened to be homegrown giants of the game. They set the standard. And we were expected to emulate what they achieved without players of that calibre. O'Gara you could say, set the template for what a Munster outhalf should be. If we couldn't find a similar level at home, maybe the organisation should have had the ambition to go out and pay for one.

Same principle for Paulie's position: an absolute force of nature at lock forward. What about the front row – could we have powered it up with one or two elite international players? You need them in that position too, if you're going to be serious about winning the Champions Cup. You just won't get away with it in Europe if you don't pack your squad with really formidable, world-class operators. Financially, I think we were far too conservative, we ended up skimping on the talent that's needed to win the big one. Or, maybe it was just a basic lack of ambition, I don't know.

A friend of mine, a massive Munster fan all his life, recently sent me a list of about 50 players who've come and gone over the last decade and more. A few were great while we had them, the likes of Damian de Allende who was outstanding. A fair few more were good pros who did their job without setting the world on fire. But Jeez, when I looked at that list and saw some of the duds we signed over the years, it kind of reinforced what I'd been feeling for a long time about our recruitment policy.

Another basic oversight was that none of us senior players were ever consulted in advance about various potential signings, not that I can remember anyway. I mean, the likes of myself and the other lads who've been on the international circuit and being part of Lions squads and all that. We get to hear a lot of stuff about all sorts of players from all over the world. We're plugged into that network of information. We'd have a good read on a lot of our peers in other countries. So, you'd think that maybe someone in the organisation might ask for our opinion before they go out and sign someone? What about this fella or that fella? I know there were a few where I'd have said straight off the bat, absolutely fuckin' not. He just won't fit in. Or he's overrated. Or he's not a grafter. We'll have heard this stuff on the grapevine. If we're not sure, we can make a few calls and get back to you.

Obviously, the business of recruitment is never an exact science; there's always a risk involved. But you could mitigate some of that risk by asking us fellas who might be in the know. You could end up saving a lot of money as well as bringing in the right players with the right character. Anyway, in all my time at Munster I was never once consulted about a signing.

Being locked into the same pattern every season eventually wears you down. It takes something away from your spirit. Especially among the veterans who've been running into the same brick wall for years. You'll have your end-of-season piss-up and we'll keep going back to the same themes cos we'll still be raw from the latest failure. And one of those perennial themes is recruitment. Why aren't we recruiting certain players in certain positions to help us take the final step? We can get through the group stages, most of the time, we can even get past quarter-finals, and then we hit our ceiling.

In later years, we've ended up asking the same fundamental question: are we actually good enough? Do we have the firepower? Do we have the quality? Like, we have tried our absolute best, we've prepared as thoroughly as we can, but even if we play to the max of our ability, are we actually good enough?

Personally, for the first half of my career I didn't really get into those conversations because basically, I didn't know any better. I was full of hope and optimism. I hadn't been battered by bad results for long enough. I suppose I was in denial too, I didn't want to contemplate it, because that would be an admission of defeat. And we are solution-oriented people. You don't go round too often admitting that you were just beaten by a better team. Instead, you look at what you could have done better and where you can improve for the next game. You always believe that you can make it right. But finally it ends up staring you in the face. Maybe we just don't have the players to get it done. Is our scrum strong enough, do we have a world-class ten, do we have world class centres? I mean, we can't be bluffing ourselves forever either. Because we know what the level is, we know what the standard is, and there has to be a reason why we keep falling short.

I should say that the culture in general has gotten better with regard to how players are treated. I've seen it over the last five or six years, fellas won't settle for being treated casually, even for small things like match tickets and where your family is being seated for games. They used to be seated in the corners of stadiums until players spoke up and insisted that they get put in the middle of the stand or in a corporate box. They're your family, they've made so many sacrifices for us, the least they deserve is to be treated respectfully.

During Covid you'd have been happy to have them sitting anywhere. It was a horrible time for everyone and a pretty weird experience for anyone in my line of work. It was the strangest thing to be playing in empty stadiums. These were competitive games, but they felt more like training sessions. You could hear what everyone was saying, team mates and opponents. The whole thing was off. It didn't look right or feel right. It was artificial without the crowds.

In August 2020 they opened lockdown just enough to allow some sport to be played. We played Leinster twice and Connacht once in the space of a fortnight, all in the Aviva. Connacht's new signing Abraham Papali'i nearly took my head off in that game. It was just as well I'd been strengthening my neck muscles ever since the collisions with George North and Marika Korobeite. Papali'i clotheslined me. It could have done serious damage, but my neck was able to absorb the whiplash. The worst whiplash you can get is when you've just passed a ball and your body naturally relaxes and you're kind of limp and then wallop, a fella ploughs into you sending your body one way and your head whiplashing back the other way. You could end up with a concussion from one of those tackles and you haven't been hit in the head at all. As it turned out, I was okay after this one, I just got lucky. Bundee was friends with this fella and he told me that Abraham had asked him to pass on his apologies and hope there were no hard feelings. Grand, no problem, it can happen in this game.

A week after Connacht, Leinster beat us in a Pro 12 semi-final for the third year in a row. JJ Hanrahan knocks over a penalty for us after five minutes and we don't score for the rest of the game. I'm box-kicking all day because those are my orders. After this no-show the outside rumblings around Johann's stewardship start in earnest. He is such a genuine, nice bloke that I think everyone does their best for him, but you can feel the stagnation in the set-up. It's not necessarily his fault. The whole organisation has been treading water long before he took over. One man on his own isn't going to turn it around unless he's a genius. And every season we pull off performances that break the cycle and leave people believing that we've really turned the corner this time.

In December 2021, we had one of those games where you could be tempted into thinking that the future really looked rosy. A fresh Covid outbreak had left a load of our players stranded in South Africa. The scheduled games against the Bulls and the Lions had been postponed. The rest of the touring party that were lucky enough to get out of the country had to quarantine for ten days when they got home. Thankfully, myself and the other Ireland players in our squad had been spared the trip because we were being rested after the autumn internationals.

CLOSE BUT NO CIGAR

While Johann and the other coaches were serving their time in quarantine, Ian Costello stepped up from his role with the academy to manage the ship for our Champions Cup game against Wasps in Coventry. A rake of his players came with him to make up the numbers. Suddenly us veterans were struggling to put names on young fellas who were now our team mates. But they did brilliant. They were thrown in at the deep end and they did more than survive. It was a cracking Munster performance on the road. We beat Wasps by 21 points. Fellas like Pa Campbell, Scott Buckley and Daniel Okeke all stepped up and acquitted themselves admirably. In the absence of the coaches, myself and Joey Carbery at ten had to take on the responsibility for planning the attack that week. We had to put on presentations at team meetings and walk them through our ideas. We stripped it back and kept it fairly simple for the newcomers. Everyone mucked in together.

Joey was really good at explaining to the lads what he wanted. He'd been going through his own injury struggles on and off for a couple of years by then. Your heart would go out to fellas you see in rehab for months on end trying their hardest to get back playing again. Any player can tell you that it's a lonely station. It takes an awful toll on your mind and body. When Joey arrived from Leinster in the summer of 2018, we were all incredibly excited to have him on board. He was a natural ten; he was absolute class. And, in fairness to Munster, credit where it's due, they pulled off a big coup with this transfer. Looking at him in training early in that 2018/19 season, I was thinking this could be the final piece in the jigsaw for us. We have a Champions Cup calibre flyhalf here. If everything else falls into place, we could go the distance.

I can remember a load of moments that season when we were building our relationship at halfback and thinking, this is working, this is working really well. He had this quirky habit of sometimes playing himself into trouble and in the same moment playing himself out of trouble with this really quick, agile footwork that he had. And then we played Gloucester in Kingsholm in January 2019 and he went up another level in my estimation again. He ran the game, he controlled it. He showed the full repertoire of an elite flyhalf. And a week later, against Exeter at Thomond, he nailed a crunch penalty from 45 metres with seven minutes left to edge us into the lead. It was the kick that took us into the Champion Cup quarter-finals that season.

It was obvious to us all that we had the right man in the key position. Then seven months later he damaged his ankle playing for Ireland in a World Cup warm-up game against Italy. As far as we could tell, that ankle injury plagued him on and off for the next couple of years and I don't know if it took away some of that magic that he had in his footwork. I do know that it was a desperate stroke of bad luck for Joey and for Munster.

But that week against Wasps in December 2021, he was good to go and so were we. Munster weren't given a hope of winning in England, but you could feel the anticipation around the place in the days before. And then afterwards the buzz in the dressing room was magic. You had all these young lads who were absolutely loving their moment in the sun. And it gave us old-timers such a great lift too.

We beat Castres at home a week later and a month after that, in January 2022, we go to their place and grind out a tough, hard victory that goes down to the wire. I might add in passing that I'd hope, before this era gets completely written off by

CLOSE BUT NO CIGAR

Munster fans, there might be some bit of recognition for these performances on the road. Even in lean times, we generally mustered a few of them every season where we turned up in rough weather against powerful teams and hostile fans, and stood our ground. The pride in the jersey was always there. The spirit and commitment to our tradition was upheld; sometimes in victory, sometimes in defeat, but I don't think we ever lacked for bottle and heart.

In May we hit our ceiling again at the quarter-final stage, this time against Toulouse at the Aviva. This is the day of the penalty shoot-out after extra time. The match is a classic in front of over 40,000 people, most of them wearing red. Myself and Ben Healy missed kicks in the shoot-out. But my big regret from that game is that we let a ten-point lead slip through our hands in the last fifteen minutes. I didn't beat myself up over the missed kick. I had done my practice religiously, I hadn't skipped any kicking sessions, my technique was in good order. On the day, my second kick had to be taken from the ten-metre line and I just pulled it slightly.

A month later we turn up in Belfast for a URC quarter-final against Ulster and we are unrecognisable from the side that took the European champions to extra time. It's a horror show at the Kingspan. We've had these mood swings in form for years where we can go through the roof for major one-off fixtures and then fall through the basement when we're not switched on. Maybe we were just papering over the cracks as best we could and then, finally all the shortcomings inside the culture are bound to get exposed at other times. But this is another example where we don't really fire a shot in a knockout game.

That was Johann's last game in charge. He'd announced

months earlier that he would be leaving at the end of the season. We can't say that we didn't have stability during this period. He was nearly five years in charge. By the time he left we were more or less back at square one. We were at a certain level when he started and we were still at the same level when he finished. So, it's probably fair to say that while we liked him as a human being, there wasn't much emotion one way or another when we heard he was on his way out. We were kind of neutral about it. We hadn't won anything under him so we just kind of shrugged our shoulders and moved on.

If I'm being honest, maybe some of us were thinking that we might have a better chance of silverware with someone new in the hot seat.

Chapter Sixteen

LEADING THE PACK

WE WERE IN OUR HOTEL in Edinburgh the evening before the British & Irish Lions squad flew out to Johannesburg for the 2021 tour of South Africa.

We had played Japan earlier that day in a warm-up game. Alun Wyn Jones had to come off with a dislocated shoulder after seven minutes. Gats had lost his Lions captain before the tour had even properly started. Alun Wyn was an all-time great of Welsh and Lions rugby. He had toured with the Lions in 2009, 2013 and 2017. Suddenly, on the eve of the 2021 series, there was a giant vacuum left by our captain and leader.

Back in the hotel, we were all milling around the foyer in various groups before we were called in to a squad meeting. I happened to be chatting with Jamie George, Owen Farrell and Elliot Daly. They were sitting on a couch, I was round the back of the couch leaning in, genuflecting on one knee. I get a tap on the heel and I look round and it's Gats tapping me with his foot. He's beckoning me to have a chat with him.

We find a pocket of space to ourselves and he says, how would you feel about captaining the squad for the tour? Sorry, say again? He says Alun Wyn is out and that he's had a discussion with the other coaches and they've agreed that I'm the right man for the job. I don't know what to say, so I say, yeah, sure, a hundred percent. Gats says, cool, I'll announce it at the meeting. And he drifts away. Just like that, I'm appointed captain of the British & Irish Lions.

I drift back to Jamie and Elliot and Owen, a bit stunned. I blurt it out to the lads. Their reaction is great, congratulating me and wishing me well and offering their support in every way. But I haven't even begun to get my head around it. And I'm trying to figure out why they chose me when they could have chosen Owen himself or Maro Itoje or Ken Owens. It's a situation where you're kind of swept along because you've had so little time to plan for it. Gats stands up and announces the news to the squad and there's a really generous reaction from everyone.

Later that evening, he revealed it to the media and the next day we flew to South Africa. This was the Covid tour with all the social distancing, the restrictions on movement and everyone wearing masks and the daily tests to see if anyone else had contracted the virus. It was a horrible time in so many ways. Inside our bubble we tried to carry on normally as best we could. At my first press conference as captain, I explained I would have to be me and not someone else. I couldn't be Alun Wyn or Paulie or Sexto or Pete O'Mahony.

I was 32 at this stage. I'd long ago learned that you shouldn't try to put on another personality. The Munster culture in my early years was driven to a huge degree by passion and emotion. I tried to replicate that in myself, but it never worked. It wasn't me. I didn't need to be banging on tables and shouting and roaring. I'd seen fellas giving it the big lash over the years with speeches and the eyes bulging out of their heads and you just knew there was an element of performance about it. The fellas who could do it for real, you'd follow them into hell. The fellas who were faking it a bit, you wouldn't follow them into the pub.

If a fella is hamming it up, it'll be spotted straightaway in a group of 30 or 40 players. We're desperate gossips anyway and at the end of the day everyone talks about everyone. There's no hiding place in that environment. So, a player putting on a front – pretty soon there'll be a bit of bitching about him behind the scenes and when the time is right, a few jokes fired at him in front of everyone, to get him to cop himself on. So no, I'm not going to turn into Braveheart. I'll stay who I am, just with added responsibilities and obligations.

In going with me, Gats was going with someone he'd gotten to know in his first stint as Lions head coach in 2013. I was a Lions rookie back then and third in the pecking order of scrumhalves, but he put his faith in me by bringing me off the bench in the second and third Tests against Australia.

He started me in all three Tests against New Zealand in 2017. I happened to play some career-best rugby during that series so I'd imagine that was one reason he chose me for the leadership role in 2021.

Modern Lions tours are not the leisurely campaigns of old. They are compressed into ridiculously tight windows. In New Zealand that time in 2017, it was particularly helter-skelter. After 24 hours travelling, we landed in Auckland and the next day we were sent road-tripping north to Whangārei in a fleet of branded Land Rovers. We had to stop off to make various community visits along the way, in schools and hospitals and care homes and local rugby clubs and anywhere else the sponsors wanted us to go. We were all split up into different groups and assigned our gigs. Myself and my group visited an old people's home. We shook hands, signed autographs, stood in for photos and handed out Lions merchandise.

The overall strategy was to get all these social commitments out of the way early. The next day we had our first match, against a provincial barbarians team in the Toll Stadium in Whangārei. This was literally just three days after we'd arrived in New Zealand. It was a totally unreasonable ask of the players. Thankfully, I was left out of that squad. But we all travelled on the team bus to the match and I remember looking over at Sexto at one stage and he was fast asleep. He was out for the count. Our sleeping patterns were upside down from the jet lag. We were lucky enough to get out of the place that night with a win.

From there it was planes, trains and automobiles up and down the North Island and South Island and back to the North Island. It wasn't a huge surprise that we were beaten by the Blues in Eden Park. We weren't being shown much mercy off the field, in terms of the itinerary, and the host teams certainly weren't going to show us any on the field. The Blues were straight-up proof of that.

I started my first game in the next fixture, against the Crusaders in Christchurch. That was another massive landmine in a venue that was a fortress for the home team. We eked out the win. We felt like we'd stopped the rot before it got too serious, but then the Highlanders clipped us by a point in Dunedin. These games were coming thick and fast, you barely had time to think before you were packing your bags and hitting the road again. Finally, our form found a bit of traction against the Maori All Blacks in Rotorua. The outside consensus was that we were vulnerable

LEADING THE PACK

to a beating here from a high class Maori team. Lowey was on the wing for them that night. He had to deal with a fair few high kicks, and in the pissing rain too. You could hear the noise from the crowd, but you couldn't really see them. The pitch was floodlit but the surrounds were in darkness. It was an unusual ambience and kind of cool. Anyway, we won going away. Gats' tactics were starting to take shape. We were starting to bond together as team mates and friends.

Plus, the Test match squad was becoming clearer to everybody. But the overall unity wasn't compromised, as can happen occasionally when fellas realise that they're going to be featuring in the midweek fixtures instead of the blue riband games. On the Tuesday before the first Test, the midweek lads, led from the front by Besty, put in a storming performance against the Chiefs in Hamilton. That was the night James Haskell had everyone in stitches with his famous riposte to Gats. James, the England flanker, was part of a brilliant performance by the forward pack. In the dressing room after, Gats was praising the lads and telling them how good they'd been and that he'd be announcing the Test squad a few days later. But we all more or less knew by now who was in and who was out. So, while Gats was in the middle of his spiel, Haskell shouted out from the back of the room, "So, you're saying there's still a chance?!" And the whole room erupted because everyone knew he had next to no chance, barring injuries. A well-timed punchline in a dressing room – there are professional comedians out there who couldn't do it any better.

We weren't laughing after the All Blacks stuffed us in the first Test in Eden Park. Pete was chosen by Gats to captain that side. It was an incredible career honour for my old Munster buddy.

Drico came into camp that week to present us with our jerseys. When Gats announced that Pete was captain, I remember looking over at him and seeing how moved he was in that moment. He held his head in his hands for what seemed like several seconds. Personally, I believe Pete was unfairly treated for us losing that first Test. Almost like he was scapegoated a bit for it. He went from being captain to being dropped completely for the second and third Tests. In my view, that was a bit too harsh. But as usual, we had to move on and get our heads sorted for the business to come.

We weren't given a chance for the second Test. But we came back off the ropes down in Wellington. If we were going to go down, we were going to go down swinging. Instead, we won swinging in the pouring rain. And I'm glad to be able to say I threw a few punches of my own. We were trailing by seven points with about twelve minutes to go. Jamie George made a brilliant carry. I arrived at the ruck; it was about ten metres from the try line and ten metres from touch on the right hand side. And I can remember clear as day Anthony Watson out on the right wing: I was eyeing him up for a pass as I came to the ruck and he was roaring at me to go back to the open side, there was nothing on over his side, the short side. But I already had the ball in my hands and was about to fling it to him when I noticed a black jersey drifting slightly left, as if anticipating the pass. Suddenly there was this little gap and I shot through it and next thing I was diving over. A Test try for the British & Irish Lions against the All Blacks is something I will always cherish. Especially in the circumstances of that match.

Owen landed the conversion and then a superb penalty from long range to leave us three in front with three minutes to play.

LEADING THE PACK

The ironic thing was that the penalty came off a terrible pass I threw to Kyle Sinckler. My left-to-right passing had been off-kilter since George North ploughed over me three and a half months earlier. The net effect was what should have been a standard pass came out of my hands way too high. Sincks had to jump to catch it. But Charlie Faumuina was already committed to the tackle and inadvertently hit Sincks while he was in the air. Hence, the penalty.

New Zealand came roaring back at us to try and salvage the game. In the 79th minute we had a lineout on our own 22. The tension in the crowd was insane at this stage, the noise was deafening. The lineout was a messy contest; the ball bounced back to me randomly. I was tight on the touchline and the All Blacks were piling through. I hadn't a fraction of a second to get ready. I just put boot to ball and for some reason it came off my foot sweet as a nut. It just pinged off it, as if my boot was a trampoline, and it travelled way downfield. In those situations you'd be lucky to get five metres on a kick before it goes into touch. But there was a bend on the trajectory, like a banana kick, that kept it in play until it bounced on their 22 and bobbled on for another ten metres or so before it finally limped into touch. We had gained nearly 70 metres in the dying seconds of this incredibly pressurised game. That is one of my favourite memories from my three Lions tours. It was the best kick of my life. And God knows I've kicked a lot of balls over the last 15 years. But that particular one is number one. I have never connected sweeter with a ball.

The third Test finished level, the series finished level. At the final whistle we were all a bit bewildered by the way it turned out. Both sets of players were flat, we didn't know what way to react. It felt like a big anti-climax all round. It's why I think that the third Test of a series should go to extra time if necessary. There should be a winner on the day one way or another. But looking back on it now, I'm more than happy to have a drawn series with the All Blacks on my CV. That was the 12th Lions tour of New Zealand in history. Only the famous 1971 squad actually won a series down there. So, to come away with a draw is a pretty significant achievement in the record books.

By 2021, a lot of my Lions colleagues from 2017 were now friends as well as team mates. They couldn't have been more supportive when I was promoted to captain, the England lads in particular. Owen Farrell, for example, went out of his way to be a source of advice and help. It was really nice to realise how much respect you had from your international peers. You could tell it was genuine. It meant a lot because one of the most important things for me as a professional was having the respect of your team mates. I always wanted to earn the respect of every team I played on and I felt I had it from a group of fellas who were the best rugby players in Britain and Ireland at that particular time.

So, while I was out of my comfort zone as captain, I felt I was settling into the role fairly smoothly as we did the rounds of early games and social engagements. Then, lo and behold, Alun Wyn being the warrior that he is, made it back to South Africa less than a month after he'd been ruled out of the tour. He'd made a phenomenal recovery from his shoulder injury. Once we heard the big man was coming back, I was happy to step down and join the troops again. Gats thanked me for my service. In fact, he was so grateful for my service that he ended up dropping me for the first Test match. I'd gone from being

LEADING THE PACK

Lions captain and a so-called automatic starter in the Test 15 to sitting on the bench! Ali Price got the nod ahead of me. I came on for the last 27 minutes, we eked out a great win in a ferocious battle in Cape Town.

I started the second Test and for my troubles got wiped out in the air by Cheslin Kolbe. Handre Pollard launched a huge up-and-under in the 25th minute. I had to come from a long way, but it meant I had a great launch pad to get airborne. I sailed up for it and grabbed it and Kolbe came right under me and flipped me upside down. I crash-landed from a height. I was just about able to get a hand down to take a bit off the impact, but it was a hard fall and I needed medical attention. Kolbe was a lucky boy; he only saw yellow. The Springboks were in no mood to take a backwards step that day. They obviously had the hump after being beaten in the first Test. Rassie Erasmus went on a rant about the officiating and a lot of other things a few days after that game. We knew they were going to be wound up for the second Test and that was how it transpired. They got away with some decisions that day.

Ali Price was restored to the starting line-up for the final Test. A late Morné Steyn penalty won the match and series for the Boks. Between trips with Munster, Ireland and the Lions, I've toured South Africa nine times. I've always loved it down there, I've a load of great memories of the games we played and the cities I got to visit. But this time round, between playing in empty stadiums and the whole Covid nightmare and the way the final two Tests panned out, I was happy to get back home.

At the airport your luggage would include the mountains of clothing you get given by the Lions organisation. I mean, they give you so much stuff that they have to give you a huge wheelie bag and a big holdall to pack it all into. They give you a customised bag too for your boots, and one for your gym visits, and a backpack for when you're strolling around town. The formal wear alone would nearly fill up a wardrobe and the playing and training gear would nearly fill a sports shop. From the field in the morning to the swanky hotel in the evening, you are kitted out from head to toe for every occasion, several times over. It's actually way over the top. If I'd kept everything I was given from the 2013, 2017 and 2021 tours, you'd be able to kit out a whole rugby squad with it. Add to that the mountains of gear I've got from Munster and Ireland over the last 15 years – you'd need a warehouse for it all. You couldn't possibly store it at home. And I hate clutter anyway. So, I've given most of it away to family and friends and charities. I have held onto my Ireland and Lions Test jerseys.

I have heaps of jerseys too from opponents I swapped with. I've also kept the Lions formal wear, the blazers and ties, protected in that plastic wrapping you get from the dry cleaners. I've also kept my medals and awards and special gifts such as a few bottles of rare whiskey and vintage champagne with customised messages on the labels. It will be nice to have these mementoes, but I won't be putting them on display for everyone to see when they walk into the house.

I have framed photos of Ireland teams and the Lions teams I played on, but they won't be plastered all over the walls either. I'd hate to be one of those ex-sportsmen who builds a shrine to himself and wants everyone to admire it the minute they walk in the door. All this stuff will be kept in one private room and anyone who asks to see it, I'll show them. Other than that, my past will stay in the past. It's all there in my head anyway. I know

LEADING THE PACK

what I've done, I have thousands of memories stored away in my soul, and I don't need to prove it and I don't need to be living in the past either.

In the spring of 2025, the speculation started again, as it does around that time every four years without fail. Who would make the Lions team, who would make the squad and who might be in with a shout from leftfield? A few well-meaning friends mentioned to me that I might be in with a squeak, not least because of the relationship I'd built up with Faz and his Irish backroom team over the years. Not a chance. That was never a runner. I knew that. Instead, I was lucky enough to be asked to do a bit of TV punditry work and I really enjoyed getting to see how sports TV works from the inside. I've spent a lot of my life sitting on sofas watching sport, so it was a cool experience to end up actually giving my views on camera. Television is an option that appeals to me.

But, bottom line, you know for sure that when they're asking you to pick up a microphone and talk, you have officially become one of yesterday's men. Come in, Lion number #790, your time is up. That's fine by me too. Three tours of duty with the British & Irish Lions, plus eight Test caps, was more than I could ever have hoped for when I was flinging balls off lampposts as a kid back in Patrickswell.

Chapter Seventeen

SLIP SLIDING AWAY

BACK AT MUNSTER, AND BY the time we were falling apart against Ulster at the Kingspan in June 2022, we knew that our next head coach was going to be Graham Rowntree.

Wig had joined Munster as forwards coach in October 2019. When he took over, he brought in a new coaching ticket with Mike Prendergast as attack coach, Denis Leamy on defence and Andi Kyriacou for the forwards. Personally, I hadn't needed to have a huge amount of interaction with him during his time as forwards coach. And pretty soon I discover that I'm not going to be having a huge amount of interaction with him now either. As usual, the internationals have a late start to the domestic season because we've been away on summer tour.

This one wasn't just any old summer tour. We'd gone down to New Zealand and won a series there for the first time in the history of Irish rugby. Jamo by this stage had nailed down the number nine jersey with Ireland. He'd made his international debut against Italy in October 2020, replacing me for the final 13 minutes. He took to it like a duck to water and he just kept getting better and better. He was incredibly consistent too, so when I got bumped down to number two I couldn't complain.

Jamo proved himself to be a class operator and a good bloke

and there was a lot of mutual respect there from the start. But Faz kept the faith with me too. As I said earlier, he's got exceptional levels of emotional intelligence. There is just a sensitivity and truthfulness about him that makes you feel you can trust him. So, despite him dropping me down the pecking order, I still feel very much valued. And in each of the three games in New Zealand I'm thrown into the fray in the last quarter. It is one of the highlights of my career to have been part of an Irish squad that achieved something so prestigious.

Back in Munster however, it doesn't cut much mustard with Wig. I'm 33 and a half at this point. I guess like a lot of new managers, in any sport, he wants to turn the page and make his own mark. Out with the old, in with the new, and all that. The international crew are all available for the game away to Dragons in September 2022. Pete and Earlsy are selected to start, Tadhg and Joey are on the bench. And me? I'm the designated 24th man, the travelling reserve. More often than not, your travelling reserve is going to be a squad player or an up-and-coming young talent. It's not normally something you'd impose on a longstanding servant who's done World Cups and Lions tours etc. Ask him to travel to Newport as a non-playing reserve at this stage of his career? It's kind of disrespectful.

Craig starts and Paddy Patterson is on the bench. Craig has been knocking on the door for three or four seasons so he's entitled to his shot at the jersey too. But to me there's something very odd about being effectively demoted to number three scrumhalf – and then rubbing salt into it by dragging me over to Newport as the non-playing reserve. And I'm still a centrally contracted player with the IRFU. Wig fobs me off when I approach him about it. He tells me I need to get a pre-season under my belt first. But like I'm flying fit. I'd been training down in New Zealand until the middle of July. And I have a few weeks of training done anyway. I've done the same prep as the other internationals who've been picked for the Dragons. But he has his mind made up so I leave it at that and go away and fume in private.

The last thing you want to be seen doing is moping around on the training ground. That's a big no-no in my book. I've seen it too many times. It drags everyone else's mood down. You can't be bringing negative energy like that to the group. If you're hurting about something that's been said or done, you keep it to yourself and act like a professional. You can vent about it when you get home. I'm very conscious of that. I'm not clear about what their plans are for me, but I'm clear about how I should conduct myself when I'm at work.

For the next two months I'm in and out of the picture. Meanwhile, I get my 100th cap for Ireland against South Africa in the autumn internationals. In December they announce the squad for the first Champions Cup match of the season, against Toulouse at Thomond Park. Again, I'm dropped from the squad completely. Again, there's been very little communication from the boss.

A few days before Toulouse, we're having a run-out at Thomond and I approach Wig for a word. As in, what's going on, I'm fit, I'm raring to go. And his reply leaves me stunned. You don't deserve to be in, he says. Or, you don't deserve to get on. Something close to those words. But it's so blunt and so dismissive. I don't know what else to say to him so I just leave it. I'm really hurt by what I feel is a basic lack of respect. Then, seven days after Toulouse, we're away to Northampton and I'm picked to start. It all seems a bit random to me. A couple of weeks later, I'm back on the bench for the return game away to Toulouse.

With Ireland it's a totally different story. It's amazing what an arm around the shoulder can do for your morale. At Munster I'm starting to feel like a piece of meat that can be discarded and recalled at somebody's whim. In the Ireland set-up I feel taken care of and appreciated. As it happens, Jamo does his knee before the first game of the Six Nations and I'm brought in to start. Faz has no doubts about me at all. I start against France too, come off the bench against Italy, start against Scotland and come off the bench against England in our final game. While I'm getting messed around at Munster; I've won a Grand Slam with Ireland. You feel on top of the world after contributing to something like that, but then when you're coming back down the M7, that euphoria is replaced by a growing anxiety about the treatment you're facing down in UL.

In Munster, I'm back on the bench for our Champions Cup last 16 game against the Sharks in Durban. They run riot on us in the second half and that's us dumped out of Europe for another season. Two weeks later, we're back in South Africa for a URC showdown with the Stormers. They rarely lose in Cape Town and we know it's going to be a brutal contest. So, they pick me to start in this one and as it turns out we pull off a brilliant win against the odds. We're back in Durban a week later and we come from 19 points down to draw a match against a Sharks side that had hammered us three weeks earlier.

Typically enough, with our backs to the wall we get the dander up and end up coming away from South Africa with two huge performances. There are times when it seems the harder a job is, the more we like it. And now we're on the road again, away to a tough Glasgow side in the URC quarter-final. I'm starting my third game in a row. I finish it a bit too early for my liking. Tom Jordan, their flyhalf, poleaxes me with a shot to the head after 25 minutes. It's a fuckin' serious hit. He catches me right on the chin with his shoulder at full velocity. He sees red, but I can see nothing because I'm sparked out on the ground. It's as bad a concussion as I've ever got.

I manage to get up and walk off, but I'm all fuzzy in my head. One of the medics puts me through the protocols, the memory test and numbers test and balance test. I fail the balance test. RG Snyman has already been taken off with a HIA and Malakai Fekitoa follows us for the same reason in the second half. So, we're sitting together in the seats in Scotstoun and I've still got my wires crossed. Joanna and I are getting married in the summer and we're in the middle of making all our plans for the wedding at that time. But there in Scotstoun I have this thought running through my head that we got married the week before. I'm there looking at the game and there are these images running through my mind of our wedding day last week! Basically, I'm all over the shop. I'm away with the fairies.

The three of us are stood down for the URC semi-final against Leinster. Jack Crowley's late drop goal swings another huge battle of wills our way. I've been watching Jack's development since he joined the academy in 2020. He is the real deal. I rate him very, very highly. He already has a Six Nations title under his belt and I'm looking forward to the battle between him and Sam Prendergast for the Ireland ten jersey in the coming years. He has a cool head and it showed in his composure for that winning drop goal.

SLIP SLIDING AWAY

Wearing my Munster heart on my sleeve, I'm incredibly excited that we're going to be playing in a final, my first in eleven years, a first final of any description for the vast majority of my team mates. Wearing my cold, analytical hat, I think we've caught a break here because Leinster are playing La Rochelle in the Champions Cup final a week later and they've rested most of their frontline players for that one. Mind you, they've got such a stacked squad that their second string would be a match for most teams in the URC.

Our lads were put to the pin of their collar to get past them in the semi-final. But that's their problem, not ours, and now we're heading back to South Africa to take on the Stormers, the defending champions, in the final. It's our sixth game in a row away from home. I'm returned to the starting line-up. I think I've earned it over the previous six weeks or so. I've held my form as best I could throughout the season and bitten my tongue and gotten on with it.

Stephen Archer is starting too and we joke among ourselves that this is definitely a case of the old dogs for the hard road. Because generally it doesn't get much harder than South Africa. Johnny Hodnett comes up with the winning try with five minutes left. Craig has taken over from me in the 66th minute and those last 14 minutes watching it are agony. But our team has been in one dogfight after another and, in terms of attitude and heart, I think we've rolled back the years. There isn't an ounce of quit in us. We hold out for a famous victory. For the likes of myself and Pete and Earlsy and Archie who've been there for so long, the relief is just massive. To finally have some silverware to show after eleven barren seasons, it's such a sweet feeling. I can feel it deep in my bones, how satisfying it is.

The craic that night and the next day is outrageous. The party continues back in Limerick, but I've to bail out when we land back in Dublin airport and catch a flight to Portugal for the wedding. I get changed out of my Munster gear at the airport Radisson, pick up my wedding suitcase and head for the Algarve. The big day is a week away and we have loads of logistics to sort out in the meantime. Joanna is delighted because I've arrived in one piece and because the whole Munster contingent is going to be in great form, they're going to be on a high since Cape Town and a fabulous day will be even better still. It's going to be one hell of a party, that's guaranteed.

I've been down in the dumps for a lot of the season, but it finishes with two fairytale endings, not one. I get back in the team and we only go and win Munster's first trophy in eleven years. And then I get married to the woman I love in a beautiful setting surrounded by the best of people, my family, friends and team mates. I'm not in Scotstoun anymore. The wedding is for real and I don't think I could be any happier.

But, by the end of 2023, it seriously looks like I'm heading for a divorce with my head coach. I'm 34 and a half now, so maybe from the outside people might be thinking that Murray has had his day. The thing is, though, I don't want to fade away. I want to be relevant right until my last game. I want to be competing for the jersey. It runs too deep in me. I don't like being marginalised because it's the first time it's ever happened to me in my career and I don't like it one little bit. I can understand now why RoG fought with Johnny for the ten jersey to the bitter end. We're competitive animals. We're proud of who we are.

So, I'm going to maintain my standards until the last training session before the last Munster game of my life, whenever that

SLIP SLIDING AWAY

will be. I've no interest in being a sort of elder statesman around the squad, just there to pass on my advice and experience to the young lads. I'll do that anyway, but in my head it's not what I'm there for. I'm not there to be sitting on my laurels. As long as I'm there I want to be playing and competing and doing what I've always done. That's the long and the short of it.

The situation is bringing back memories for me of the 2013 Lions tour that I mentioned earlier when I was selected as the third-choice scrumhalf on that tour and in our third game was the only sub who didn't get played. Fast forward ten years later and I'm down the pecking order again and I'm not accepting it. Well, I'm not accepting it meekly. I have to accept the selection decisions when they go against me, but I'm not resigned to my fate.

I understand that I'm at the other end of my career now, but that's no excuse as far as I am concerned. I'm not here to freewheel to the finish line. I'm not here to pick up the money and coast along. No. I'm determined to keep my side of the contract in terms of my fitness and conditioning and general professionalism. I'm ticking every box, up to and including my ice baths and massages, my sleeping patterns and nutrition, my application in the gym and on the training ground. I don't want any slippage on my part. Faz and the staff in the Ireland set-up are monitoring me too and they're still keeping the faith. You won't meet a shrewder judge of players than Faz and if I was slackening off in any way, he'd spot it. I'm involved in every Ireland game at the 2023 World Cup. I get a generous amount of playing time.

In mid-November, I'm back with Munster and the pattern from last season resumes: in and out of the team and not really knowing where I stand. In early December, I have a chat with Wig and he tells me, "You're not there yet, mate, you're not there yet." I take it to mean that he figures I'm still dealing with the emotional hangover from the World Cup. He might have a point. I've found it very hard to climb out of the dungeon for a good few weeks after that crushing disappointment. The only thing is, I was getting the same treatment last season, long before the World Cup.

I tell him I think the situation goes deeper than a World Cup hangover. I tell him I've been thinking deeply about this for the last twelve months and I reckon there's a changing of the guard going on. I'm being eased out, irrespective of my fitness or form. Wig says that's not what's happening. He's adamant about that. He promises me that that is not what they're planning. He promises me, "When you're back at it, I'll pick ya." And he tells me I'm going to have to take his word on that. So, I say, okay, I've no other choice but to take his word for it.

You can only have these conversations a couple of times a season. You can't be banging on their door every week looking for explanations. That's a mug's game. You don't have a winning hand of cards here. The coaches have the power to pick whomever they want whenever they want. You can't talk yourself into getting a game. Ultimately it comes back to letting your actions do the talking. And if your actions are positive and you're showing up well in training and they're still not selecting you, it means that they're not listening. You just have to play the waiting game and hope it will turn around at some stage. It's a head-wrecking place to be but it's your lot.

I know from seeing other lads in the same situation down the years that trying to bargain with coaches isn't the way to go, no matter how much you want to get stuff off your chest. Because coaches will give you any old excuse to explain themselves. They'll make up all sorts of reasons. They can pick any aspect of your game apart and say that's the reason. Because no one ever plays a perfect game, there's always something they can isolate if they want to. "Oh, you missed a tackle on your left shoulder against this team and we want you to work on that." It can be any old sort of random bollocks. The bottom line is, if he wants to drop you, he'll drop you. If he thinks the other fella is going better, he'll pick him and drop you. It can be very subjective. He might just fancy another player's style more than yours. Or, he might be seeing something that isn't there at all. Doesn't matter. You don't have any power here. If they're giving you feedback that you know is bullshit, you have to take it. And that's why I keep my counsel for long periods of time under this regime. The irony is that in the pre-season just gone I've run my fastest time ever in one of our sprint exercises, I'm clocked at 9.40 metres a second. That's quick, it's not Earlsy quick, but it's fast. Athletically, I've been absolutely blessed all my life. So, I'm in great physical shape but, at this moment in time, I could be Usain Bolt and I don't think it would matter much.

By Christmas of 2023, I'm thinking I'm done here. My contract with the IRFU will expire in the summer of 2024. All the indications are that my time with Munster is up. I don't think Wig is for turning. Maybe it's time for myself and Joanna to leave Limerick and look for pastures new. The only light at the end of the tunnel is with Ireland. Faz and his coaches are still showing me the love. Sure enough, I'm very much included for the 2024 Six Nations squad and, being honest, heading up to Carton House for every camp that spring is such a joy and such a contrast to my situation back at home. But then, out of the blue, in February, I'm offered a one-year extension with Munster. After a decade with the IRFU my central contract will be terminated. But I'm still categorised as "a player of national interest" so this will be a hybrid deal, half-funded by the Union and the other half by Munster. It's the first time in over ten years that Munster will have to pay a penny for my services.

Part of me is pleasantly surprised by the offer and another part of me recognises the cold reality here. There's a position-specific criterion at work here. Munster have Craig at nine for the foreseeable future, but after that, they're possibly not convinced about their cover. It's a specialist position and it's not like the back row, say, where they have loads of options. The decision regarding me, I figure, is determined by the roster. They're maybe a bit nervous of being a little bare in this department if Craig gets injured and I'm gone.

I don't for a moment believe it's out of loyalty to me for services rendered. I have seen players of my vintage and younger being let go without a second thought. It's a hard school, but that's the way it is. I'm on the verge of 35 so I'm grateful to be getting a good deal at that age when I've seen so many friends and team mates over the years scrambling around looking for one last gig before they retire.

And there's another reason why we're glad to be staying at home for another season, albeit we're keeping it under wraps for now: we are expecting a baby in the autumn. We're both thrilled with the news and it's a weight off my shoulders that I'll know we'll be at home surrounded by family and friends when the happy day comes to pass.

So, I sign on the dotted line in March 2024, but I can't pretend

SLIP SLIDING AWAY

that I'm feeling any fresh burst of affection in UL. Rowntree is an old-school prop forward with the cauliflower ears to prove it. He's hardy. He's not one for modern, holistic man-management. But funnily enough, any time we've to play South African teams in South Africa, he seems to want me. Once again, I'm starting games where he knows the going will be tough. I end up scoring the winning try against the Bulls in another bruising encounter at Loftus Versfeld. Of course, the dressing room is buzzing afterwards and one of the coaches comes up to me and he's gushing about how well I've played and how much it reminded him of my performances in South Africa twelve months earlier. Lovely, thanks for saying it, but in my head I'm like, I've been capable of this all season so why have ye been marginalising me for months on end?

Fuck it, let's move on. Northampton have knocked us out of Europe two weeks earlier, but we've found our mojo again and maybe we can put two URC titles back to back. We finish the regular season on a hot streak of form and end up with a home semi-final against Glasgow. We are heavy favourites and we blow it. We bloody well blow it. Glasgow, in fairness, were really tough and resilient on the day. They had two players yellow-carded in the first half but we still couldn't take advantage. They turned up not one bit fazed by our fans or our famous home venue. Sadly, it's been a long time since Thomond Park was a fortress. The aura it used to have for visiting teams has become a thing of the past too.

Munster teams used to have an aura about them as well. You certainly know how much it has diminished when you get beaten by Zebre, of all teams. It has never happened before. Munster have won all 20 previous encounters. Zebre have been cannon fodder for years against virtually every other team in the league. But, in September 2024, they turn the tables on us at the Stadio Sergio Lanfranchi. It is a shock result, one of the most embarrassing defeats for Munster in the professional era. I'm sent on for the last ten minutes. We don't know where to look at the final whistle. It wasn't a fluke, they were better than us. Our defence was abysmal. Some of the mistakes that let them in for tries were so basic that you couldn't pin this one on the coaches. When coaches keep drilling good habits into players day in day out and then some of those players go and do the exact opposite in games, the buck stops with the fellas on the pitch. You can't be spoon-feeding professional players all the time. They're supposed to have learned the ropes by now. They have to take responsibility themselves for schoolboy errors.

But there's one issue beyond our control that probably played some part in this shit-show and that was our travel itinerary. The penny-pinching has been going for years at Munster, a sort of a mindset of doing things on the cheap here and there and hoping to get away with it. In this case we were down to play Zebre in Parma on the Saturday at 4pm. On the Friday morning we drove to Dublin – two and a half hours. Waited in the airport – two hours. Food was a problem, lads had to get food in the airport and you should not be eating airport food. Fly to Milan – two and a half hours. A coach from Milan to Parma – 90 minutes. Get to the hotel about half seven, eight o'clock on the Friday evening. We have our dinner and head to bed, everyone wrecked. The next morning it's breakfast, pre-match meetings, and then the bus to the venue. And we're supposed to be fresh in ourselves and firing on all cylinders after that? It is not the way a professional team should be travelling. Straight after the game

SLIP SLIDING AWAY

we have like 20 minutes to get showered and dressed because we're rushing to get back to the airport in Milan for the same journey in reverse.

This travelling on the cheap has become an issue in the last few seasons. The players' leadership group has brought it up with Wig a number of times, but his attitude is more or less, just get on with it. Overall, it's another manifestation of the ongoing financial spiral. They don't buy big-time players because they'll cost too much so you end up with fewer box office talents who'll get supporters coming through the turnstiles. Your squad becomes progressively weaker season upon season and inevitably, then, results start to suffer. That in turn affects the gate receipts which in turn means the quality of the recruitment goes down and the vicious circle continues. An air of stagnation starts to hang over everything. And eventually you end up sending your squad cattle class to Italy and the Munster brand name takes another embarrassing hit to its prestige.

The downward loop continues into October when we're outclassed by Leinster in front of 80,000 at Croke Park. They run amok in the first quarter and for us it's a salvage operation after that to try and keep the scoreline respectable. I drove up that morning because I was going to be staying in Dublin overnight for Sexto's big book launch at the Bord Gáis Energy Theatre the next evening. I made sure to get to Croke Park early. I've had the privilege of playing in some historic venues around the world and finally I was getting the chance to tick this box too. I'd grown up steeped in Gaelic games, so I wanted to take it all in good and proper, rather than just arriving in the team bus and heading straight to the dressing rooms. I wanted to sample the whole ambience, the enormous scale of the place. They sent me on for the last 20 minutes and it was such a lovely bonus experience to get to play in this hallowed stadium in my last season.

Then it's down to Cape Town where we're beaten by the Stormers. Once again, I'm picked to start in South Africa. We have the Sharks in Durban a week later, but I have other things on my mind. Our baby is due in the next couple of days so I get a flight out of Cape Town the day after we play the Stormers, arrive back at home Monday evening and in the maternity hospital in Limerick, on Tuesday 22nd October, Alfie Murray comes into the world. It is an amazing, indescribable emotion to see him born and to hold him in my arms.

A week later, Wig, after the squad has got back from South Africa, is relieved of his duties. By this stage a parting of the ways was unavoidable. I won't be two-faced here and say I was sorry to see him go. In all honesty, I wasn't. I will let other players speak for themselves, but the way he'd spoken to myself, and one or two of my close friends in the squad was, at times, unacceptable.

I'm not sure he was cut out to be a head coach. He'd always been an assistant coach in his post-playing career. Munster was his first job as a number one. Sometimes a staff coach will struggle to make the transition to the top job. Wig when he was in the mood could make a good connection with the lads. He showed a bit of charisma from time to time. He could come into a meeting after a win when the vibe was good and do a sort of a stand-up comedy routine for ten minutes, slagging the young fellas and slagging the old fellas and getting the laughs. But as a head coach I didn't rate him and, in his last season, even the younger, more innocent players were starting to see through

SLIP SLIDING AWAY

him. Personally, I didn't see a lot of rugby knowledge there. He knew his scrums alright, but after that, he left a lot of the heavy lifting to Prendy and Leams, two great fellas and really good coaches. Rowntree got a lot of credit for us winning the URC title in 2023, but in reality it was Prendy and Leams and the senior players who drove the momentum in those weeks and put that winning streak together.

You wouldn't get much inspiration from Wig in the dressing room, before games or at half-time. Leams and Prendy would lead the talks about defence and attack. At half-time when you'd be needing an emotional lift, you'd get practically nothing from him. Again, it would be his two deputies lifting us and then the players ourselves would say what needed to be said. Wig was just a figurehead a lot of the time. In all honesty, I was relieved when he left. I felt a weight off my shoulders and I don't think I was the only one either.

Cossie steps up as interim head coach and fair play to him, it's a really difficult situation to come into and try and manage now. It is not easy to take over the reins in a scenario like this. But I learned long ago that irrespective of who's in charge, I have to take care of my own business anyway. You can't be waiting on the boss to whip you into shape. That's on me. I have to stay on top of my fitness and conditioning, my gym work and skills practice. It's a fundamental obligation about being a professional. Keep on top of your own shit first and foremost. Maintain your own standards. Apart from anything else, it's your best chance of keeping control of your own destiny. Don't ever give anyone the chance to say that you've let things slip. So, another coach is gone, but you still have to do your weights and your ice baths and your passing drills.

CONOR MURRAY

By Christmas of 2024, I know I have only five months or so left in a Munster jersey. All I want to do now is remain the best version of myself until the final, final whistle. I don't want to fizzle out and fade away to the margins.

I want to finish as I started nearly 15 years earlier, by making a contribution on the field of play, the only place that ultimately matters. I think it would be a travesty to my overall career if I took the foot off and let my standards deteriorate in the dying months of my life with Munster. That's not going to happen.

Chapter Eighteen

LAST TANGO IN PARIS

I AM SENT INTO BATTLE in the 61st minute. And by battle I mean war. My team mates are giving the All Blacks a ferocious pounding and the All Blacks are giving it right back. It is the mother and father of a Test match. The atmosphere in the Stade de France is sensational. The noise, the lights, the pressure, the desperation, it's an absolute furnace of emotion. Both sides want this win so badly. The 2023 World Cup quarter-final is one of the most extreme pressure situations I've ever witnessed on a rugby field. And now I'm not witnessing it: I'm off the bench and dropped into this massive battle of wills and I've to hit the ground running.

I know I won't have time to catch my second breath, that moment in every match when you're no longer blowing hard and you've settled into your aerobic rhythm. Any player will prefer to be starting but at scrumhalf in particular it can be hell coming into a game because you're going from sitting on the bench to running around like the proverbial blue-arsed fly. In other positions you might be able to take a breather but in my job you're straight in at the deep end. If your team has the ball you have to be there for every phase, and you have to get there as fast as your legs can carry you because you're the link man. Virtually every move will go through your hands. And they can't be waiting around for you to turn up at the next ruck. You have to be there as soon as it's formed, if not sooner. And that's just for any routine match.

But the pace and ferocity of this game are at another level. This is so intense that you're going from 0 to 90 in a flash and you don't have time to settle your lungs. If anything, it's getting even more frantic the longer it wears on. The lads are fighting with every fibre of their beings to claw back the deficit on the scoreboard. We're down 25-17.

I'm not sent in with any specific instructions. The basic message is, just keep playing. We've had it drummed into us over the years when it comes to New Zealand. Keep playing rugby irrespective of the scoreline; don't go into your shell if you're ahead, keep taking it to them if you're behind. They will never stop playing and competing, so we have to do exactly the same. Especially when you're in possession. They will come at you in waves and you can lose your nerve and go for the safe option. Don't do that, if you can avoid it: throw it out the back, get it out wide, trust your skills and hold your nerve under the blitzkrieg.

My first job is to take the ball from a lineout and feed it back. After a few phases, Hugo Keenan makes an incision into their 22 and there's another series of recycles and, sure enough, after about ten phases, I'm blowing hard, I'm sucking in oxygen to get to the next ruck and the next one. We've had the ball the whole time I've been on so far and we're hammering away at their defence. Lowey makes a good carry inside their 22 and

LAST TANGO IN PARIS

Johnny and me work a little one-two round the corner and I'm brought down by Sam Whitelock and he's pinged for not rolling away. Johnny kicks the penalty to touch and I finally get a chance to fill my lungs. The lineout works like clockwork and so does the maul until it's sabotaged by Codie Taylor just inches from the line. Wayne Barnes is decisive: penalty try to Ireland, yellow card for Taylor. It's the 64th minute, we are one point down and one man up. It's all on a knife edge. Everyone is feeling it. Even Jordie Barrett is feeling it because four minutes later he pulls a penalty kick left of the posts when normally you'd expect him to make it. That's a big let-off for us in a game of these tiny margins.

Unfortunately, he doesn't miss the next one. Even more unfortunately, I'm the one who's given up the penalty. Johnny launches the restart from Barrett's missed kick. Beauden Barrett gathers and puts up a high one and this is where the problems start. I can see he's got under it a bit, the ball isn't going to go long, it's hanging up there. But it's not a little dink over the top where you know you've got to cover it. A short little dink and sometimes it's the scrumhalf's job to contest it. Longer kicks straight down the field and obviously that's the full back's gig. But this particular one, it's neither long nor short. Is Hugo Keenan too deep to come and claim it? It's hard to tell because I'm looking up into the sky like everyone else. But I'm sort of caught in between and next thing I can sense a player in black charging by me to challenge for it as the ball comes down.

So, I decide to "cradle" our catcher. I'm not sure which of our players is going to challenge for it, but if you're in the vicinity you're supposed to try and cradle him by forming a protective wall of bodies around him. Then another thought runs through my mind. When we played New Zealand at the 2019 World Cup I was beaten by Beauden Barrett to a high ball. I can't remember if they scored off it, but all of a sudden I have a flashback to it and now, four years later, I'm thinking, I'm not going to be beaten in the air by him again in another World Cup quarter-final. There's a ripple of anxiety in my mind, on top of all the anxiety of the occasion. The ball is in the air for three to four seconds but in that space of time I've processed all these thoughts and calculations.

It drops and Hugo makes a spectacular catch and next thing Barnes blows his whistle. Penalty to New Zealand. It's Jordie Barrett who's on the floor. It was Jordie who was chasing his brother's up-and-under. I didn't know that until I saw him lying in a heap. Hugo has sailed up and over him to make the catch and naturally he goes to Barnes looking for an explanation. So, Barnes gives him one and I'm within earshot: "Conor. Conor's caught number twelve off the ball." Oh fuck. He's fingered me for it. At first I didn't even know what I'd done. I was escorting Barrett back alright, but I thought the contact was minimal to non-existent. Tadhg Beirne and Andrew Porter are joining me in the cradle too. Tadhg gives him a bit of a bump as well.

I couldn't look at the video for months after, but when I did I saw that I've put my hand on Jordie's shoulder just as he's about to get airborne. It's the most harmless, innocuous touch you'll ever see on a rugby field, but technically speaking it probably is a foul. I probably kept my hand on him for a fraction of a second too long. I was just a bit too anxious to prevent him from beating me in the air. The thing is, he was so crowded out by green jerseys at this point that he probably wouldn't have been able to win it clean anyway – and Hugo was coming like a steam train to make it his own. But it was such a harmless bit of contact that I think other referees in other circumstances would have let it go. It didn't help either that Jordie went down like a sack of spuds.

Anyway, the ref blows his whistle and I hear him saying my name and it's a horrible feeling. I've given away a penalty at this stage of this match. Soon as Barnes names me, I get the glare from Johnny. The what-the-fuck-are-you-at glare. He doesn't say anything, but that's what his eyes and his face are saying.

Jordie Barrett nails the kick this time. Their lead is out to four. It gives them breathing space. It means that realistically a penalty or a drop goal isn't going to get it done for us. We have to score a try to save our World Cup. We have eleven minutes left to do it. So, it's not a fatal blow. Eleven minutes is enough time. This is my 112th international cap. It's ingrained in me by now to put a mistake behind you and look to follow a negative outcome with a positive one. That is standard operating procedure. But there's nothing standard about these circumstances. This is a match with implications for your career, for everybody's career. And for a lot of us there's not going to be another chance of cracking our World Cup quarter-final hoodoo. We're running out of road, we're not going to be around for another four-year cycle. So, think positive? Sure. But I'd be lying if I said that here and now I wasn't thinking of my own predicament. I did not want the outcome of this match, above all matches, hanging on a stupid fucking mistake that I had made.

In my head, I'm like, Christ, please let this work out and I can get away with it. The trained, professional side of my brain is telling me to park it straightaway and move on to the next task. The secret, personal part of my brain is desperate for me to be let off the hook by us finding a way to win.

CONOR MURRAY

Immediately, we get back down to work. I nudge a grubber into their 22 on the right hand side, Bundee is the first to the breakdown and wins the penalty. We're going to have a lineout on their 5m line down in the right corner. The Irish crowd erupts. Johnny gives me a high five: all is forgiven. We're feeling good about ourselves again. Tadhg wins the throw, the maul starts grinding for the line, arcing left as the All Blacks get their counter-shove going. We're paused and there's a brief stalemate. Ronan Kelleher is holding the ball at the back and I've arrived behind him. I reach in and put my hands on the ball without taking the ball off him. I'm just communicating with him, letting him know I'm there as an option. But the lads get a second drive going and it's moving fast now and we pile over the line, me pushing Ronan as he flops down and scores the try. I mean, I'm sure it's a try. It can't be anything else, can it? But Wayne isn't blowing his whistle to confirm it. I'm sitting down on my backside looking up at him and he's not confirming it. And he's not confirming it because Jordie Barrett has managed to get himself under Ronan as Ronan falls for the touchdown. Barrett has prevented the ball from touching grass. The All Blacks start yelping and cheering like they've won the World Cup. For them it's a huge moment. I get up and jog back. You can hear Barnes on his ref mic saying, "It's held up, mate." It's not a try; it's a goal-line drop-out. It's a huge let-off for the All Blacks and a huge let-down for us.

But there's eight minutes left on the clock. We still have time. It's getting a bit desperate now, but we still have time. Let's follow a negative action with a positive one now. We're going to get possession off the drop-out, get into our shape, start playing again and win a penalty or we might get a line break. They launch the drop-out, Caelan Doris is there to receive it and he drops it. A knock-on. Caelan is all alone receiving that catch, he has loads of time and space. I can't speak for him, but I presume it's the pure pressure of the moment that has forced that error.

Speaking for myself, I know I'm going to be feeling more pressure if I'm under that ball. Like, I know I can catch this all day long if it's a league game in Thomond Park. But this is eight minutes to go in a World Cup quarter-final and we desperately need a try and now I have to catch this ball. The anxiety is heating up your brain, your calmness is compromised, so your technique is compromised and you end up taking your eye off the ball for a split second and next thing it's on the floor. In these circumstances, a glitch in your technique can happen because there's a glitch in your mind. Barrett's freakish act in defence has flooded them with relief and it has piled even more pressure on us. So, now we have followed one negative outcome with a second negative outcome. And all the time the clock is ticking.

New Zealand manage the clock for the next four minutes, recycling over and over. With three minutes left Aaron Smith hoists a high one and Jimmy O'Brien makes a brilliant overhead catch. We have the ball back. We're between our own 22 and our 10m line. It's a fairly long way from their try line, but at least we have a chance. We throw it across our backline, we come in wave after wave down the field. I take a little bit of pride in the fact that we kept playing under this mind-bending pressure, kept throwing passes and gaining yards. After 20 phases we're tiring and the All Blacks are getting closer to a turnover, but we manage to keep it alive as the clock ticks into the red. Bundee and Garry Ringrose make half-breaks inside their 22, but are brought down. The Irish crowd is going mental in the stands.

My lungs are screaming going from ruck to ruck. It's been non-stop relentless for three full minutes without a breather. We keep charging, they keep tackling, and on the 37th phase Sam Whitelock gets in for the poach and gets the decision and it's all over. You could argue that Whitelock doesn't release in the tackle before going in for the poach but you can only shrug your shoulders at that now.

The All Blacks go off on one at the final whistle. I've never in my life seen them celebrating like that. They're euphoric. They normally keep their emotions in check. They just can't contain their relief at surviving.

I've never seen an Irish dressing room as devastated. The numbness in there is sick. The silence, the pall of gloom, the awful silence, the shell-shocked numbness, the haunting silence. It always seems way too inappropriate when somebody in sport describes a defeat as like a death, a bereavement. This is one time where I'd make an exception. It was like we were all suffering this stunned reaction to news of a sudden death and we don't know what to think or what to say because we just can't take it in.

We were convinced we were going to win this one. And that wasn't wishful thinking on our part, far from it. I'd never been with a squad more grounded in reality. We were hard taskmasters on ourselves. We were big into self-criticism and self-improvement. There was nothing airy-fairy about our conviction. We had the work done, we had the results in the bag, we had the talent in the squad. We'd won the Grand Slam seven months earlier. We'd beaten New Zealand two times in a row in New Zealand in 2022, winning a tour there for the first time in Irish rugby history. We'd beaten South Africa in our pool game three weeks earlier. We'd won seventeen games in a row. So, we weren't imagining things. We knew we had the stuff to beat the All Blacks and get to the World Cup final.

Instead, it's over. We're out and it's over. The magic carpet ride is over. We'd had a fantastic six weeks in France. The Irish fans had been incredible all tournament. The singing, the craic, the atmosphere, the sound of 'Zombie' and 'The Fields of Athenry' reverberating around the stadium, we were on this incredible high from the day we landed at our base in Paris. The next day we'd be packing our bags and going home.

I can't remember what Faz said in the dressing room afterwards. I can't remember anything really cos the numbness had taken over. I know he had a few words for Mick Kearney, our long-serving manager who was retiring, and for Johnny and Earlsy who were also retiring after their epic careers. The room was heavy with emotion. Fellas were shedding tears. Most of us just sat there in our gear drinking a beer, not able to move to the showers. There's pizzas and chicken wings brought in, as there usually is after a match. I didn't have much of an appetite.

Eventually, we go through the motions of showering and dressing and we head back on the bus to our hotel. It was late when we got back. Between the dressing room and the bus I had a good few beers already and at that stage all I wanted to do was to go to bed. Everyone deals with it differently in their own way. Some lads went on the piss, I had a few glasses of wine and went to bed totally wrecked. Up the next morning, get a late breakfast and then the day-drinking starts straightaway.

The hotel has an internal kind of plaza, like a square with a garden in the middle of the building, and when I get down there a load of the lads have already started drowning their sorrows.

CONOR MURRAY

All the wives and girlfriends and family connections are hanging around too, but they stick to a separate part because the lads, we just need to be on our own, together on our own. And, of course, once a few beers are had, the black humour starts to come out, the bit of messing and slagging, the gallows humour. What else can you do? We head into Paris that night on the team bus with the girls and hit a few bars and keep the wake going into the small hours. That's how we put in the Sunday. On the Monday we packed our bags and flew back to Dublin that afternoon. There were buses laid on at the airport for the Ulster lads, the Munster lads and the Connacht lads, and me and Joanna are back in our house in Castletroy later that evening.

A few days later, we're back to Dublin for a barbeque party in Johnny's house. It's the final farewell among his team mates for this out-and-out legend of a player. We'd started as halfback partners together in 69 international matches stretching back to the 2011 World Cup. Apparently the Australian legends George Gregan and Stephen Larkham hold the world record at 78. Johnny and I played together for Ireland a total of 82 times. So, that's a long era in which to be throwing passes to one man. He got used to me, I hope; I certainly got used to him. It was a pleasure and a privilege.

They say opposites attract: I was the calm one, Johnny was... the less calm one?! In fairness, it'd be easy to write him off as a cranky bollocks, but that's a bit of a stereotype. Obviously, he had far more dimensions to him than that, as a player and a human being. He is one of the most decent, loyal friends you could have. As professionals, as team mates, yeah, sure, I got my share of bollockings from him, especially in the early years. But more often than not he was right and I'd be like, fine, fair enough. And when I felt there were situations where I was in the right, I'd stand my ground and make my case. The few times I did argue back it was because I knew I was fully in the right – you had to be sure you were fully in the right before you made your argument. And he'd accept it, "Sorry, sorry, wrong call", or whatever. And we'd move on straightaway because we're adults not children and because we're professionals and we've a job to do.

If some ex-team mates come out down the line and say he was too harsh or too demanding, then, I dunno, my opinion would be that maybe they weren't able for it. Sexto had very high standards; we all know that. He wanted the team to be the very best it could be, and he was arguably harder on himself than anyone else. And the other thing was, same as the likes of Michael Jordan or Roy Keane, he'd never ask you to do anything that he wouldn't do himself. He was first to put his body on the line.

Virtually every single member of the squad was at his house party that day. It was important because, number one, we were all going through the same grieving. We were the only people who understood what each other was going through, who were hurting in the exact same way. And number two, because we'd never share a dressing room together again. All of us who were there, we'd never be in any room all together again. Johnny and Laura were incredibly generous hosts, as usual, the food and drink flowed for the afternoon. That evening we all went out to a restaurant in Ranelagh to continue the night and bring this journey of many years to the last stop, the end of the line, the final parting of the ways.

A few days later, me and Joanna flew out to Dubai for a

holiday. In between times, I stewed in my own thoughts back in Limerick. I wasn't due back with Munster for a couple of weeks, but I didn't want to stick my head outside the door anyway. After a defeat of that magnitude, I find I just want to hide myself away. I'm afraid to meet people. I'm kind of embarrassed. You're well aware that the whole country had massive high hopes for us reaching a World Cup final and maybe winning the whole thing. And as a player you want to give them that high. You want to make them feel proud, you want to help to give them this national celebration. And in that little child's part of your brain where you still hold onto your dreams, you've pictured in your head the open-top bus parade back in Dublin with hundreds of thousands lining the streets; the reception back in Limerick, in Thomond Park, everywhere you go. But now you come home to your quiet house on your quiet street and you hide away, basically. You don't want to talk to anyone. That's how I feel about it anyway.

And, in the quietness of your own house, you have too much time to think about the what-ifs and the maybes, the things you could and would have done if you could just turn back time. In my case, if you could turn back the clock to the 71st minute. Because when our maul gets paused, I'm at the back of it and I'm looking at Aaron Smith, my opposite number, and he's covering the narrow side with one other player and it crosses my mind that I have an option here. He's standing on the try line and he has his hand up calling for a team mate to come over and cover his side because he's thinking what I'm thinking: Ireland have a three-on-two here. I'm thinking, if I go now, Johnny is going to come with me and we have Jimmy O'Brien there on the wing so it's a three versus two. And in the same stream-of-consciousness I'm looking at Smith and thinking I'm a bigger, stronger man. He's an unbelievable player, but I'm definitely bigger and I could crash through him. But I don't do any of these things because after those few seconds the maul gets moving again and we're driving for the line and Ronan is crashing over. And I don't do it because the golden rule is, if the maul is making headway you leave them at it. You don't try to fix it when it's not broken. If the maul is grinding away and inching closer to the line, you leave them at it. There's the risk, I've seen it happen, where you try to take it off the hooker, but the hooker doesn't want to let go of it and next thing there's a fumble and a knock-on. There's also the risk that if you take the ball, someone in their maul will be close enough to scrag you and bring you down. And the other thought that stops me is, for as long as I've played the game, if the maul is going forward and you take it out and you don't score, you're going to get fucked out of it by the forwards.

This whole maul lasted about twelve seconds. It was held up for about three seconds before it got moving again. That was my window of time. That was my fork in the road. And for months afterwards it was eating me up about the road not taken. That I didn't just grab the fuckin' ball from Kelleher and plough through Smith if he came for me and dot it down. I was so tantalisingly close to doing it. Next thing the maul is moving again and I'm latching onto Ronan and falling on top of him as he's grounding the ball. I'm convinced he's grounded the ball. Nine times out of ten the hooker scores there. Except he hasn't grounded it and that's the game right there. That's our World Cup right there. That's the end of our World Cup dream. For many other lads they will get another shot at it. But for Johnny,

Pete, Earlsy and me, it's written in stone now and no amount of what-ifs and maybes will ever change it.

The 2023 World Cup quarter-final is the most hurtful result of my career, bar none. The pain of it is almost physical, like you can feel it in your bones. I wake up with it in the morning and go to bed with it at night. I can't get a proper night's sleep for weeks.

One night in Dubai we're out for dinner, this is about a week later, maybe more, and I just start bawling crying. The shock and the numbness have thawed out and all of a sudden, without any warning, I'm a mess of tears and emotion.

Joanna is like, "I've been waiting for this." She knew it was coming, it was only a matter of when. And I am not a crier. I'm more of a get-on-with-it kind of fella. Sports psychology has taught me that it's way better to talk about something straight away, face up to it and get it out of your system. But this was just too big to talk about immediately. I needed time to process it and even now I'm not sure if I fully have. But the dam burst that night. It took me a week to break down, basically, and begin the long process of making peace with it.

Naturally enough, the hurt has faded between then and now. But in this game you pick up a fair few mental scars, some worse than others. This particular scar cut so deep, I think the track of it will always be there in my soul.

Chapter Nineteen

SPIRALS

YOU'RE SUPPOSED TO SAY NEVER SAY NEVER. You never know what's going to happen in the future so you should never rule anything in or anything out. I'm gonna break that rule here. I will never go into coaching. I am one hundred per cent certain about this. I will never be a rugby coach of any description. Never.

I'm just not cut out for it. I can't ever see myself doing that job. The idea of it just doesn't float my boat at all. I love the sport, but I'm not so obsessed with it that I will never want to leave it behind. As soon as I hang up the boots, they'll stay hung up. I won't be taking them back down again to stand on the sidelines shouting at players to do this, that and the other. I'll just go back to being a civilian.

Someone said to me recently that it's going to be an awful waste of your knowledge. That I've been a scrumhalf for 20 years and that that's a huge amount of know-how and experience to be wasting without passing it on. It's maybe a valid point. But there's no guarantee I'd be any good at it anyway. Playing is one thing, teaching is another. Would I be any good at teaching what I know? I can't make that assumption. Those are two different jobs. You could have a fella who had a middling career as a player who happens to be great at teaching. He could have a vocation for it that I would never have. He might just have the right personality for connecting with young lads, for explaining the nuts and bolts in a way that makes them listen and helps them improve. That's a separate skill set altogether.

Anyway, for what it's worth, I'll try to share some of what I've learned here, on the off-chance that there's a young girl or boy out there who loves the game and might be interested in picking up a few tricks of the trade.

In this particular trade there are two obvious fundamentals – passing and kicking. It goes without saying that these are your primary skills. You cannot do the nine's job well if you can't do these well. Believe me, I've seen scrumhalves who were incredible athletes, but fell short of the international level because their basics weren't good enough. Especially their passing. What makes a scrumhalf is their pass, essentially.

Next is kicking. They are non-negotiable basics of the trade. When I came into the Munster academy in 2008, Ray Egan was one of our skills coaches. I can remember Ray saying to me one day that I would sink or swim based on my passing and kicking. It was one of my first sessions in the academy at UL. We were standing on the edge of the second basketball court, near the Munster Rugby offices. And Ray said if I wanted a career in the game, "it's your passing and kicking that will earn you your contracts and your money". They would be the two building blocks. I remember it clear as day. And thank God it clicked with me when he said it. In my head I was like, right, that's exactly what I need to do. I have to develop a world-class passing and kicking game. Ray also said that "you sharpen the knife on both of them all through your career".

SPIRALS

And I did. I've never let them out of my sight. Of the two, passing is the number one priority. Every set piece move starts with the first pass. If it's off by a couple of fractions it has a domino effect on everyone else's movement. It's nuts-and-bolts stuff, but it's very important. If the nine is out of kilter with his pass, the attack is out of kilter. You grow into the job knowing that your margin for error is tiny. To some degree, everyone else is dependent on you doing your job efficiently because the nine is the link in the chain between his forwards and backs. So, in a nutshell, get to the ball early, get it away fast and get it away accurate. That's essentially the job. Speed and precision. Do it again and again and again in a game. Do it over and over and over in training.

I've been trying to take a wild guess at how many times I've thrown a rugby ball in my life. I haven't got a clue really. But say I've thrown it 100 times a day for 300 days of the year over 20 years; that would be 600,000 times. Let's round it down to half a million. I could be way off with that figure. But maybe it's plausible enough.

When Ray passed on that advice to me, it was music to my ears because I'd already been practising since I was fourteen or fifteen anyway. I was already obsessed with spinning a ball out of my hands. I'd fallen head over heels in love with rugby when I went to St Munchin's in Limerick for secondary school. The place was and is a hotbed of the game. An oval ball became my constant companion, maybe like a comfort blanket or something. I was a contented kid when I was playing with it, I'd be in my own world. How far can I throw it? Can I hit that spot on the wall? Can I get a nice spiral on the throw? Can I get an even nicer spiral on it? So, unbeknownst to myself, I guess,

I was putting in the famous 10,000 hours of practice before I'd even heard of the 10,000 hours concept. And naturally the more I practised, the better my pass was getting.

When I left Munchin's, I joined Young Munster because most of my mates were there and that's where the craic was. One night I was out training with the Munsters Under 20s at Derryknockane and John Broderick was our coach. This was 2007, I reckon. John had coached loads of us at Munchin's too. It was a foul night, filthy with muck and rain and darkness. The floodlights were shining. We were running a lineout move, I got the ball off the top and ripped a long pass out to our inside centre. He was miles away, but soon as the ball left my hands I knew it was a zinger. It was right on the money for speed and trajectory. Broderick stopped the session and called to one of the coaches on the sideline: did you see that? We could use that pass now. We could make a new move out of that. We could use it in a game.

And the session resumed, but it dawned on me there and then that, Jeez, this is actually a real strength of mine. The main man has noticed it. I must be good at it, or getting good at it. And when you're that age it's gold when you get feedback like that from a coach, absolute gold. It fills you with confidence and it encourages you to do it even more and to do it even better. I was all in on trying to master the mechanics of my craft.

A small bit of personal resentment went into the mix too at this time because I was tall for a nine and, in the view of a few experts, I was a bit too tall. There's never any shortage of rugby experts in Limerick! And there can be a lot of traditional mindsets, people with fixed ideas about the game. The scrumhalf is supposed to be a small, nippy sort of a breed. Being low to the

SPIRALS

ground, they don't have to bend as far to fish the ball out of the ruck. I was only vaguely aware of this opinion starting out. But I switched to Garryowen after a season with Munsters and there was a match report in a local paper that season about this new scrumhalf on the block. And there was a line in it to the effect – I'm paraphrasing here – that the ruck ball was unusually slow from the unusually tall scrumhalf. Or words to that effect. Basically, the perception was that because I was taller, I was bound to be slower. I don't know how it got back to me, but it did. And, naturally, it pissed me off.

Now it might only have been the opinion of one person, but as far as I was concerned, it was one person too many. I knew myself that physically I was elastic. I was really agile and flexible. I had no problem getting low to a ruck, none whatsoever. I could do any number of squats, I could nearly do the splits in fact. One of the coaches started timing me just to be sure that his eyes weren't deceiving him. Soon as I'd bend down at a ruck he'd put the stopwatch on me and time it until the ball hit the outhalf's hands. That full motion was timed and he found my speed of pass was elite standard.

And as for the pace perception, short scrumhalves tend to look quick because their legs are going nineteen to the dozen. But it doesn't necessarily mean they're going any faster than a leggier player who is covering more ground in fewer strides. You can look busy, but you're not doing anything faster or better than the next fella. Anyhow, because of all those preconceived notions I made it my business to be seen zipping from ruck to ruck at training every day. I wasn't going to have that stereotype hanging over me.

Some early mornings in the academy you'd have a pure passing session with the other scrumhalves in the squad, up to and including Stringer, O'Leary and Gerry Hurley. Those sessions were real sharpeners because we were all being compared to each other and we were all really competitive. Strings was a brilliant passer. His ball would be travelling almost upright, which makes it easier for the catcher to kill in his hands. He had quite an arm-driven technique whereas I was obsessed with being wristy. O'Leary's pass wouldn't have been as fast as Stringer's, but it was still a high-quality delivery and he was also a really good kicker and very physical around the breakdown.

When Greig Oliver came into the academy as a coach he really helped me evolve to another level. Greig, Lord rest him, died tragically in South Africa in July 2023. He was only 58. It was a terrible shock. It saddened me a great deal because I remembered him so fondly. He'd been good to me. He'd taken an interest in my development. He was innovative as a coach and we always appreciated a bit of innovation because so much of our work is just pure repetition.

In my case, he studied my technique, broke it down for me and helped me smooth it out without taking away my own natural habits. For example, I never had a textbook follow-through on my pass. You look at Aaron Smith of New Zealand and you'll see a picture-perfect pass where he will follow straight through, like his two hands pointing perfectly at the target as the ball is released. We were always taught to finish with our two hands pointing at the target. I tend to use more wrist in my action and a bit less arms and shoulders, to get more spin on the ball, so I'm usually a bit more hunched and compact rather than at full extension on the follow-through. It has its advantages, though, and Greig, in fairness to him, never tried to rebuild my whole technique. As a good Scotsman, he was into his golf and there's a saying in golf known as "Swing your swing". In other words, use the swing that suits you best. Greig used to say to me, "Pass your pass."

And I'll tell you what, when Greig had one of his passing sessions on the basketball courts at UL, you knew all about it when you were finished. You'd be pissing sweat. He'd have you in at seven in the morning doing footwork drills, passing circuits and back-pedalling exercises, flying into rucks from all sorts of different angles, sometimes wrestling with him like he was an opposition forward trying to sabotage the nine. Then at the end of all that, could you still rip a pass? Could you ping it out at full speed and accuracy in a state of exhaustion? Because that's often when it matters most in a real-life game: can you provide a top-class service to your flyhalf when the arms are hanging off you and you're panting for oxygen? Greig prepared me thoroughly in my apprenticeship; he was my mentor, and I will always be grateful to him for it.

You had to do all of this work left-handed as well as right-handed. I had to learn to be completely ambidextrous. Your weak side had to be developed until it was as good as your strong side. This was an essential part of your daily learning too. You wouldn't get away with it at the highest level if you couldn't pass properly off both sides. It's like a soccer player I suppose who can control and pass the ball equally well off either foot. I didn't like the idea of not being as good off one side as the other. I have a perfectionist streak in me and it wouldn't accept being more dependent on one side than the other. In my head, it wouldn't look good at all. I wanted to be perfect off both sides.

Right-to-left was my natural strong side and the temptation

when you're young is to revert to your strong side all the time and that becomes a bad habit. You can easily become frustrated when you're trying to do something that doesn't come naturally to you and you keep failing at it. So, you revert to your comfort zone. In fairness to myself, I tried to stay out of my comfort zone as much as I could. I worked incessantly on my left-hand passing. For me it was a new skill that I would have to learn. No shortcuts, just keep repeating it over and over, day after day.

The funny thing was, although right-to-left was my dominant tendency on a rugby pitch, in everyday life it was a bit more mixed-up. Sometimes I was right-sided, sometimes I was left. Like, I write left-handed. I brush my teeth left-handed. If I'm stirring a sauce or flipping steaks on the barbeque, it's all left-handed. A bowl of soup? The spoon is in my left hand. I wouldn't be able to hit my mouth with my right. But I play golf right-handed. Holding the steering wheel in the car, right-handed. When I was a kid skimming stones across water, it was right-handed. It was never a conscious decision either way, I just did whatever came naturally to me.

During my apprenticeship years I kept working on my left side and, in the end, I actually became a more accurate passer off my left. By the time I had gotten it up to scratch, I actually preferred passing off my left because I had practised it so much it overtook my natural ability on the other side. I had built in the muscle memory. The pay-off came in game situations where I never had to adjust to a favoured side. Whichever way the ball came to me, I would fire it away from that side without having to think about it.

You can see scrumhalves who are weaker off one side than the other and they'll be adjusting themselves to throw it off

SPIRALS

their stronger side. That's where you lose fractions of seconds. I've seen nines not wanting to run a move from a certain side of the pitch because it would require a longer pass off their weaker hand. And if they have no choice, but to do it, you can see the pass is more awkward, more laboured. It doesn't happen as much nowadays in professional rugby, but you can still see it from time to time. The bottom line was that being equally proficient off both hands helped me cope as I moved up the levels; I had the tools I needed to adapt to the next standard. I didn't get exposed for technical flaws – if you weren't sound in the fundamentals you would get exposed somewhere along the journey between club rugby and the British & Irish Lions. Ray Egan was right: the pass was my passport into the paid ranks. It wasn't the only thing you needed, far from it, but in my trade you were going nowhere without it.

In all honesty, when you've been doing it for 20 years it's not going to have the same excitement that it did when you were setting out on this adventure. Eventually, it becomes a job of work. It's your daily bread and butter. You don't have the same innocence, you can't have the same innocence that you had when you were young and you were mad for road.

You've been through the mill, you've seen it all and done it all. But still, I find, if you're watching a match on the telly and you see a scrumhalf throwing a perfect ripper, I'll be purring along in appreciation. The same if you're down at training and one of the young nines makes a peach of a delivery, it'll get your juices flowing again. And, even to this day, if I rip a pass absolutely plumb, it's still one of the most satisfying feelings I get from the game. It just feels very good. And they don't all have to be big, long, raking deliveries. In a match situation, if you can manipulate the defenders around you, fool them with a dummy and put your fella through the gap with a short pop-pass, that's very satisfying too. But ripping a long pass to your winger on the edge is lovely when it comes off. It looks great, for one thing, because the speed and trajectory have to be top drawer. If you've done it right, the ball will stay on the same plane from your hands to his hands. It can't oscillate in the air because that will slow it down and make it vulnerable to an interception. It has to stay on the same plane all the way. It has to spiral perfectly. The spiral on it has to be symmetrical. There can't be any wrinkles on either end of the ball as it's travelling.

If everything is on the money, you have a pass that looks really stylish, but is also really efficient. Your winger is in business then. You have taken out three or four defenders with one pass. He's got the ball in time and space. He can make serious ground with it. Ideally it will enable him to beat the cover and run it in for a try. And you as the scrumhalf have put it on a platter for him. You have unlocked their defence. So, here's my advice to any young nine who has given his winger a Rolls-Royce of a pass and he ends up with all the glory: if he doesn't buy you an expensive drink that night, you're entitled to take the piss out of him big time. You'll be well within your rights!

For some reason, Jordan Larmour's try against Samoa at the 2019 World Cup sticks out in my memory. It was early in the second half. We'd put the ball through a fair number of phases and we weren't really getting anywhere. We're at a ruck about sixteen metres from touch on the right hand side of the field. Johnny, of course, is roaring at me to hit him with the next pass. And I hear him loud and clear, but then I spot Jordo on the edge and I'm like, fuck, this is on here. So, I pick the ball up and

SPIRALS

bullet it out to him left-handed. It has to be bullet speed cos the Samoan defender can nearly touch it with his fingertips as it goes by him. The ball smacks Jordo bang in the chest and he's in near the corner. The TV commentator calls it "a beautiful pass" and who am I to disagree with him.

Part of the thrill when it comes off is that it's so risky. You see those passes being intercepted all the time and suddenly it's seven points down the other end. In this particular case, fast and all as the pass was, Johnny still had time to throw a few fucks into me before Jordo caught it. Of course, I was all smug about it after cos Johnny's like, if we didn't score there I was going to fuckin' kill you. And I'm like, yeah, but we did score. Chill the beans there, Johnny!

I wasn't so smart four years earlier when I saw Damien Hoyland disappearing into the distance on an intercept off my pass with the clock on 80 minutes and Munster leading by two points. We were playing Edinburgh in Murrayfield in November 2015. We were just trying to kill the clock, but we ended up making a big break and we got to about five metres out from their line and I tried one of those flashy passes and next thing Hoyland was sprinting away in the opposite direction. Oh, Christ. Anyway, thank God, some of our boys scrambled back and dragged him down, but it set up a siege on our line for about 20 phases. Edinburgh were battering us and we were all hands to the pump. We should have been back in the dressing room by then, but here we were busting a gut trying to hold onto our lead with time deep in the red. And it was my blunder that had us in this predicament. They kept battering, we kept holding them out and eventually they went for the drop goal through their scrumhalf Sam Hidalgo-Clyne. It was dead straight in front of the posts and only about fifteen metres out, but CJ Stander somehow got out to block it down. We got away with it. Or I got away with it, although it didn't spare me a bollocking from Axel in the dressing room afterwards. I think it went something like, "You fuckin' eejit, what the fuck were you at there? Don't ever fuckin' do the like of that again." Something gentle and diplomatic like that!

You win some, you lose some. Same when you're trying to connect with your wingers through your boot not your hands. It happens routinely that you have to go to the air to gain ground. It's not what you'd call the most artistic form of attacking play, but it often gets the job done, not unlike soccer where you've a longball team that instead of playing it through midfield launches it direct up to the centre forward. It's not very cool nowadays, but it can still be very effective. It's a similar principle in our game: if you go to the air you've a bigger chance of giving possession away but it's less risky, it's simpler and it's more direct. And if you get the kick right and your wingers win the contest in the air, you've got serious momentum without huffing and puffing your way through a dozen phases. As with passing, I've spent 20 years working on my kick, to the point where I'll know as soon as it leaves my boot what sort of distance, height and hang time I've got on it. I won't need to look up, I'll know straightaway.

In Ireland camp the last few years, myself and Craig and Jamison, for a bit of fun, have been doing a rugby version of the crossbar challenge, where we stand on the 22m line and try to hit the crossbar with our kicks. The twist is, you can't look at the ball after you've kicked it, you've to try and predict where it's gone by the feel off your foot: that one's gone a bit right, that one's a bit short, this one has a chance, this one will go close, and so on. And usually you'll be spot on because we've been doing it for so long, we'll know instantly without even looking at it.

Before I specialised in rugby, I played a lot of Gaelic football and the habits I acquired there were transferred across, for better or worse. It meant I didn't have the most orthodox kicking style with an oval ball. I'm a right-footed kicker. My ball drop from hand to foot came from Gaelic which meant I didn't keep my left hand in contact with the ball until the boot met it. I would release it from the hand a fraction earlier, which gave me less control over the point of contact. In Gaelic, I loved launching it into the sky. I could be 20 yards out from the posts, where all it would need is a clip to get it over the bar. But I loved hoisting it high and watching it drop down. My GAA coaches in Patrickswell would be telling me, you don't need to put snow on it! You just need to clip it over the bar.

So, there were imperfections in my technique and it's one reason why I never developed a good drop kick. But the Gaelic probably meant I had better all-round ball skills and spatial awareness and footwork. Once again, Greig didn't try to re-invent the wheel with me. It was the same principle again. "Kick your kick." He would work with the kicking action that I already had. And, actually, I found that a box kick is similar in set-up to a Gaelic kick in that you make contact with it more or less at hip height, you keep your head over it and stay aligned on the follow-through. Greig figured out anyway that even if my release was too early, by the time ball met foot I was pretty much perfectly aligned and I could do whatever he needed me to do in terms of distance and hang time and accuracy.

The rest of it was down to the chasers. And to their opponents on the other side. Contests in the air often come down to the speed and athleticism of the jumpers. But courage is a big part of it too. There's going to be a mid-air collision and some fellas fancy it a lot less than others. We'd always keep an eye on every opponents' back three and also their flyhalf if he covers the backfield. If they're weak in the air, you go after them. They're targeted all the time. You could have a winger who's really dangerous with ball in hand, but doesn't fancy the aerial stuff. We'll definitely be going after him with a few bombs to see how he copes. If you can get a few mistakes out of him it gives us momentum and sometimes it has the extra bonus of knocking his confidence with ball in hand too. Wingers tend to be flair-driven and attack-minded; they love beating defenders with their pace and sidesteps; they love scoring tries. The downside is that a lot of them don't fancy the dirty work, the basic defensive job of competing in the air, which often involves collisions and then a heavy fall.

It became a real weapon for us during Joe's time with Ireland. We had fellas out wide who loved going up for the high ones, the likes of Trimble and Bowe and Conway. Rob Kearney was incredible in the air. Eyes on the ball all the way, the timing of his jumps, and how secure he was in his handling. The crowd loves a spectacular catch and Rob was just an expert at it. Felix Jones was good at it too. Earlsy used to be saying to me, "Gimme a small one. A small one! Don't be fuckin' giving me a big high one." He used to get a bit dizzy if he was running after a skyscraper and looking up in the air for several seconds trying to track the flight of it. His sat-nav would be inclined to go on the blink!

Conway loved chasing these ones. All he wanted was a 50-50

chance to get it back. Make it a contestable kick. "Just fuckin' get me into the contest," he'd say. "Get me after it, get me after it!" And then he'd go chasing it like a greyhound after a hare.

In December 2017, I duly sent him chasing after one against Leicester in the Champions Cup at Thomond Park. Conway had a lot of physical courage, he'd back down from nothing. But he used to get very nervous before games. And I'd be trying to get him to relax a bit. I'd be saying to him stuff like, "What's the worst that can happen? What's the worst that can happen, Andrew? We lose the game. That's the worst that can happen." Then, against Leicester, he goes tearing after one of my kicks, but their fullback, Telusa Veainu, gets to it first and poor old Conway runs straight into him and is knocked out cold. It's a high impact collision. Veainu ends up with a broken jaw and Conway is stretched out on the ground, in the tonic posture. And that's the end of his chasing days for a good while.

Eventually, he arrives back at training one day and he comes up to me and starts imitating me, "What's the worst that can happen, Andrew? What's the worst that can happen, eh?!" All we could do was laugh. You have to have a fair old streak of black humour in this line of work.

Anyway, as Conway will be the first to tell you, getting your timing right can be very tricky for the jumpers. Sometimes the aerodynamics will do funny things with an oval ball too. You think you're under it, but the flight path has deceived you, the ball has moved in the air, there's a drag on it, and it deviates off course. A spiral bomb is horrible to deal with. I got caught badly against England at the Aviva during lockdown. I ended up in the fullback position at one stage. George Ford was on the ball and I knew by the way he was shaping up to kick it that he was going to put up a huge spiral bomb. So, I scrambled into position, about five metres in front of the posts and reckoned I had it under control. But it suddenly wilted in mid-air; there was a drag force on it, like it had been sucked back and it actually landed about five metres in front of me. Because the stadium was empty I could actually hear the thud off it as it hit the ground. And I was nowhere near it. Bundee saved my bacon. But I was made to look a fool just by the way the ball deviated off course.

For the chasers, it's far from simple to judge the flight path perfectly, especially when you're looking up at it and you don't know what's happening around you with defenders trying to get in your eyeline and bump you and take your ground. But it's my job to give them the best chance of winning the contest. You have to kick it far enough to make some decent ground, but not so far as your winger hasn't a chance of competing for it. You need to get it high enough to give them a few seconds chase-time and long enough to gain some territory – and try to keep it the right side of the touchline also. You're not always going to get them on the money. But as far as Joe was concerned, you should be getting them right more often than wrong. The hang time you got on the ball was a big thing. Vinny Hammond, our video analyst, used to put the stopwatch on your efforts. Four seconds of hang time and about 25 metres distance was considered more or less ideal. It would give your chasers a fighting chance to get up in the air and hopefully bat it back down on your side. It worked a lot during Joe's time, it was an important weapon in our armoury.

If you're on the front foot and you've got good field position, a nice little subtle kick in behind will give your runners a great chance of scoring. The defenders have to turn back while your winger already has a head of speed up; if the ball arrives nicely in front of him, he should have an open goal, so to speak. It's mainly the outhalf's job to put those nice little dinks in behind, but sometimes the nine gets his moment too. I still have fond memories of the cushioned kick I put in for Bowe against South Africa at the Aviva in 2014 – even if it did bounce and Joe said it shouldn't have bounced! Because a lot of your kicking is just the mundane stuff of clearing your lines and basically hoofing it downfield as far as you can. So, it's always nice to show a bit more creativity when you get the chance.

I'm still irritated by one that got away against Argentina. It was the autumn series, 2017. Adam Byrne was making his international debut. It would've been an absolute dream for him to score a try on his first cap. About ten minutes in we were on their 22. I bounced out of the ruck and I could see that Adam was completely open on the right wing and I just needed to nail a dinky, low crossfield kick. But I snatched at it a little bit and the ball came off my foot a bit wonky. It wasn't turning through the air the way it should, but I thought it still had a chance, I thought he might be able to catch it clean at the corner flag. But it just died late in its flight path and hit the deck and because of the way it was rotating, it ricocheted backways off the turf and over his head and into touch. It was like there was massive backspin on it. It was tantalisingly close. I felt bad about it because that should've been a try for Adam on his first Ireland cap. I apologised to him after, but he's a very nice fella and just said don't worry about it.

Because we used the tactic so often, by the end of Joe's time in charge I was being pigeon-holed as a box-kicker. It pissed me off no end. As far as I was concerned, I could do the lot. Throughout my career, I always wanted to be a complete scrumhalf. When I first started playing with Munster and Ireland I was a running threat; I was breaking the line and scoring tries. But the game was becoming a bit more systematic in that decade. With all the video analysis and pre-planning that went into matches, coaches were coming up with more and more pre-rehearsed moves. Every situation was being legislated for in advance. If you're here, you go there, and if you're there you go here, sort of thing. The general culture of the game was becoming a bit more risk-averse. That was fine by me because under Joe we started winning things.

Then we started getting a reputation as a systems team rather than a spontaneous team and that was partly down to the amount of box-kicking I was being asked to do. There were a lot of times when it was the right thing to do, but the narrative started to form that Murray was a one-dimensional, box-kicking nine. I was well aware of that narrative. For a long time, I ignored it, but in the end it got to me, it definitely got to me. There was far more to my game than that. In my head, I was a universal scrumhalf, there wasn't one part of the job that I couldn't do. There was far more to me than just bloody box-kicking, which let's be honest, is one of the most boring parts of the whole game of rugby. But we overused it, we definitely overused it for both club and country, and I ended up stuck with the stereotype.

As an option, though, while it mightn't be cool, it will never go out of fashion. A lot of the time you've no choice but to use it, especially in defensive situations where you're under the cosh. You just have to get it out of your 22 and get your team up the pitch. Simple as that. It's the safe, sensible thing to do. Even

SPIRALS

then, if the opposing team is dictating terms at the breakdown, you're often in danger of getting blocked down and then you are really in a world of shit. You could have a six foot ten second row with his big long arms coming over the top trying to get a block on your clearance. Opposing forwards are always trying to harass the scrumhalf. It's an occupational hazard. They'll be scragging you and slapping at your arms and hitting you late and, basically, doing anything they can to get into your head and put you off your job. Tadhg Beirne loves doing it in training and it's so fuckin' annoying! It's why he's an absolute beast at the breakdown. I love it when he's doing it to other teams, but he gets his practice in by doing it to us. Fair enough too.

Along the way you have to learn a few tricks of your own to survive in that dog-eat-dog environment. Like, you'll never pass straight from the base of a ruck if you can feel them breathing down on top of you. If you know there's a danger you're going to get scragged, you roll the ball out with your foot, step backwards and then kick it or pass it. If there's a heap of bodies fighting for it at the ruck, you might have a stray hand poking through – a sneaky forward looking at you and looking at the ball and you just know he's thinking strongly about flicking at the ball or flicking at your hand if you go to pick it up. You don't want to be giving a fella like that any encouragement whatsoever. Because there's nothing worse than someone clipping your arm as you try to make a pass and the ball goes to ground and then you're pinged for a knock-on. You look stupid and it's unbelievably aggravating. The fella on the ground will be thinking along these lines. Sometimes he just can't resist the temptation. But he knows that you know what he's thinking. And you can't just let him have his own way.

So, in that situation, as you're planting your feet to crouch down over the ball, your foot might accidentally-on-purpose end up on top of that stray hand – just to keep it honest. Then you can throw your pass knowing that your backswing isn't going to be hampered. It's not that you're stamping down on him with force. He's just getting rapped on the knuckles – quite literally – for his trouble! And he will understand that it's not just the forwards who have to learn a dark art or two in this game.

But us backs are only in the ha'penny place when it comes to the dark arts. Those fellas end up with PhDs in the subject. The worst one, I find, is when you've released your pass and you're in a hurry to get to the next phase. Especially if it's a wide pass, say out to the touchline, and you've a lot of ground to cover to get to the next ruck and one of their fellas blocks your run. He body-checks you, he obstructs you in some way that will stop your run. That's what we call getting "spannered". The ref hasn't seen it because he's been following the play. It's usually the first defender on the open side. You're in motion as you release the ball and he stops all your momentum. You have to restart your run and it's so fatiguing to deal with. You've lost two or three seconds and you're late getting to the next ruck and that gives their defence enough time to realign and get set. Worst case scenario, the ball is sitting there at the back of the ruck waiting to be played, but because you're late getting there, the opposition piles through and wins the turnover. You have just been properly spannered. It takes its toll on your body and mind.

In the latter part of my career, I've stayed clear of the warzone. But the first few years I loved getting stuck into the

SPIRALS

battle at the breakdown. I was big enough and strong enough to make a difference. I enjoyed being able to make good hits on big forwards. I loved the feeling of driving a fella backwards. I didn't love it quite so much when it was me who was being driven backwards – and then being trampled over by a pack of rhinos. You'd stagger back to your feet after one of those stampedes and, for a moment, you wouldn't even know which direction you were playing. Anyway, various coaches decided it wasn't worth the effort. If you got stuck into too many wrestling sessions you ended up being too fatigued to do your number one job properly. Nowadays, the nine will usually end up defending on the edge with his wings and centres. So, more often than not you end up a spectator at these unmerciful poundings between the forward packs.

When it comes to scrums, I've had a close-up view for 20 years and I still don't know what the hell goes on in there. As the saying goes, I might as well be staring into a field of thistles for all I know. My job is just to feed the ball in and go round the back and wait for it to emerge. There's no such thing as a crooked feed anymore. It's years and years since I've been pinged for that. Every feed nowadays is crooked, pretty much. You are supposed to roll it in fairly straight, but I'm actually allowed to be in line with my front row when I put it in so the feed automatically favours your side. It should be underneath your hooker's foot. Often times you can roll it straight into the second row and no one passes any remarks. Currently there's no contest for the ball between the hookers. When I was young and naive I'd occasionally feed it in proper straight and an odd time the opposition hooker would strike it back on his side. I quickly learned not to do that because of the amount of fucks I got from my own forward pack when that happened. In fact, I remember getting blamed when it had nothing to do with the feed at all. Our pack was just horsed off the ball. It'd be a bit embarrassing for them so to make light of it afterwards they'd be saying, "Ah the feed was shit!" Our lads could get absolutely hosed in the scrum, but it was the nine's fault anyway!

The important relationship here is with your number eight. You both have to know what your next move is going to be when the ball comes back. You have a variety of options that are pitch-specific and gameplan-specific. The eight and nine absolutely have to be on the same page in those situations. With the opponents' scrum, if we know that their number eight likes to pick and go, it's my responsibility to get to him first. Get the first set of hands on him. Same with their nine or ten: whichever of them is making the play, he's your man. Stop the move at source if you can.

It just so happens that, as my own career is winding down, the most famous rugby player in the world is a scrumhalf. Antoine Dupont is an alien. He's like the next generation of robots. He's ahead of his time. For me, Mike Phillips was the greatest nine of my lifetime – until Dupont came along. Fourie Du Preez, George Gregan – incredible players. Ruan Pienaar was outstanding. Another South African, the late Joost van der Westhuizen, was just a bit before my time but I saw a lot of his old footage and understood why he was such a revered player. He was unbelievably good. I actually met him once, a day or two before we played South Africa in that match in 2014. The poor man was in a wheelchair at the time. He died from motor neurone disease in 2017. But he was brought into the Shelbourne Hotel that night in 2014 and I was called over to say hello to him as a fellow international scrumhalf. His illness meant he couldn't verbalise much, but he raised his eyebrows in recognition, I think, and smiled and we shook hands. It was a very nice moment.

Just imagine how great all these players were. So, if you're going to put someone ahead of them, he has to be phenomenally special. Dupont is the one. He is already the greatest scrumhalf of all time, I believe. His athletic talent is just a complete freak show. Sometimes he'll make the wrong decision, he'll go down the wrong side of a ruck, for example, but he's so strong and so explosive that he'll end up doing something incredibly good to get himself out of trouble. He can turn a wrong decision into a moment of genius. That's what's unique about him, in my opinion. Even the nuts-and-bolts stuff looks special when he's doing it.

What Dupont makes you realise, I suppose, is that every dog has his day and then the show moves on. I have had my day and the show has moved on. Dupont has taken the job I do to another level. But he's a once in a lifetime player. I don't think it would be right or fair to say to any young aspiring rugby player that he should be your role model. That would be asking far too much.

Instead, what I would say is to maximise what you have. Get every ounce out of your talent, if you can. Learn the fundamentals. Do them thousands and thousands of times until they become second nature. Then keep doing them anyway, right throughout your career. Never lose sight of them. In my opinion, that's how you give yourself the best chance of going as far as you want to go. There's no great secret to it. I found that out for myself. And what I have learned, I hope I have passed some of it on here.

Never say never. I'm not going back on it now! But while I'm certain I'll never go into coaching, I suppose I can't deny that if by chance, years from now, young Alfie ever happens to show a bit of interest in an oval ball, I might have to go up to the attic for a pair of my old boots after all. In fairness, that would be sweet.

Chapter Twenty

TROLLS

WE HAVE SIX-AND-A-HALF MINUTES TO SURVIVE in Twickenham. We haven't played well, but that's mainly because England haven't let us play well. They've thrown the kitchen sink at us. But we've hung tough and weathered the storm and now Lowey has given us a two-point lead with his try in the corner. It's a slick move, clinically executed. It's Round 4 of the 2024 Six Nations. We are six-and-a-half minutes away from the win that will leave us just one game away from back-to-back Grand Slams.

And we've had setbacks throughout this match. Calvin Nash is gone with a concussion after five minutes. A reshuffle is needed. Ciarán Frawley replaces Calvin, but moves to full back and Hugo Keenan goes to the right wing. Then Frawley gets a knock on 50 minutes and I replace him. I go to scrumhalf, Jamison Gibson-Park moves to the right wing and Hugo reverts to full back. All this chopping and changing can destabilise a team, but it looks like we've dealt with the problems. It looks like we've survived England's massive effort in front of a very vocal home crowd too. It's a matter of game management now. They get a breakdown penalty on halfway in the 75th. Elliot Daly has a boot on him that can make a kick like that, but his strike sails wide and that has eaten up another 100 seconds on the clock. They run back the kick-off, get a few phases, Marcus Smith makes yards with a good incision into our 22, but we turn it over and Lowey clears long. There's two-and-a-half minutes left. They run it back again and get it out wide left, but Jamison makes a tackle and I bundle George Furbank into touch. It's our lineout on our 22.

There's a break in play for treatment to one of their lads. That gives us a chance to get into a huddle and talk through our next play. We're joined by various support staff, a couple of medics and the fella in charge of the water bottles. At least one of them will be wearing an earpiece that's wired up to the coaching box. If the coaches need to get instructions to the players, they'll relay it via earpiece to the person on the sideline and he'll relay it to us during the next break in play. You'll know it's coming from the coaches box, but the messenger will often point to his earpiece to make it clear that's where it's coming from.

On this occasion, I get the message from one of them, something like, "Ball off the pitch." I pass it on to Jack Crowley at ten. We'd have known ourselves that the percentage play was to put the ball into the touch, but this was confirmation anyway. Both Lowey and myself with our previous kicks had gone 'long and on', which basically means when you're inside your 22 you clear the ball downfield as far as you can. If it goes into touch, fine, but the first priority is maximum distance. But England were counterattacking really well that day, making a fair bit of ground and getting line breaks and putting us under pressure. That was another reason why touch was the option here. It would eat up more seconds and we would get our defence set for their lineout.

TROLLS

Iain Henderson claims our throw at the tail, Jack Conan makes the carry and sets up the ruck. I drag the ball back with my foot and clear it into touch about ten metres inside the halfway line. There's another break in play for treatment to Jack. The clock is stopped at 78:55. "Swing low sweet chariot" is ringing around the stadium. Maro Itoje goes up and catches it and throws it down to Danny Care and they sweep across midfield and Daly gains ground before transferring it to Tommy Freeman, who makes a good ten metres before being brought down. England all of a sudden have made rapid yards and have big momentum. The recycle is fast, Marcus Smith receives at speed and pops it to Immanuel Feyi-Waboso on the edge and somehow in no space at all he manages to skip a tackle and flies up to nearly our 5m line.

Next thing, the referee is calling penalty advantage for an infringement at the ruck. It all unravels as quickly as that. They work it infield through four or five phases and we're scrambling desperately and the ref blows for another penalty advantage, this one just left of the posts and a banker three points. So, with nothing to lose, they switch the ball back to Marcus Smith and he has a dolly of a drop goal from underneath the posts. Twickenham erupts, the England players go berserk, our history-making Grand Slam is gone in 60 seconds.

Back in the dressing room, I have a quick chat with Faz and turn on my phone. It starts beeping with message alerts and notifications. That's normal enough for big games, especially after a win. You'll have family and friends and all sorts of randomers who think they're your buddy sending you compliments and congratses and well dones. But I've never seen the phone lighting up like this. WhatsApps, Instagram, texts, they just keep pouring in. There's hundreds of messages arriving. I go into my Instagram account and there's reams of them and they're nearly all abusive. Effing idiot, effing retard, useless effing c**t, an absolute tirade of filthy language; the tone is vicious; people are raging at me. At first, I don't know what to make of it because I don't think I've done anything wrong. I can't remember making a glaring error. But there's a theme emerging among the ranters: why did you kick the effing ball out you effing prick? These particular rugby experts have decided we lost the game because Murray kicked the ball into touch.

I'm the scapegoat. I'm on the receiving end of this toxic stream of personalised abuse. Not having a clue about what happened and why it happened obviously doesn't stop any of them. It's bad enough getting abuse when you actually have made a mistake because you're already feeling guilty and beating yourself up about it. You don't need a load of strangers beating you up about it too, but I understand that it's part of the price you have to pay. If you've missed a tackle or made a bad decision in a high profile match you have to hold your hands up and you have to accept the nasty comments that are going to be coming your way online.

But it's horrible getting abuse when you've done nothing wrong. I got the order from the coaches box to kick that ball to touch and that's what I did. But even if I didn't get the order I probably still would have done it anyway because it was the logical, rational thing to do in those circumstances. I've played international rugby long enough to know that you can't hold onto the ball on your own 22 for over 60 seconds or so when you have such a slender lead. It's just too dangerous. The rugby authorities made it clear years ago that they don't like teams sticking the ball up their jersey and counting down the clock. It's considered negative, cynical play and referees are told not to tolerate it. They'll be looking for a reason to ping you. And because there's something illegal going on at nearly every ruck, they'll find something if they want to. If we start picking and going on our 22 we can easily get done for sealing off or something. It's just too high risk.

So, we know what the play is in this scenario. We've trained for it, we know the drill. We clear our lines, give them the lineout and get our defence set for the last series of phases. The problem was after the lineout. They made rapid yards up the middle because we were maybe a bit too passive for fear of making a mistake and when they get it to the edge we miss a tackle and Feyi-Waboso makes the line break. When we reviewed that last few minutes in the Monday video session, my kick didn't even come up. It wasn't even mentioned. It wasn't relevant; there was no reference to it in that conversation. What did come up was how we defended off that last England lineout.

But the damage was done by then. By that, I mean the damage done to your family and loved ones. They are seeing all this vile stuff on social media and it upsets them really badly. It upsets me to see them so upset. That's what I find really painful about an episode like that. I have the support of my team mates and the coaches. And we all know the facts of the situation. But Joanna, my parents, my sisters, they're not clued into the planning and decisions that go into a match scenario like this one. They can't be. And straight after the game they're seeing all this bile pouring out on various platforms and, of course, it's going to worry them because they're not sure whether you've made a big mistake or not. Thousands of punters online can't all be wrong, can they? Well, sometimes they can. I get a text from Joanna's dad telling me not to look at social media, but it's impossible to avoid it completely. You only have to turn on your phone and it comes pouring in.

In the old days, coaches would advise players not to look at the newspapers, but in this day and age you can't not turn on your phone. I only looked at a fraction of the shit that was posted at me – and that was more than enough. But in my heart I knew I'd done nothing wrong and that helped me cope with it. I'm only on Instagram; I'm not on X/Twitter. I'd imagine I was buried on that forum. If you're in the public eye at all you get exposed to the dark side of human nature, but the evil part of it is that innocent people like your wife and parents become part of the collateral damage. Some of the worst messages were directed at my wife, really dark, nasty material, a lot of it from people hiding behind anonymous profiles, of course. But some of it came from users with their actual names and photos up, including people who were saying crazy stuff about my family. Like, people with good jobs who seem to consider themselves very respectable and successful.

In a few of the worst cases, I was sorely tempted to forward these messages to their employers and say like, this is what your employee is doing at the weekend; look at who you're hiring here. Harry Maguire, the Manchester United player, was getting a bad doing that week too online, only it was multiplied by a factor of a thousand for someone as famous as he is. But I felt like I got a glimpse into the life of a big-name Premier League footballer. It must be hellish at times for their families.

In my case, I know for sure that if there's this much criticism about me online, it will spill over into real life too, in homes

TROLLS

and pubs and offices and workplaces. It's all borrowed talk. An opinion spreads online and suddenly thousands are agreeing with it. It can be totally wrong, but it becomes gospel anyway. To give you an idea of how far this particular one spread, I was in Thomond Park three weeks after Twickenham for a Munster game against Cardiff in the URC. I wasn't playing, I was struggling with a neck injury. But myself and Killer were down to do a meet-and-greet organised by the Munster Supporters Club. There was a minis game at half-time for kids from a couple of the province's rugby clubs and you're brought into the dressing room to say hello and shake hands and stand in for a few selfies. It's a really nice thing to do, the kids are buzzing and their coaches are well pleased too.

I come out of the dressing rooms underneath, back into the crowds and next thing a voice pops up, "Why did you kick the ball away?" It sounded like a young fella, it came from a group so I couldn't see him. There's safety in numbers. But I heard it loud and clear and it really stung me. I'm a fairly even-tempered fella, but in that moment I was really tempted to turn round and have a go back. I was so close to pulling the trigger and confronting whoever said it. But then the camera phones would be out and if you make a scene it'll be up online before you know it and that'll go viral too. I bite my lip and ignore it. But hearing it in your home place among your home supporters wasn't nice. It undid all the happy vibes with the kids a few minutes earlier. At the end of the day, I guess the only way you can tolerate it is just by accepting that some people are fucking idiots. It's no more complicated than that. Some people are fucking idiots.

We have Scotland in the final round a week after England. On the Tuesday in between, Simon Easterby meets the rugby press at the IRFU's High Performance Centre in Abbotstown. I haven't spoken to Simon about the furore online but, of course, he knows all about it. Simon is asked specifically by the reporters if the call for the kick to touch had come from the coaches box.

"Yes," he replies. He elaborates a bit more on the whole debate. "Listen, you know what, those decisions will always be reflected [upon] and hindsight's lovely, isn't it? 'It was the right decision because we didn't concede', 'It was the wrong decision because we did concede'. It's such fine margins. Had we kicked it long and they'd broken us and made 90 metres then you'd say, 'Well, you should have put it out'. You can pick holes in every decision."

In the meantime, I've been having a rough few days. I've made a flying visit home and the mood is low with everyone. They're all feeling for me, but I'm not too bad, I just hate to see my loved ones suffering for no good reason. They have nothing to do with this, it's completely out of their control.

On the drive back to Carton House, I'm alone with my thoughts and the whole thing gets in on me a little bit. Like, we've all had abuse in our careers; I've had it before, but it's just the sheer scale of it this time that rattles me. I mean, just the bloody volume of it. And the thought goes through my mind, like, what's the point of playing on? It only lasts very briefly, but it does hit me: what is the point of playing at all, if this many people think you're a waste of space? I mean, there's just hundreds and hundreds of messages with wild abuse in them. Why are you having to justify your presence to these people? Why are you even trying to explain it to them? And why am I putting myself through this? Anyway, I snap out of it and tell myself again that I didn't do anything wrong. I put my professional head back on and drive on up the road.

TROLLS

Faz knew I was suffering in myself during the next few days of training. As I've said, he's very emotionally intelligent, he can pick up one person's mood out of a big group of people. He just has that sort of sensitivity radar. He comes up to me in Carton House a night or two later and says, "I hear you're getting a bit of flak." We talk about it for a while. And he's like, the way we defended that lineout is why we lost the game, it wasn't because we kicked to touch. And that's all I needed to hear. I knew it anyway, but it was nice to get a bit of support one-to-one from the main man.

A few days after Simon talked to the press, Faz went public too with his support. You just can't buy that kind of loyalty from your coaches. It's one of the reasons why the Ireland camp is such a happy place to be. We all feel valued by the coaching staff. It's a caring environment. Their rugby knowledge is off the charts, but they are brilliant at the soft skills like communication, human warmth and general emotional intelligence. They set very high standards, but they make you feel safe and secure too.

Faz goes in to bat for me when the question about social media abuse comes up at his press conference. In his own understated way, he doesn't hold back.

"The more successful some people are, the more that people – I don't know what the word is, other than [they] get pissed off with success, longevity, people staying at the top as long as they possibly can. Everybody always wanting somebody else to come in, a new fresh young rookie to light everything up. It takes an unbelievable amount of dedication and courage to stay at the top and keep riding with the punches throughout a long career that's been so successful for somebody with 120-odd caps like Conor. I can only marvel at somebody like that and when you ask me to describe what I think of him, it's right there in all that, isn't it?"

I am really grateful for those words, not so much for myself as for my wife and family. It really helps to lift the cloud that's been hanging over them. Someone of his stature coming out in public and defending me like that, I don't know if he knows it but it's a great act of kindness for my folks. It just relieves a lot of the pressure they've been feeling. But that's Faz all over – a proper leader of people in my view. I owe him a lot. In the next few days, I start getting messages from genuine fans expressing their support and telling me not to pay any heed to the trolls. It makes a difference, a small difference, and it restores my faith in people a bit. I appreciate that these good supporters have taken the time to reach out to me. But the experience has made me more hardened overall. There are an awful lot of people whose opinion I just won't value anymore. There's only a select few I'll take advice from now. The whole episode has told me to switch off the external noise and only allow the few people that really matter into your circle of trust.

After the video review on the Monday you're supposed to close the page on that game and move onto the next one. But we're not robots either. There's an emotional drag from the England match that lingers on for a couple more days. It's hard to let go of what-might-have-been. We were just seconds away from sealing the deal. In theory, you're supposed to turn the page, but the regrets are too raw to be erased like they're tabs on your laptop that can be closed with a click. I think the hangover was carried into the Scotland game. We were feeling the pressure, there were a lot of nerves about. It took us a long time to finally wear them down.

TROLLS

I replaced Jamison in the 69th minute. I was very happy to be there. Before the tournament I think a lot of followers would've reckoned that Craig might get the nod ahead of me. I was facing up to that possibility too. Craig was number one at Munster and he was in good form. Faz had a bit of a juggling act on his hands. But I was chosen as back-up to Jamison for the France game. I got the last ten minutes of that sensational performance in Marseille. Then I was dropped out of the 23 for the second round match against Italy; Craig started, Jamison was on the bench. I was sent back to Munster and played against the Scarlets five days later in Llanelli and got a bad bang to the neck for my troubles. It could've been touch and go at that point. But I was brought back in for the next game, against Wales, and held my place in the 23 for the rest of the tournament.

It meant the world to me to be on the field when we clinched the championship against Scotland at the Aviva. It's just not the same when you're standing there in your tracksuit and you haven't played your part. Add in the week I'd just had and this feeling was particularly sweet. It was my fifth Six Nations title to go with 2014, 2015, 2018 and 2023. But because of the circumstances, I felt personally vindicated. It was an eff you to the people who'd hurt my family. It was huge for me, it was very, very satisfying.

Back in the dressing room, I'm loving the shenanigans. There's nothing like it when there's a trophy in the middle of the room and everyone's singing and dancing and spraying the champagne around. It's not often in your life you get to be in one place where every single person in that place is beaming with smiles and laughter. You're in a place where everyone is happy. It's just intoxicating, with or without the beer and the bubbly.

CONOR MURRAY

I'm conscious that Joanna and my parents will be waiting to see me. It can often be a long wait by the time you get out of the dressing room. There's always delays of some sort. And it can be longer still if the commercial manager nabs you to do a few meet-and-greets in the corporate boxes. I hear my name being called for the gig. But I've done lots of them in the past and I've been around the block a few times and I know there's an exit route that brings you into the underpass beneath the stand. And from there I can go up the back stairs and find my folks. So, I sneak out and sadly the corporate boxes will have to do without me on this occasion.

The Saturday night is the usual round of banquet, speeches, formal wear and finery. But most of us are wrecked as well and badly in need of a good night's sleep. The Sunday is the best day if you're celebrating a trophy. It also happens to be St Patrick's Day so, of course, everyone is mad for action.

The Shelbourne Hotel is hopping from midday and earlier. Myself and a bunch of the lads saunter over to O'Donoghue's, the famous pub that has hosted generations of Irish rugby players. The manager there has a room set aside for us upstairs, away from the madness in the main bar below. From there you can look down onto the street at all the people milling around and just relax and drink pints at your leisure all day if you want to. It's the next best thing to that golden hour in the dressing room when everyone is at their happiest.

The next day we went to Derry to collect our dog who was being minded by Joanna's family. Went out in Derry on the Monday night, back to Limerick on the Tuesday, and then a few days later over to Cashel for Robbie Henshaw's wedding. Then, Pete O'Mahony in the middle of it all, decides to throw a big party at his house in Cork on the Saturday. After a week in hell, it's a week of bliss. It's been a brilliant seven days.

Mind you, I don't totally let myself go. In the window between Derry and Cashel I did a weights session, a run and a session on the stationary bike back in Limerick, just to keep myself ticking over. Since I turned pro I've been super-conscious of my fitness. Summer holidays, winter breaks, long weekends, I'll always be doing some sort of maintenance work at a minimum. I love feeling fit and healthy. If I've done a few days on the beer, I'll generally sweat it off on the bike or in the gym the first chance I get. I've always done the extras too, like ice baths and massages and prehab and stretching routines. Nutrition and sleep as well – I keep on top of all of it. I'm convinced it's one reason why I've managed to last so long in the sport. I don't think I've ever taken a shortcut with my fitness in my professional career. I love it too much to take any chances with it. Being fit isn't just part of the job; it long ago became a way of life.

I'd like to think that being trusted by someone of the calibre of Andy Farrell to play a part in the 2024 championship season, at the age of nearly 35, was fair reward for going the extra mile all those years when no one was watching.

Chapter Twenty-One

FINAL CURTAIN

ANYWAY, BACK TO WHERE I started this story. March 2025, and we beat Italy in the Stadio Olimpico in my final appearance in a green jersey. After saying slán to my Ireland mates in Rome with a few bars of the 'Summer of '69' on the team bus, it was back to my Munster buddies for the final curtain in red.

Those were the best days of my life. Some of the best days of my life happened with my hometown team too. But, sad to say, those days were already behind me. I would be romanticising it if I said otherwise. In all honesty, my last few seasons with Munster were not the happiest of times for me. I could see the decline in the club's stature continuing year by year. I could see the standards slipping, slowly but surely. You didn't have to be on the inside to see it. Every supporter could see it in the results. That was just the reality.

On top of that, I felt I wasn't getting a fair crack of the whip in terms of game time. But, for most of my last season, I'd made up my mind to try and not let the situation get to me personally. I sort of numbed out that side of it. I tried to resign myself to accept I wouldn't be getting many starts and that I would be getting fewer and fewer minutes. If I didn't make that mental adjustment I'd be in a negative humour all the time and I didn't

FINAL CURTAIN

want to be that person. I'd seen it lots of times with other players and I didn't want to be that guy. You owed it to your team mates to put out the bright side and carry on as a good professional.

I owed it to myself too. I had complete clarity about that. I was not going to let my own personal standards drop under any circumstances. I would not be taking any shortcuts in my work. I would continue doing all my extras in training and at home. I'd made that promise to myself for the sake of my own professional pride. And I certainly did not want the fans to see any deterioration on my part. I wanted them to remember me as they'd seen me in my prime. So, regardless of how the interim coach was judging me day to day, I would be my own judge. I wouldn't be letting the side down and I wouldn't be letting myself down. That was the bottom line.

It seemed that during those final months there was a milestone to be marked nearly every second week. After my 125th and final cap with Ireland, my next game back with Munster would be my 200th cap. And, for an added bonus, we would be playing Connacht at a new venue for both sides, MacHale Park in Castlebar. It would be the first time that the famous home of Mayo GAA would be hosting a rugby match. The fixture was scheduled for 29th March 2025. The week before, the word went out that it was a 27,000 sellout. It would be the biggest home crowd that a Connacht rugby team had ever played in front of. It was going to be a special day.

At our squad announcement earlier that week, they put the team and subs up on the screen as per usual and my name was highlighted in a different colour to the rest for my 200th Munster game. But it was in the subs, not the starting fifteen. I was expecting that. I was hoping for something different, but

CONOR MURRAY

I was expecting what happened. Again, I'd resigned myself to it. A couple of my veteran team mates came up to me after and said it was a disgrace that I hadn't been picked to start for the occasion, just to honour me properly. Yeah, I felt that too. But the main point for me was that I wouldn't weaken the team if I did start. I was playing as well as ever. I didn't want to start because of what I'd done in the past. I was hoping to start because I felt I was still relevant. I was hoping for it because I felt my form and fitness could justify it. I was three weeks away from my 36th birthday at that stage, but I hadn't allowed myself any slippage in standards at all. And once I was ticking that box, I was hoping that for my 200th cap I might get the honour of starting. But it wasn't to be.

Still, I was really conscious of trying to make the most of it. In my final few months I wanted to savour it all one more time. I tried to park the selection issue, to put it into a separate compartment of my brain so that I could enjoy the craic in the dressing room down the home straight of my career. The dressing room has always been my safe space, your sanctuary away from everything else. That's where the heart and soul of your life as a rugby player is. Even in the darkest times of injuries and results, the comradeship and the humour will pull you through. I really didn't want anything to spoil my enjoyment of my last days in that special place. When you know you're running out of time, you want to cherish it all the more.

And my relationship with my team mates hadn't changed one iota. I felt enormous gratitude to them for all the times we'd had together. I felt the comfort and security of their presence around me. The coaches were over there, my team mates were here around me. The night before the game, in our hotel in

FINAL CURTAIN

Westport, Pete presented me with a customised Munster cap, in the traditional red with the gold tassels and club crest. It was a very nice little ceremony. They played a montage of my highlights on video and Pete spoke wonderfully well as he always does.

MacHale Park was a class experience, a proper old-school GAA ground. The atmosphere was top notch and we played pretty well. I got thirteen minutes. I shrugged my shoulders and moved on because we had another amazing occasion coming fast down the tracks. We were heading to France for another crack at Europe. And not just anywhere in France, but La Rochelle, European champions in 2022 and 2023, the city where RoG was king. O'Gara had transformed that club; he'd turned the Stade Marcel Deflandre into a fortress. And now Munster were coming to town. I was one of the few survivors who'd actually played with him during his pomp at Thomond Park.

What a weekend we had! It was like the vintage old days when RoG himself was leading the Munster charge in Europe. When we got to Shannon airport on the Friday morning it was a sea of red. The drummers were there and loads of other familiar faces who'd followed us through thick and thin. The airport was heaving.

On our approach to the runway in France, we passed over the île de Ré and it looked magnificent. The city was really cool too. We did our captain's run that afternoon and went for a stroll that evening. Archie had to get his ice cream; I wanted to soak up the atmosphere down at the port. It was hopping with fans from both sides. The next day our bus stopped at the wrong entrance to the stadium so we had to walk around and we were serenaded by hundreds of Munster fans along the way. They were lining up either side of us and cheering us through. Inside, the atmosphere was electric. And Munster rolled back the years with one of our greatest performances ever in Europe. It was exceptional, really exceptional. Again, I was given thirteen minutes. I had an involvement in the build-up to Jack Crowley's drop goal which put us eight points in front with ten to play. We held out for a massive win on the road.

Bordeaux Begles stuck a big fat pin in the balloon a week later. We fought like lions in the second half to try and salvage it, but Bordeaux had essentially taken the game away from us in the first 40. To win back-to-back games against two stacked French teams away from home was probably asking too much. We didn't say it at the time when we were preparing for them, but it was a big mountain to climb. With that defeat, myself and Pete and Archie had reached the end of the road in Europe. There would be no holy grail for us. We would be checking out of Munster without the silverware that was the dream all along. That was the big vacuum on our CVs that we would have to take into retirement with us. In your heart, it was all you ever wanted with Munster. In your head, you'd have to admit that we never had the squad to get it done. For that decade and a half we just were not strong enough or good enough. End of story.

And as if to prove the point one last time, we finished the season with a serious struggle to even qualify for the Champions Cup in 2025/26. There was a time when failing to qualify for the knockout stages in Europe was seen as an absolute disaster. But we started to get used to that too by the middle of the last decade. And now, here in May 2025, we were staring down the barrel of not even qualifying for the tournament at all. We were

FINAL CURTAIN

in danger of not finishing in the top eight in the URC league table, which would mean not making the Champions Cup for the following season. Financially, it would have been a bad blow. In terms of our standing in the game as a brand name, and as a club, it would have been desperate. We ended up needing to win our final two games of the league, against Ulster and Benetton, to save our blushes.

Ulster in Thomond Park would be the last appearance there for myself and Pete and Archie. But obviously everyone's priority was winning the bloody match first. A crowd of almost 18,000 turned up and you could feel the warmth from them for us in the match preliminaries, which was lovely. Archie had reached the monumental total of 300 caps against Bordeaux. He and Pete started against Ulster. I came on with fifteen to play and, to be honest, I was embarrassed. We had the match in the bag by then, we were well ahead on the scoreboard. The game was in garbage time. I wasn't going to be contributing to the result. I felt a bit embarrassed being sent in like that, like I was an afterthought. In my head I was going, just let me onto this famous field one last time for a decent amount of time. I'm not here for the ceremony, I'm still a competitor. I'm not going to play badly, it's not going to affect the result, just give me a decent amount of game time in my very last game at Thomond Park; that's all.

Against Benetton in Musgrave Park, I got the last five minutes. The two Cork lads got the send-off in front of their home crowd that they so richly deserved. I was very happy that Pete and Archie were getting the chance to go out on their own terms. We got the win that saved our bacon for Europe the following season. In the dressing room afterwards, Micheál Martin came in and spoke a few words. He congratulated the three of us on our careers and wished us well for the future. It was really nice to have the Taoiseach of your country speaking about you like that. When that was done, I quickly showered and quietly exited the dressing room. I wanted out of there. I wanted to go home to Joanna and Alfie.

The final shake-up in the league table meant we'd have to head to Durban to play the Sharks in the URC quarter-final a fortnight later. Once again, we fronted up in a hostile venue a long way from home. I thought our boys were magnificent on the night. That was a Sharks team packed with Springboks. The intensity of the battle was incredible. And we hung tough to the bitter end. I came on in the 65th minute. They were throwing the kitchen sink at us in the last quarter. We were three points down with four minutes to play when we won a penalty a few metres inside the halfway line. Myself and Jack and Tadhg had a brief huddle. We had options. We could go down the line with it or Jack could take the kick, or I could. Tadhg made the captain's call, "No, Murr, you're kicking it." And that was that. It was a vote of confidence in me which made me feel good. In the warm up I'd been kicking smoothly so I knew my technique, my kicking action, would be sound if the pressure didn't get to me.

There was a bit of an irony going on here because I'd been practising kicks my whole career while very rarely being called upon to take them in a game. It was rarer still that I'd have a kick to save a game. But, after training every day, I went through the routine anyway. Maybe the last few seasons not quite as often because I was stiffening up regularly now after sessions in the gym or on the pitch. I had to be a bit more careful about minding my body. But I had my process nailed down anyway,

FINAL CURTAIN

like a golfer with his swing. I'd always remembered Fla saying after the 2006 Heineken Cup final how happy he was that his darts had stood up to the pressure. His throwing technique hadn't buckled under the pressure. That always stuck with me.

Mossie Lawlor came on with the kicking tee. I went into my routine. I was aware of the situation, of course, but you couldn't allow that to invade your thoughts. I was nervous, but I zoned the context out of my mind. I settled into my stance, regulated my breathing and lined up angle and distance. It was about 46 metres out and in front of the posts. Soon as it left my boot I knew it was on its way. It sailed between the posts no bother at all.

Extra time was stalemate. No one wanted to make a mistake. Fatigue had set in on both sides. We all knew a penalty shootout was on the cards. Jack, Rory Scannell and myself were going to be our designated takers. It's a cruel business; it's just you and the ball, the whole spotlight narrows down from the team to the individual. I was gutted for Rory that he missed his first kick and proud of him that he landed his second. Jaden Hendrikse showed no class at all. The Sharks scrumhalf took the first kick of the shootout. Soon as it went over he was mouthing to Crowley, trying to put him off. Then, after Hendrikse takes his second one, he goes down with cramp right beside where Jack is going to be taking his next kick.

It's obvious what he's doing. It's horseshit, he's hamming it up; it's blatant. I go over to him and his physios and let them know that I know what's going on here. I say it to the referee, but he's not sure what to do. I hate this kind of behaviour in rugby. And especially in this situation where the kickers on both sides are all in this together. We're the ones putting our heads on the block. May the best man win is my attitude.

CONOR MURRAY

I actually went over to their third kicker, Bradley Davids, and offered him my hand before the shootout started. Now I was seriously tempted to grab Hendrikse by the collar and drag him away from the scene. I weighed it up in my mind. But I knew if I did that, there'd probably be a melee with players piling in from both sides and that would delay Jack's kick even longer. Instead, I shouted at Hendrikse to get the fuck off the field. Jack kept his cool and nailed his second shot, this one from 40 metres. Rory on the occasion of his 200th cap did likewise. Davids knocked over the winner. And, with that, my Munster career was over. Competitive debut, 18th April 2010, two days before my 21st birthday; last game, 31st May 2025, aged 36 and 41 days.

We all went out for drinks in Durban that night. There was no great emotion. We were still caught up in the drama of what happened; most of us physically and mentally drained. We arrived back in Dublin the next day and I drove home with a few of the lads for company. The following Thursday we had our end-of-season debrief in the High Performance Centre in UL. I didn't have to be there, I suppose, but strictly speaking I was still on contract until the last day of July and I wanted to be there anyway. I wanted to say a proper goodbye to all the staff and all the squad and to the other lads who were leaving alongside myself and Pete and Archie.

But for me personally, I felt my proper sign-off was with that kick in the 77th minute in Durban. I was lucky to get that moment. The dying minutes of a fifteen-year career and you have a clutch situation right at the end of a clutch game. Nailing that kick was symbolic for me. It meant I had kept my promise to myself. It was my way of saying that I hadn't let my standards drop. I'd maintained my standards right to the last. I

FINAL CURTAIN

felt it validated my decision to play on deep into my 30s. I felt it vindicated my hunger and desire to keep competing, to keep fighting for my place in the squad and in the first fifteen, right until my last breath as a Munster player. Basically, I think I can say that I died with my boots on in the red jersey.

Any professional sportsperson will have to admit that it's not the most grown-up of environments in which to spend the first phase of your working life. You were only playing a game instead of playing the game of life. But I guess you can always catch up on the serious stuff. There's plenty of time for that after you put your gear in the wash for the final time. There's plenty of time for life after you have lived the dream. I have lived the dream for almost half of my time on planet Earth. I am well aware that most people don't get to live it at all. So, the dominant emotions I have now are gratitude and fulfilment. I am so grateful for getting to live this dream for so long. And that at the end of it all, I've come out the other side safe and sound.

You can't live on Cloud Nine forever and you wouldn't want to either. All good things must come to an end. But how blessed was I to live up there and take in the view for all those years. It was lovely up there. But it's not so bad down here either. I have landed on solid ground. Instead of Thomond Park it'll be walks in the park with Joanna and the wee man. The professional sportsman dies twice. But I have been blessed twice over, once for 20 years and now, fingers crossed, with my family for the rest of our lives. Sure, those were the best days of my life – apart from all the days that I hope are still to come.

ACKNOWLEDGEMENTS

YOU DON'T HAVE TO WAIT until you're retired to start appreciating the people who've helped you along the way. You will know it at the time. But when you're looking back with the benefit of a bit of distance, it really hits home how much your career was shaped by people who were good to you.

When you're starting out, the mentors you have are particularly important. But I found I needed help and encouragement right throughout my career. Getting sound advice at 30 can be just as valuable as the advice you get at 13.

Andy Farrell was a rock of support for me during the latter years of my time with Ireland. Faz kept the faith and I will always be grateful to him for that. Joe Schmidt before him took my game to a different level. He was incredibly influential in helping me to think differently about my job and what we could achieve as a squad. His predecessor, Declan Kidney, believed in me when I was a rookie pro and took a leap of faith with me when I still had so much to prove. Tony McGahan did likewise at Munster. Before Munster there was St Munchin's where John Broderick instilled into me his love and passion for the sport. John planted the rugby seeds in me that continued to grow for the next 20 years. Brian O'Donoghue was another teacher at Munchin's who encouraged me to believe I had a future in the professional game. But back then I'm not sure any of us really believed I'd end up going on three tours with the British & Irish Lions. It was Warren Gatland who selected me for all three tours and I will always thank him for granting me those priceless life experiences. The foundations for those amazing high points were laid at the Munster academy. Once again, I was blessed to have had people who minded me and nurtured me there. I am deeply grateful to those coaches, among them the late Greig Oliver who spent hundreds of hours building me into the player I became.

In the dressing room and on the training ground, I had colleagues who weren't just team mates but who doubled up as friends, confidantes, advisors and comedians – Earlsy, Paulie, RoG, Pete, Conway and Sexto among them. Those fellas would never let you down, on or off the field. I will savour forever the times we shared and the memories we forged.

Andrew Burke and I more or less began our rugby journey together and the friendship that started then is as strong as ever now. Senan O'Sullivan remains a great buddy too, having supported me from my first days with Munster and Ireland to my last.

On international duty we were taken care of by coaching, medical and logistics staff who went out of their way to do their best for you. Ger Carmody and Mick Kearney were unstintingly generous with their care and support. They always had your back, you always felt supported, and I thank them both sincerely for their years of friendship.

When you hit your thirties you have to start planning for life after rugby and I have been so lucky to receive a great deal of practical advice and moral support from Brian Crowley and Alan Clancy, experts in their field who have become good friends.

ACKNOWLEDGEMENTS

My agent Dave McHugh has been representing me diligently for over a decade at the coalface of the rugby business. I want to thank Dave and Reach PLC for making this book possible. Tommy Conlon had the job of turning all my recollections into words on the page. We worked hard to make it as good as we could. I hope that between us we have delivered an entertaining and insightful story. I am grateful to Tommy for his professionalism and patience.

One of the great things about Mum and Dad was that they never weighed me down with too much advice when I was a kid. I will always be profoundly grateful for everything they did for me, including, when it came to sport, just letting me get on with it. They supported me every step of the way while at the same time giving me the space to follow my own instincts. I played everything and anything and they were happy as long as I was happy. When I started to specialise in rugby, they were always there for me in the background and I always had the security of knowing that. My sisters also came along to every game they could to cheer me on and encourage me in every way. Our beloved auntie, Lily Woulfe, lived right next door to us in Patrickswell. Lily was my godmother and a wonderful lady. She bought me brand new boots every Christmas and never complained when we knocked slates off her roof when we were kicking the ball around. So, it was never my journey alone; it was Gerry and Barbara, Sarah and Aisling, and Lily and Con when they were still with us. My family were the ultimate foundation for everything I did.

In 2024 Joanna and me began our own family. Alfie coming into our lives has changed everything. It was one of the greatest joys of my whole rugby career that I could bring him onto the field at Lansdowne Road right at the end of that career. I am looking forward to the day when we'll be able to show him the photos and explain to him what his old fella did for a living once upon a time.

I met Joanna in 2017 and it was the start of a relationship that has brought so much happiness and contentment into my life. She has been there for me through some rough times – and lots of great times too. Joanna's love and support kept me going in those later years when my confidence was low and I was really questioning my place in the game. As a mother and life partner, she has been everything I could hope for and more.

Finally, I don't think I'll ever be able to thank enough all those Munster and Ireland supporters who for fifteen years lifted me, energised me and inspired me. Playing in empty venues during Covid made you appreciate even more the atmosphere they provide week in week out. I was blessed and privileged to experience that emotion and that commitment so often for club and country. It never went unnoticed and I know how special it was.